SUPERCHARGED
MERCEDES
In Detail

SUPERCHARGED
MERCEDES
In Detail
1923-1943

BY JAMES TAYLOR

Herridge & Sons

Published in 2013 by Herridge & Sons Ltd
Lower Forda, Shebbear
Beaworthy, Devon EX21 5SY

© Copyright James Taylor 2013
Designed by Ray Leaning, MUSE Fine Art & Design
Colour photography by Simon Clay

ISBN 978-1-906133-48-1
Printed in Hong Kong

Contents

Introduction and acknowledgments

1935 Special Roadster on the 500K chassis

The story of the supercharged Mercedes-Benz racing cars, the Silver Arrows of the 1930s, has been covered dozens of times. To my surprise, however, the story of the supercharged road cars whose initial development preceded that of the racers has not. One reason, I assume, is that so very few of the early (and less glamorous) cars survive today. Another is surely that the surviving later cars (from the more glamorous period) now change hands for such huge sums of money that they are simply beyond all but the wildest dreams of most car enthusiasts. Well, as I have been intrigued by them since boyhood, there seemed to be ample excuse to attempt a book about them myself.

For cars which have such a high profile in the classic car scene today, surprisingly little factual information was easily available although a lot of contradictory information has been published in magazines over the years. Of course, a great deal is available through the Mercedes-Benz archives, and I am grateful to the keepers of those archives for the material they have provided to help me tell the story. Even so, not even they know everything, as I am sure they would readily admit; it is also not their policy to

1930 SS tourer

comment or pass on some types of information.

Some of the books on the subject are now out of print and very expensive, which is a dreadful shame. I was able to consult Herbert Lozier's 1967 *The Car of Kings*, which tells the story of the Porsche-developed six-cylinders through a lot of pictures, in the fashion typical of the period. Halwart Schrader's 1979 *The Supercharged Mercedes*, with illustrations by Carlo Demand, was a good source of some information, and I have great respect for the research that lies behind Jan Melin's two-volume *Mercedes-Benz, the Supercharged 8-cylinder cars of the 1930s.*

Other books illuminate particular aspects of the subject, such as Blaine Taylor's *Mercedes-Benz Grosser 770 Parade Car.*

As will be readily apparent, most of the contemporary photographs of these cars have come from Mercedes-Benz themselves. However, I am also specially grateful to Simon Clay, who took the series of magnificent colour pictures which, in my opinion, do so much to bring the physical reality of these cars closer.

James Taylor
Oxfordshire
May 2013

Chapter One

THE BACKGROUND

The supercharged cars from Mercedes-Benz in the late 1920s and throughout the 1930s played a huge part in establishing the marque's image both within and outside Germany. By the end of the Twenties, supercharging stood for high performance, and the supercharged Mercedes stood for the glamour and excitement that came with their achievements on the race tracks. But this was only half the story: the cars were also associated with celebrities, with the rich and successful, and with the lifestyle that was characteristic of 1920s high society. As high society and its expectations changed during the 1930s, so did the supercharged Mercedes, largely forsaking the race tracks (where specially-designed supercharged single-seaters nevertheless carried on the great tradition) but remaining in the forefront of the new and glamorous age. Only the 1939-45 war put an end to their lineage and even then, there were supercharged Mercedes in German government service throughout the hostilities.

However, the supercharged Mercedes did not spring forth fully formed in the late 1920s. It could trace its origins back to experiments carried out in the aftermath of the 1914-18 war, when Germany had been barred from developing engines that could power new war planes and its engineers were bursting to find an alternative outlet for their ideas. In those days, Benz & Cie and the Daimler Motorengesellschaft that owned the Mercedes marque were separate and rival companies, and it is important to recognise right from the start that supercharging was a line of research initiated within Daimler; Benz was a less adventurous marque and did not become involved until the two companies had merged as Mercedes-Benz in 1926.

In the beginning, the Daimler company used racing cars to develop and refine the technology of the supercharger. Though they promised roadgoing cars with supercharged engines as early as 1921, in practice none were available

Gottlieb Daimler.

until 1923. It was perhaps an odd policy to offer supercharging on the cheaper, everyday models, and perhaps the additional cost was a factor in its early demise. There is no reason to suspect that the technology was deficient: a much more likely reason for the failure is that Germany was gripped by massive inflation from 1923, and the buyers simply were not there. So Daimler withdrew its supercharged models in 1924 and changed tack. For the future, supercharging (and that attendant cost) would belong only to the expensive models at the top of the range.

When Daimler merged with Benz & Cie to form the Daimler-Benz Aktiengesellschaft in 1926, it was more than a mere business arrangement. These were the companies founded by the two inventors of the motor car, Gottlieb Daimler and Karl Benz. Both men had come from the gas engine industry and, even though they were working independently, the two great minds were thinking alike by the start of the 1880s. It was 1883 when Daimler made the world's first petrol-powered internal combustion engine, and 1886 before he put it into a modified horse-drawn carriage to make a self-propelled vehicle. In the meantime, Karl Benz had created a water-cooled four-stroke petrol engine which he had installed in a purpose-designed three-seater vehicle in 1885.

Daimler and Benz before the supercharger

It was less than 30 years after his father had built that petrol-powered internal combustion engine that Paul Daimler began experimenting with supercharging in the Daimler workshops. He had become the company's chief engineer in 1907, taking over from Wilhelm Maybach, who had left that year to set up his own engine company.

In the meantime, Daimler had become one of the leading German makers of cars. It had also taken on a new identity, replacing the Daimler name with that of Mercedes from 1902. Not that there had been anything wrong with the Daimler name: it was simply that the board recognised a good marketing ploy when they saw one. What had happened was that in 1901, Daimler had produced a new 35hp model which was quite ground-breaking in that it not only embodied a host of technical innovations but also owed absolutely nothing in appearance to the horse-drawn carriage. Arguably this was the first "real" car, drawn up by Wilhelm

Paul Daimler, who became Chief Engineer in 1907 and was responsible for the company's first forays into supercharging.

Maybach but using some elements of a Paul Daimler design. A 35hp Daimler was entered into the 1901 Nice Week trials by Emile Jellinek, a wealthy motoring enthusiast who had become a member of the Daimler board and held a sales franchise for France. To avoid legal difficulties with Panhard-Levassor, who held the licence to build Daimler engines in France, Jellinek decided to name the car after his 10-year-old daughter, Mercedes. It sold well and performed well in competition, and the Mercedes name struck a chord, so the Daimler board decided to adopt it for all their new car models.

A Mercedes 18/28 of 1904, known in Britain as the 60hp model and a formidable machine.

A Mercedes military ambulance of the type introduced in 1914.

Karl Benz.

Just six examples of the "Blitzen Benz" were built. In the hands of Barney Oldfield, one was timed in 1911 at a record 141mph/228kmh over the measured mile.

The Mercedes marque went on to make a name for itself through racing, and notably with international success achieved via the 1908 and 1914 Grand Prix cars. So high performance was part of the Mercedes DNA from a very early stage. Even so, the range of cars with which the company emerged from the 1914-18 war was relatively mundane. Most customers, after all, did not want high-performance cars; their interest lay in cars that were durable and reliable, and in those two areas the Mercedes name was already riding high.

Meanwhile, the company that Karl Benz had founded in Mannheim originally to build gas engines had also done rather well in the motor car business. By the turn of the century it had built 2000 cars and had a production capacity of 600 cars a year. In addition, it had sales agencies in several overseas countries. All this was sufficient to make the Benz company the world's leading motor manufacturer of the time. However, Benz himself was very conservatively minded, disinclined to think about designing for mass production and especially opposed to any association with motor sport, even though it was this that attracted the customers he needed. So the Benz designs rapidly became outdated as motor car development surged ahead, and sales began to slump. When Benz's sales director engaged another engineer to produce a more modern design, Benz was furious, and left his own company in 1903. Though tempted back briefly in 1905 to help the now ailing company get back on its feet, he left for good in 1906.

This left the old Benz company under the guidance of its chief engineer, Hans Nibel, who recognised that a move into motor racing would put the company back on equal terms with its arch-rival, Daimler. The comeback began in 1907, and by 1909 the company had developed the streamlined Blitzen-Benz ("Lightning Benz"), a 21.5-litre monster that trounced its opposition

on the race tracks and held the World Land Speed Record from 1909 until 1922. Its exploits increased public regard for the Benz company no end.

In the last years before war broke out in 1914, Benz introduced a wide range of road cars, which sold to an increasingly broad market. Though wartime saw the inevitable focus on trucks and aero-engines, Benz found the market slow to pick up when peace returned. Despite some fine engineering, Benz & Cie were finding the going hard by 1924, the year when their bankers suggested a merger with Daimler. A period of co-operation ensued, followed by a full merger in 1926. It was an act that saved both companies and founded one of the world's leading makers of motor vehicles – the Daimler-Benz Aktiengesellschaft, with headquarters in Stuttgart.

A change of focus

Even though some sort of shake-up within the Mercedes and Benz model ranges was inevitable once the two companies had merged, the strategy for the supercharged types had already been planned out. New supercharged models appeared at the top of the range, based on earlier Mercedes designs and still guided by Ferdinand Porsche, the man who had replaced Paul Daimler as the Daimler company's chief engineer in 1923. These new cars had six-cylinder engines.

This new product strategy certainly worked. The new supercharged models became image leaders for the recently merged company, appealing to the wealthy playboy type who simply sought performance as well as to the more conservative wealthy buyer who simply wanted the best of everything. Bodies by the world's leading makers began to appear on Mercedes-Benz chassis, and the cars became as fashionable on the road as they were successful on the race tracks. Paul Daimler's 24/100 chassis developed through the Model K to the Model S and SS, and from these would later be derived the formidable SSK and SSKL competition machines.

So by the end of the 1920s Mercedes-Benz was confident that it could aim for the very top of the market and earn prestige by designing a car for royalty and heads of state. Just four years after it had become a single company, it therefore introduced the supercharged 770 model,

better known as the Grosser Mercedes, which enabled it to compete on equal terms with the "old-money" prestige makers such as Rolls-Royce, Bentley, Bugatti and Duesenberg. This was the first of the supercharged eight-cylinder Mercedes though not the company's first eight-cylinder model. That it was otherwise quite disappointingly conservative in its engineering was of no concern to the company because it was of no concern to potential customers either. Prestige was the name of the game, and the Grosser Mercedes played it well. Open models soon became favourites as parade cars with the new German government after 1933, ensuring that the company's cars would be associated with the top strata in the minds of the German people.

In the meantime, the S, SS and their bred-for-racing derivatives had given way to a new approach. The cars of the 1930s no longer had to compete for prizes in concours d'élégance competitions and win races as well, because these tasks had been divided between two separate types. On the road, glamour and high performance were combined in a line which began with the 380 in 1933, and went on through the 500K of 1934 and the 540K of 1936. On the race tracks, the company now fielded world-class single-seaters, with the full support of the regime, which saw them as an important element in its programme to re-establish Germany as a world power of consequence.

By 1937, there was no doubt that Mercedes-Benz was pandering to German government requirements. It was providing them with cars that won international races – cars ultimately derived from the supercharging technology

A Benz saloon of the early 1920s, a worthy but pedestrian vehicle typical of the company's output of the time.

A Mercedes chassis plate of the 1920s, in this case indicating that the car to which it is attached is a 26/120 model.

The catalogue of the 1921 Berlin motor show, at which the unblown versions of the first Mercedes models to be supercharged were exhibited.

pioneered in the top-model road cars – and it was providing them with cars that added the right amount of theatre and impressiveness to their parades and major political events. It is almost certain that the 1938 and later 770 models, completely redesigned from the 1930 original, were intended primarily for German government use and were therefore designed to meet that customer's requirements. The cars were also offered to other customers, but it was probably a matter of indifference to Daimler-Benz whether they bought any or not; in practice, very few did.

But all good things come to an end. When war broke out in 1939, Daimler-Benz had just two supercharged models in production – the 540K and 770 – and it was of course working on some new designs for future introduction. But the market for such fabulously expensive pieces of machinery quickly disappeared, and the Daimler-Benz factories were directed to produce

war materiel of various kinds rather than non-essentials such as luxury cars. Development of new supercharged models was halted, and the last cars were probably built in 1943.

Once the war was over, Daimler-Benz had been bombed to ruins and had to re-start by making kitchen utensils. There was no market for the grand cars of earlier times, and such was anti-German feeling that the company had to feel its way very carefully back into the world car market in the late 1940s and 1950s. By then, fuel injection had taken over as the latest engine technology, and supercharging did not re-surface in Mercedes-Benz cars until 1995, when it was applied to some smaller engines in other-wise mundane saloons in order to improve performance and competitiveness.

In context

The glamorous supercharged Mercedes so dominated public perceptions of the marque in the 1930s that it is easy now to get the idea that the company only built supercharged models. Nothing could be further from the truth; as the foregoing makes clear, the supercharged cars were by this stage small-volume models at the very top of the maker's range. Below them were many relatively mundane family saloons that sold in far greater numbers and were the real fillers of the Daimler-Benz coffers.

However, the supercharged cars were enor-mously important in establishing public perceptions of the marque outside Germany. Once Daimler and Benz had merged, they embarked on a sales push abroad, using the glamorous supercharged models to reel in Hollywood celebrities and British aristocrats alike. This they were able to do because the supercharged cars had unique qualities that made them appeal to such customers, whose high public profile provided the Mercedes marque with free and very positive publicity. The more mundane cars may have been solidly engineered and dependable, but outside Germany they were competing with locally-made products and did not carve them-selves much of a niche in overseas markets. All this helps to explain why countries such as Britain and the USA today see Mercedes-Benz as a prestige marque, while to others – in Africa and the Middle East, for example – a Mercedes is primarily a reliable, long-lived but unglamorous taxi.

UK MODEL DESIGNATIONS

In the UK, a great deal of confusion has arisen from the names used for the supercharged models. The importers – sensibly, as far as potential buyers were concerned – gave them names that conformed to the RAC horsepower rating system which then governed the amount of annual road tax to be paid on a car. The problem arose because the horsepower ratings under the RAC system were not the same as those under the German fiscal horsepower system.

It was also German practice, for a time at least, to give the supercharged cars a designation made up of three numbers – the fiscal horsepower, the actual horsepower without the super-charger engaged, and the horsepower with the supercharger engaged. The British importers tried to make things simpler, by giving only the maximum figure with the supercharger engaged. It was indeed simpler at the time. The problem lies in matching UK model designations to their German equivalents.

So to avoid further confusion, these are the two sets of names:

UK model name	German model name
12/40	6/25
16/60	10/40
24/100	15/70/100
33/180	Model K
36/220	S
38/250	SS

After the arrival of the 380 models, the German type designations were also used in the UK.

SUPERCHARGED MERCEDES AS A PERCENTAGE OF TOTAL PRODUCTION

In some cases, the exact annual figures for supercharged models are in dispute. The figures given here must therefore be seen as very approximate, and are intended only to give an indication of numbers.
Figures for 1923-26 (before merger) are for Daimler only.

Year	Total supercharged	Total car production	Supercharged percentage of the total
1923	280 (est)	1020	27%
1924	280 (est)	333	21%
1925*	0	1406	0%
1926*	210	627 (before merger)	33.5%
1926	32	1886 (after merger)	1.7%
1927	446	7922	5.6%
1928	590	6963	11.8%
1929	339	8461	4%
1930	56	6130	0.9%
1931	52	3635	1.4%
1932	22	6057	0.4%
1933	101	8282	1.2%
1934	187	11,640	1.6%
1935	202	15,759	1.3%
1936	182	22,409	0.8%
1937	170	28,039	0.6%
1938	135	27,793	0.5%
1939	131	26,628	0.5%

* The 1925 and pre-merger figures for 1926 should probably be combined to give a more accurate total. The figures then become 210 supercharged cars out of a total production of 2033, making a more realistic 10.3%.

The cars now

It is astonishingly difficult to get at some of the truth that makes up the story of the supercharged cars. Inevitably, the cars created their own myths, and some of these have passed into legend, which can be hard to distinguish from fact without hard evidence. The hard evidence is not always easy to find: some of the documentary evidence, and a lot of the cars themselves, simply disappeared during the 1939-45 war. Some material may still exist but may be kept out of sight for commercial reasons: Daimler-Benz today is, after all, primarily a business.

Nevertheless, Daimler-Benz has certainly made a great deal of material available in public, and at its own archives and museum in Stuttgart. It has also made a great deal of information available on the world-wide web, but unfortunately its pronouncements over the years have sometimes been either delphic or downright contradictory. This has not helped the genuine seeker after truth, and of course well-intentioned enthusiasts have built their own theories on these "factory truths". It is necessary only to visit a few web sites purporting to have information about the supercharged cars to see what a mass of half-digested and contradictory information there is that masquerades as fact. There is, of course, nothing that Daimler-Benz could do about this even if it chose to.

One of the big problems that still exists more than 60 years after the last of the great supercharged Mercedes was built concerns build quantities. Jan Melin, who has spent many years researching the eight-cylinder cars, has shown that the "official" Mercedes-Benz production figures drawn up in 1940 were amended in the 1960s and 1970s, but has been unable to find out all the reasons why. Needless to say, the different versions of these production figures have all found their way into print, and various theories have been based upon them. It is not possible at the moment to disentangle the resulting mess, and it will not be possible until a definitive set of figures can be established. That

Hans Nibel, the former Benz Chief Engineer who took over from Ferdinand Porsche in 1929.

Ferdinand Porsche replaced Paul Daimler as Chief Engineer in 1923. He is seen here (second from right) in front of one of his later creations, the mid-engined Auto Union racing car of the 1930s, with driver Von Stuck (in white overalls).

may never happen.

Undeniably, though, the myths that have arisen around the supercharged cars have fuelled the ultra-high prices that abound in the collectors' market today. These cars are, quite rightly, treated like prized works of art and priced accordingly when they change hands. The absence of hard information in some cases simply adds to their appeal by allowing imagination and rumour to take hold. These are not cars for the average enthusiast, but what average enthusiast can be unaware of their huge importance in the history of motoring?

Key names

In the chapters that follow, the names of many key individuals in the Mercedes-Benz story will occur over and over again. To those unfamiliar with the story, this can only be confusing, and so it is worth some explanation here.

The man who was primarily responsible for developing the first supercharged engines of interest here was Paul Daimler. He was the son of Gottlieb Daimler, founder of the firm, and he became the company's chief engineer in 1907. By 1923, when he resigned from that post after a disagreement about policy with the Daimler board, he had firmly established the principles of supercharging that would remain in place at Stuttgart for the next two decades.

Paul Daimler was succeeded as chief engineer at Daimler by Ferdinand Porsche. Porsche would later become responsible (as a consultant engineer) for the basic design of the car that became the Volkswagen Beetle, and he would go on to found his own car company that focussed on sporting machinery. When he joined Daimler at the start of 1924 he was already recognised as a brilliant engineer, and it was under his leadership and at the request of the Daimler board that supercharging was applied to the top models in the Daimler range to produce chassis that were successful in sporting events.

However, the merger of Daimler and Benz created an intolerable situation in which Hans Nibel, the former Benz chief engineer, was obliged to work alongside Porsche. Porsche's notorious irascibility soon got the better of him, and he left in 1928 after falling out with the management. Nibel took over, and it was he who guided the supercharged cars into the new era of the 1930s, when the emphasis switched from sporting ability to glamour. Not that Nibel himself would have pushed things in this direction, for he had been a strong supporter of motor sport while at Benz; it was changing times that dictated the change of direction. However, Nibel died young in 1934.

His successor was Hans Gustav Röhr, the former chief engineer at Adler. Röhr had a difficult time at Stuttgart, for a variety of reasons, and also died young, in 1937. Increasingly prominent since Nibel's time had been Fritz Nallinger, his deputy who retained that post under Röhr but became the driving force behind new designs for the later 1930s. It was Nallinger who led Stuttgart's engineering teams when war broke out in 1939, and in May 1948 he again took over as engineering chief of the passenger car division.

Key places

While the big names came, quarrelled, and went, the factories at which the two formerly rival companies built their cars remained the same.

As far as the story of the supercharged models were concerned, there were just two factories that mattered. One was at Untertürkheim, to the east of Stuttgart. The other was at Sindelfingen, a little over 16 miles away to the south-west of the city. Both had formerly been Daimler plants. (A third factory that occasionally enters the story is the one at Mannheim, just over 80 miles to the north-west of Stuttgart and formerly a Benz plant.)

The design and development of the supercharged cars was carried out at Untertürkheim, and the engines and chassis were also assembled here. However, body construction was carried out at Sindelfingen, and it was normal practice for bodies built there to be transported by road to Untertürkheim, where they would be fitted to chassis. This was the case for most of the supercharged cars built in the 1920s.

However, if this system worked well for cars that were produced in volume and therefore had standardised dimensions, it was less well suited to custom-made cars. Although Daimler-Benz was happy to supply its grander chassis (which by this stage included the supercharged types) to outside coachbuilders if that was what the customer wanted, it was also determined to maximise profits by taking as much as possible of the coachbuilding work in-house. The problem was that the wealthy buyers of the company's top models were not used to standardised designs, and insisted on stamping their own individuality on the cars they bought. Daimler-Benz bent over backwards to be accommodating, but it must have been difficult (and costly) to incorporate special design features into what were otherwise high-quality volume-produced bodies.

So in the early 1930s a new department was established at Sindelfingen. This was called the "Sonderwagen" (Special Car) section, and it became responsible not only for constructing the small-volume bodies for the most expensive cars but also for designing them. As these

An early example of Ferdinand Porsche's ingenuity was the Lohner-Porsche, in which a petrol engine drove a dynamo which powered electric motors on all four wheels – a sort of hybrid. Enveloped in his splendid fur motoring coat is Alfred (later Lord) Harmsworth, a celebrated pioneer motorist.

bodies were invariably hand-built, and as there was so much room for individual variation, the traditional build process was reversed. Chassis completed at Untertürkheim were transported to the Sonderwagen section in Sindelfingen where the bodies could be built directly on to the chassis if need be. The Sonderwagen section also took on responsibility for road-testing the finished products.

Devastation and despair: part of the Untertürkheim works in 1945.

A NOTE ABOUT CHASSIS NUMBERS

It is not at all uncommon to find the chassis number of a supercharged Mercedes-Benz misquoted, even by otherwise knowledgeable sources such as auction houses. The main reason for this seems to be the plethora of different numbers usually found on a car's identification plate, normally positioned on the engine side of the bulkhead. A secondary reason is that, without a knowledge of the German language, the meaning of these numbers is simply lost to most observers.

The Daimler-Benz identification plates used after the amalgamation of Daimler and Benz in 1926 may contain anywhere between four and nine panels, into which numbers were stamped. Sometimes, some of these panels were left blank. In addition, many 1930s cars have a separate plate carrying the "Auftrags-Nummer" (see below), even though there is also a space for that number on the main plate. On at least some cars built in 1943, the identification plate is accompanied by two separate smaller plates, one with the chassis number and the other with the (different) engine number.

In alphabetical order, then, these are the panels that may be found on a Daimler-Benz car identification plate.

1920S PLATES

Best no Mot.	Bestellungsnummer, Motor: Order number for the engine
Best no Wag.	Bestellungsnummer, Wagen: Order number for the chassis
Com no.	Commission number; orders for all types of Daimler-Benz vehicles, including lorries and buses as well as the whole car range, seem to have been recorded centrally as they were received at Stuttgart.
Hubraum ccm.	Cylinder capacity in cubic centimetres
Leistung PS.	Power output, in PS (Pferdestärke). Both the unsupercharged and supercharged figures are shown, eg 170/220.
Motor no.	Engine number
Wagen no.	Chassis number
Wag Gew kg.	Wagengewicht, kg: Car weight in kg

1930S PLATES

Auftrags-Nr.	Commission Number or Order Number; see Commission Number in the 1920s list
Baujahr.	Year of build (this is always the calendar year).
Eigengewicht kg.	Unladen weight, in kilogrammes.
Fabrik-Nr.	Literally, Factory Number. It is not clear what this relates to, and it is found only on cars from the later 1930s.
Hubraum ccm.	Cylinder capacity, in cubic centimetres. This is normally given as the familiar "engineering" figure, but may sometimes appear as the "taxable" calculation; thus a 5401cc engine may appear as a 5363cc engine, and so on.
Leistung PS.	Power output, in PS (Pferdestärke). Both the unsupercharged and supercharged figures are shown, eg 115/180.
Nutzlast .... kg.	Payload in kilogrammes. This only appears on plates in the late 1930s, when it appears that cars and light commercial vehicles shared a common identification plate. It is normally left blank on the cars.
Wagen-u.Motor-Nr.	Car and engine number. These were normally the same on the eight-cylinder cars. Some numbers are preceded by a U, which probably stands for Untertürkheim, the plant where the chassis were built. This number (less the U) is the chassis number.
Zulass. Achsdruck in kg.	Permissible axle loading, in kilogrammes. This is only found on the later plates, common to light commercials. The relevant figures are nevertheless often stamped in on car plates as well, subdivided as follows:
	Vorn. Front (ie Front Axle)
	Hinten. Rear (ie Rear Axle).
	Zulass.Gesamtgewicht kg. Permissible total weight in kilogrammes. Once again, this is only found on the later plates, shared with light commercials. On cars it is nevertheless sometimes stamped with the relevant figure.

Chapter Two

EARLY DAYS

The four-cylinder Daimler engines

Exactly when the Technical Director of the Daimler Motoren Gesellschaft first considered applying supercharging to a car engine is now impossible to say. It is clear, though, that the first recorded experiments with such an engine took place around mid-September 1919, when Paul Daimler and his engineers fitted a Roots-type blower to the four-cylinder engine intended for production in the Mercedes 10/30 car and anchored it to a test-bed.

The idea of supercharging engines had been around at the Stuttgart-Untertürkheim works for some years. The kick-start had come from the aircraft side of the business. By 1916, spotter aircraft were in quite regular use for directing artillery fire and for reconnaissance purposes over the trenches in France and Belgium, and unsurprisingly the reaction of the opposing forces was to attempt to bring them down with anti-aircraft fire. As anti-aircraft defences improved, and more and more aircraft were lost, it became clear that there was a need to fly at higher altitudes, beyond the reach of the guns.

However, there were limits to what could be achieved with existing aero engines. At higher altitudes, the air on which a piston engine depends is thinner, and the density of the air-fuel mixture drawn into the cylinders reduces, thus reducing the power output of the engine. This placed a limit on the height at which aero engines could perform reliably. In order to get the required volume of air into the cylinders, it was obvious that some kind of forced induction system was needed, artificially squeezing more air into the space available in order to compensate for its reduced density.

The Daimler company were certainly not the only German engine manufacturers to recognise this. There was no organised state oversight of aero engine development at the time, and so individual manufacturers took it upon themselves to come up with the solution. What was needed was some kind of air pump, and of course such things had been around for many years in industry, which needed air pumps for applications such as blast furnaces and mine ventilation. Paul Daimler chose to work with the twin-rotor type of air pump that had been patented in America in 1860 by the brothers Philander and Francis Roots.

Work on a supercharged aero engine began some time in 1916, based on the 21.72-litre Daimler DIVa engine that was used in a variety of bombers as well as in reconnaissance aircraft. A Roots-type blower was fitted to the front of the engine, driven by a gear on the flywheel. There were problems, though. The carburettor was located behind the engine, and was fed with air through a channel under the crankcase that also functioned as an oil cooler. When compressed, air increases in temperature, and the hotter air fed to the carburettor through the blower failed to cool the engine oil sufficiently. So a second oil pump and oil cooler had to be added.

Although the supercharged Mercedes aero engine had reached an advanced stage of development by early 1918, it did not enter production in time to be used operationally before the war ended that autumn. In the meantime, however, the Daimler engineers had recognised the advantages of forced induction for other applications. Rather than compensating for the lower density of air at high altitudes, it could be used to improve the efficiency of an engine working at sea level or below it. So one offshoot of the supercharged aero engine work had been a project to develop an engine for submarines, based on an aero engine but with as many as four Roots-type superchargers connected in series to double the engine's output. From the thinking that had led to this, it was only a small step to consider supercharging for a motor car engine as well.

Throughout the war, Daimler had built motor ambulances for the German military, and among the engines in these had been the 2.6-litre four-cylinder sleeve-valve type first introduced in the 10/30 car of 1912. The figures in that designation stood for 10 fiscal horsepower and 30PS actual engine output, and Mercedes continued to use this naming system for many years. As the smallest and least powerful of the company's car engines in production in 1919, it was arguably the one which would benefit most from forced induction. So this was the engine that was chosen for the first experiments that autumn.

Right from the start, the supercharger installation differed from that employed for the aero engines. Instead of being permanently engaged, the twin-rotor Roots blower was engaged only when maximum performance was required. This certainly reduced the stresses on the engine, and that may have been the main reason why this type of installation was chosen. So there was a multi-disc clutch and a set of spur gears, and the clutch brought the blower into operation only when the accelerator was fully depressed. The action would have been rather like the kickdown on a modern car with automatic transmission.

In early October 1919, after basic tests had been carried out on the bench, the experimental 10/30 engine was fitted into a chassis. Beginning on 17 October, the modified 10/30 was put through a 2000km endurance test over a period of six weeks. We know that the team of drivers included Jakob Krauss, Karl Schopper and Walter Schwerdtfeger. Although different versions of the story exist, it then appears that some further supercharger tests were carried out with the larger 16/45 model. The engine in this car was in effect a big-bore version of the 10/30 four-cylinder, again using the Knight sleeve-valve design and this time displacing 4080cc.

All these tests highlighted some problems. Most significant of these was that the higher temperatures generated within the blown engine overheated the oil. It cooked and solidified around the exhaust ports, so the valve sleeves overheated, and this led to breakage of the eccentric drives. It was clear that the sleeve-valve engine was unsuited to supercharging.

Two new engines

These experiments seem to have hammered a final nail into the coffin of Mercedes' involvement with Knight sleeve-valve engines. For the next generation of new engines, Paul Daimler decided to go with the basic architecture that had proved so successful in the engines of the 1914 Grand Prix cars. Though these were now several years old, their technology had been far ahead of its time and the cars themselves would remain competitive (mainly in private hands) until well into the 1920s.

The Mercedes product plan called for two new models which were to be ready for introduction in 1921. They were to replace the existing 8/22 model and were to split its market

This is said to be the very first supercharged Daimler car engine, essentially a modified 10/30 Knight sleeve-valve type. Though promising, it showed that the Knight design was not suited to supercharging.

The 6/25 chassis is seen here clothed in a fairly typical open touring body of the early 1920s.

two ways: one was to be a smaller car with a lower 6 fiscal horsepower rating and the other a larger car with a higher 10 fiscal horsepower rating. For both of these, Daimler designed four-cylinder engines with the Grand Prix-style overhead camshaft layout. The new 10hp engine was a 2.6-litre which actually shared its bore and stroke dimensions with the old 10/30 sleeve-valve engine although in a very different design of cylinder block. Curiously, perhaps, neither the bore nor the stroke of the 1568cc 6hp engine was shared with the larger power unit, even though their overall architecture was the same.

The two new models were announced as the 6/20 and 10/35 at the Berlin Automobile Exhibition that opened on 23 September 1921. But by this stage, Daimler already had plans to develop supercharged versions for later introduction. First, he needed to prove that supercharged car engines not only worked but were also reliable, and this he intended to do through the Daimler factory's racing programme.

With sleeve-valve designs now off the agenda, Paul Daimler turned to overhead-camshaft designs at the start of the 1920s. These were the engines that would later be supercharged – but they would be sold in unblown form for two years first. This is the inlet side of the 1568cc engine that powered the 6/20 (later 6/25) model, with the top covers removed to expose the valve gear.

This is the exhaust side of the 2.6-litre engine from the 10/35 model, introduced alongside the 6/20. The two engines shared major design features, although it is clear from these pictures that their cooling fans were differently mounted.

The 10/35 chassis was physically larger than the 6/25 type, and lent itself better to large, formal bodies. This was an enclosed-drive limousine from 1923.

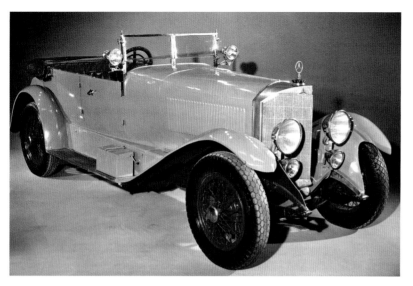

The 28/95 was Daimler's grand luxury car at the start of the 1920s, and was a revived pre-war design with a 7.3-ltre six-cylinder engine..

The blown 28/95 and 1922 Targa Florio cars

For several years after the end of the Great War, German participation in international motor sport was banned, but gradually some countries relented and by 1922 it was clear that a return to international racing was feasible. In fact, Mercedes had started to develop the cars for such a programme during 1921, in anticipation of a thaw in international relations. That year, Paul Daimler had got together with works driver Max Sailer whose day job was in the engineering department at Untertürkheim to produce a potential race-winner from the existing Mercedes 28/95 model.

The 28/95 was the Grand Mercedes of the time. Introduced in 1914, it had gone out of production in 1915 but had been re-introduced

in 1920. Its engine was a big six-cylinder of 7.3 litres with the overhead camshaft layout of the Grand Prix cars, and by spring 1921 Daimler and Sailer had a lowered, short-chassis car ready for action. On 22 May, Otto Salzer took the car to Koenigsaal and made FTD on his first time out, breaking the record as well with a speed of 55.8mph over the 3.5 miles of the track. Just a week later, Sailer drove the car in the Targa Florio, a 432km (268-mile) event over rough roads in the Madonian Mountains of Sicily. Though finishing second overall behind a 4.5-litre Fiat driven by Count Giulio Masetti, Sailer set the fastest lap time and returned home with the Coppa Florio awarded for the fastest production car. Mercedes had returned to racing.

For 1922, the plan was to ram that point home, and the Mercedes team took no chances. They entered no fewer than six cars in the 1922 Targa Florio, which opened on 2 April. Two were 1914 Grand Prix cars driven by Christian Lautenschlager and Otto Salzer, the latter with August Grupp as his co-driver, while Christian Werner the foreman of the test department at Untertürkheim who had shown promise as a racing driver was entered in a racing 28/95. But the other three cars were of particular interest, for all were supercharged.

The largest of those cars was another 28/95, further developed from the previous year's short-chassis racer and of course now with the additional benefit of a blower. Records show that it had a twin-rotor Roots-type supercharger, built under British licence from Godfrey and Partners and driven from the crankshaft. The supercharger added about 30PS to the car's claimed 95PS and helped raise its maximum speed from 80mph to almost 90mph.

The other two cars were very special indeed, and were derivatives of the new 6/25 that had been announced at the 1921 Berlin Exhibition. These two racers had a redeveloped suspension,

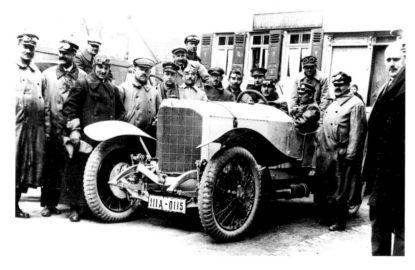

This photograph by Otto Schilling from the Daimler-Benz archives is said to show Max Sailer with his supercharged 28/95 PS before the 1922 Targa Florio. The photograph was clearly taken in Germany, and gathered round the car are a group of Daimler engineers. From the left, they are Dürrwächter, Paul Daimler, Scheib, Merkle, Heeß, Schopper, Günther, Renz, Schwerdtfeger (with glasses), Scheerer, Bauer, Sailer (at the wheel), Rieger, Krauss and Linck.

with quarter-elliptic springs at the rear instead of the conventional semi-elliptics used on the road cars. They were light, at just 1250kg (2756lb), and were capable of 135km/h (84mph).

To get their engines into the 1.5-litre capacity voiturette class, Paul Daimler had reduced the bore from 68mm to 65mm and lengthened the stroke from 108mm to 113mm, arriving just under the limit at 1499cc. He had then added a new cylinder head with twin overhead camshafts that operated four valves per cylinder to improve the engine's breathing. The camshafts were driven from the crankshaft by a vertical shaft at the rear which also drove a cross-shaft for the magneto and water pump. The crankshaft ran in white metal bearings, and at its front end were the gears for the super-charger drive. The supercharger itself was mounted on an extension piece at the front of the crankcase, and was engaged by means of a multi-disc clutch. When engaged, it ran at 2.5 times engine speed.

Arguably, these M 65134 engines were the first car engines ever designed (or, more accu-rately, re-designed) from the outset to take a supercharger. At 4000rpm, they delivered 40PS without the blower engaged, or 65PS with it working, and these figures gave them their rating as 6/40/65 models. Particularly notable was the engine's high 4500rpm rev limit. There was a dual-cone clutch, the two leather-faced cones acting in opposite directions, and the gearbox was remotely mounted and driven through a short shaft.

The six Mercedes "works" cars were all driven

from Stuttgart down to Sicily, a journey of some 2000km (1200 miles) which included crossing the Alps. Preparation was thorough, and some 20 members of the Mercedes team were in Sicily a week in advance of the race to reconnoitre the course. Yet ironically, the Mercedes that won the event was not one of the works cars. It was, instead, a 1914 Grand Prix car entered privately by Count Giulio Masetti. Masetti later said that

Hoping to take the 1922 Targa Florio by storm, this is the Daimler contingent. From left to right are the cars of Scheef, Minoia, Lautenschlager, Sailer, Werner and Salzer.

The special supercharged 1.5-litre engine of the 1922 Targa Florio racers is seen here from the inlet side. The supercharger is clearly visible, mounted at the front of the engine, and alongside the sump is the over-centre spring arrangement with its actuating rod. A pipe runs back from the blower to the carburettor mounted below the inlet manifold pipes.

This supercharged 1.5-litre car took third place in the voiturette class of the Targa Florio in April 1922. It was crewed by Paul Scheef and Jakob Krauss, who are seen here in the car.

he had painted the car red to help him; the race was run on public roads and it seems that the public were wont to hinder the progress of cars which were not in the Italian national racing colour!

Nevertheless, the other results clearly demonstrated that the new supercharging technology was reliable. Only Fernando Minoia, driving one of the 1.5-litre cars, failed to finish. The second 1.5-litre, driven by Paul Scheef, came third in its class and 20th overall. Max Sailer's supercharged 28/95 won the over 4.5-litre class and finished in sixth place overall, while Christian Werner came eighth in the unsupercharged 28/95. Of the works-entered 1914 Grand Prix cars, Lautenschlager came 10th overall and Salzer 13th.

It appears that a total of 22 racing 1.5-litre engines were built in 1922, and that one of these was built up for potential use in a power boat. Later that year, one of the 1.5-litre cars was used for a series of aerodynamic experiments, and was rebodied twice with special aerodynamic coachwork. However, these experiments were concerned more with aerodynamics than with supercharging, and need no discussion here. Much more important was that the success of the 1.5-litre Targa Florio cars led directly to a production model. As for the original racers, the car driven by Paul Scheef still survives in private ownership, and was completely restored at the Mercedes-Benz Classic Center in Stuttgart between 1997 and 2002.

In 1928, several years after that first appearance of supercharged Mercedes in international competition, British racing driver Raymond

Mays brought a former "works" supercharged 1.5-litre car into the UK. According to a report in *Light Car* for 22 February 1929, it was one of four "works" cars which had been successful in German hill-climb events. Mays had bought it with the intention of using it in competition. He had removed the original racing body and had ordered a two-seater open touring body from Corsica which increased the weight and thus reduced the top speed from a claimed 120mph to something over 90mph. The RAC rating was 10.4hp.

Even so, it was still a very fast car, with a high rev limit of 6500rpm. "The sense of power provided when one jumps on the accelerator is quite remarkable", noted *Light Car*, "the supercharger emitting a low droning note which mounts up to a very high-pitched whine as the revs build up."

A supercharged 2-litre racer

The 28/95 and 1.5-litre Targa Florio cars were only the start of the Mercedes works racing programme. During 1922, the Automobile Club de France announced that its 1923 Grand Prix would be run to a 2-litre formula, and Mercedes determined to take part in it. With a 2-litre car, they would also be able to enter the Indianapolis 500 race in the USA, which was another event that attracted international interest and would therefore maximise the publicity benefit. An Indianapolis entry would also help to support a planned Mercedes sales drive in the USA.

So Paul Daimler set to work on a racing engine which, in common with his work for production cars, had four cylinders and a supercharger. To give better breathing, it also had twin overhead camshafts operating four valves per cylinder, following success with such a design on the 1914 Mercedes Grand Prix cars. A roller-bearing crankshaft made its contribution to the rev limit of 4800rpm, and an oil cooler kept working temperatures under control at sustained high engine speeds. Daimler's principal collaborator on the new engine and the car it was to power was a Mercedes engineer named Gros, and one of the unusual steps they took was to bolt the engines directly to the chassis in order to improve rigidity without incurring a weight penalty.

Four cars, known as Type 122 models, were prepared for the Indianapolis 500 in April 1923.

Four Type 122 racers were prepared for the Indianapolis 500 in 1923, with 2-litre supercharged engines developed from those in the previous year's 1.5-litre racers.

The cars had two-seater bodies because Mercedes chose to provide a riding mechanic, even though the Indianapolis regulations no longer required one. One car was designated as a spare, and the others were allocated to the works drivers Christian Lautenschlager, Max Sailer and Hans Werner. During practice, the cars performed reasonably well but not spectacularly: Sailer set the fastest lap with a speed of 100mph, but qualified in only 20th place after hitting a wall during a rainstorm, injuring his wrist and seriously injuring his mechanic Rieger. Lautenschlager qualifed 17th and Werner 15th.

Sailer co-opted his nephew Karl as riding mechanic, and the two raced with the spare car. Their race was not without incident: the car caught fire in the pits while refuelling and, as *Motor Age* magazine memorably put it, "the Mercedes sounded like a fire department truck clanging down the line and made it more real by furnishing the fire and the explosion." Nevertheless the Sailer car finished in 8th place. Lautenschlager crashed at the South Turn on the 14th lap, after engaging his supercharger too soon; his riding mechanic Jakob Krauss broke a leg in the accident. Werner duelled for several laps with the HCS of eventual winner Tommy Milton until overcome by exhaustion; his Type 122 Mercedes came home in 11th place.

As for the cars, there are various stories of their subsequent history. One version has it that three returned to Stuttgart and that just one of the crashed cars remained in the USA. Daimler-Benz insists that the former Indianapolis cars were entered in several hill-climb events in later years, driven by Otto Salzer and Otto Merz. Another story claims that only the Werner car returned to Germany, and that US car maker Louis Chevrolet bought the other three. There certainly seem to be traces of them in the USA: one became the Schmidt Special that raced unsuccessfully at Indianapolis in 1924. By 1930, all three cars had been modified for US track racing events or for stunt driving at travelling fairs. The car that Lautenschlager had driven was restored in the 1970s, the Sailer race car existed in California in the early 1990s, but the car that Sailer crashed in practice at the 1923 Indianapolis had been lost.

As for the Werner car, it was modified and used in practice for an entry in the Italian Grand Prix at Monza that autumn. However, a combination of politics and the gloomy economic prospect persuaded the Mercedes Board to cancel their entry. Perhaps the arrival of Ferdinand Porsche as Chief Engineer in June also had something to do with it. As Chapter 3 explains, he had other ideas for racing engines.

The first production Kompressor cars

Meanwhile, things were not going very well behind the scenes at Daimler, and during 1922 the board came into conflict with its Technical Director over new product designs. What the board wanted was volume-selling products, but instead Paul Daimler had begun to focus his energies on a flagship for the marque, a new Grosser Mercedes that would presumably have replaced the resurrected 28/95. His plan was to develop Germany's first eight-cylinder engine for it.

By the end of the year, the conflict had resolved itself. Paul Daimler resigned and left Untertürkheim on the last day of 1922. Not long afterwards, it became clear that he had accepted a post with rival manufacturer Horch, for whom he duly designed his eight-cylinder engine. Meanwhile, seeking his replacement, the Daimler board approached the man who had recently walked out of the Chief Design Engineer post at Austro-Daimler after clashing with the management. Ironically, Dr Ferdinand Porsche had actually replaced Paul Daimler in that post in 1905, and now he replaced him a second time. In June 1923, he became Technical Director of Daimler.

Meanwhile, the models introduced at the 1921 Berlin Exhibition had been uprated to 6/25 and 10/40 types, and their supercharged derivatives had gone into production. It was probably March or April 1923 when the first examples of the new cars reached Mercedes showrooms, and they may actually have replaced the unsupercharged 6/25 and 10/40 altogether. By 1924, they were known as the 6/25/38 and 10/40/65 models, and it would seem logical that they took these names from the start. The designations contained three pieces of information: first, the fiscal horsepower rating; second, the maximum power without the supercharger; and

third, the maximum power with the super-charger in use.

In Britain, there was clearly still some sensitivity attached to all things German in the aftermath of the Great War. When *The Motor* borrowed a 10/40 chassis from British Mercedes Ltd, the importer based in London's Long Acre, it almost apologised for bringing up the subject. "Even allowing for racial and national feeling," read the introduction to an article called Supercharging the Mixture in the issue dated 17 April 1923, "some motorists in this country take an interest in Mercedes productions". The magazine was most impressed to learn that the chassis (for it was no more than that) fitted with a rough test body was capable of more than 70mph.

The chances are that the 70mph figure was drawn from a test by rival magazine *The Autocar*, which reported on the same chassis in its issue of dated 13 April. With two people aboard, *The Autocar* had done the flying mile at the Brooklands track at 73.77mph, "a figure which is only to be attained by sporting cars of this engine capacity, apart from purely racing cars". With four up, the car had reached a maximum of 60mph without the supercharger engaged but had run the flying mile at 66.42mph, which was undoubtedly a striking performance.

"On the road, it is sufficient to say that in normal running, and without the supercharger in operation, it is a good example of all that a docile, quiet and smoothly operating car should be... (but)... to depress the accelerator to its fullest extent is to change the character of the car completely. From a normal docile car it becomes a greyhound. There is a momentary hesitation as the super-charger takes up its work, and the mixture varies slightly; and then with a pronounced hissing sound, due to the high velocity of the air and the action of the blower, the car leaps forward with almost violent acceleration... Of the efficiency of the super-charger... there can be no possible doubt."

The Autocar also explained how the supercharger could most effectively be used in everyday motoring. "It is, for example, possible on a good road to use the super-charger momentarily to run up to a high speed, when the car may be kept at that speed merely on the ordinary induction system. By this means it is possible to maintain a very high average

The 1.5-litre engine of the 6/40/65 Sport was derived from the M65134 type used in the 1922 Targa Florio racers. It had twin overhead camshafts and four valves per cylinder, plus, of course, a front-mounted supercharger.

without at any time reaching the maximum speed of which the car is capable."

Noting that the chassis was expensive at £1100 (in 1923 a Bentley 3-litre chassis cost £895), *The Autocar* added that a smaller and cheaper supercharged 6/25 model was expected soon. As soon as British Mercedes Ltd took delivery of one, the magazine eagerly borrowed it and took it to the Brooklands track for performance testing. Once again, it was a bare chassis with a "rough test body". The test was published in the issue dated 22 June 1923, and maximum speed without the blower engaged was just over 60mph, but with the blower the magazine saw a best of just under 70mph.

On top gear, the car took 15 seconds to get from 10mph to 30mph, at which speed the blower was not engaged. This was good... but not the best of the cars in its class. However, using the lower gears to get the engine revs up and so engage the blower, the testers were somewhat astonished to find that the 10-30mph time had dropped to just 5 seconds. "It is difficult to convey in words the sensation given by this violent acceleration," they reported, and so they carried out the same test again for confirmation. Their conclusion was that "the figures for the hill-climb and acceleration are considerably better than those of much more powerful and much larger vehicles."

Under the RAC taxation system used in Britain, the 6/25 rated as an 11.5hp car, while the 10/40 was a 15.8hp. So for British buyers the cars were renamed 12/40 and 16/60, the second figure in each case representing the engine output with the blower engaged. But very few seem to have been imported. Cost was one

issue; an uneasy feeling about buying German products so soon after the war may have been another; but the major factor was that supplies dried up when Mercedes stopped making them during 1924.

With Paul Daimler out of the way, the Daimler board presumably decided that enough was enough. Supercharging added to the cost of the everyday Mercedes chassis, and this was not a time when the average car buyer could afford such a luxury, particularly in a Germany where inflation was rampant. So production of the 6/25/38 and 10/40/65 models was halted after about a year.

Even so, the Daimler board did approve for sale during 1924 a new supercharged model that was deliberately aimed at the wealthy sporting motorist. The introduction of the short-chassis 6/40/65 Sport suggested that if the board believed supercharging was unnecessary on everyday road cars, it also believed that supercharged engines could have a place in out-and-out sporting models.

The 6/40/65 Sport was essentially a production version of the 1922 1.5-litre Targa Florio cars. Although it was a 6hp car, its power outputs of 40PS unblown and 65PS with supercharger engaged were the same as could be had from the much larger 2.6-litre supercharged engine in the 10/40/65 models. With a shortened chassis to save weight, room for only two seats, semi-elliptic springs instead of the cantilever type on touring models, and four-wheel brakes, the 6/40/65 Sport was a very special and very advanced model indeed, though only small numbers can have been built before Daimler ended production of the Paul

This is a 10/40/65 Limousine model with division, dating presumably from 1924. The chassis is the 3365mm long-wheelbase type. Of interest are the exhaust pipes emerging through the side of the bonnet: this was not a stylist's caprice, but an engineering necessity to reduce underbonnet temperatures on the supercharged cars.

Both these pictures are claimed to show 10/40/65 sports two-seaters, but the ultra-short wheelbase suggest that they are actually 6/40/65 models.

Daimler supercharged cars.

Only about 360 of the 6/25/38 1.6-litre and 200 of the 10/40/65 2.6-litre cars are thought to have been made in 1923-24; as is the case with most early production figures, the exact totals are in doubt. Even the designation of the smaller car is in some doubt, and is often quoted as 6/25/40. Some authorities have hinted that further development produced an extra 2PS at the top end for the later cars, but there is no consensus about this. The 2.6-litre car seems to have disappeared by the end of 1924, although the smaller-engined model remained available into 1925.

Mercedes offered a variety of bodies for these cars. The 6/25/40 chassis was considerably smaller than the 10/40/65, with a wheelbase of 2790mm (109.8in), but bodies ranged from open four-seater Sport Phaeton types through to formal Coupé de Ville and even Limousine types. The 10/40's longer wheelbase of 3050mm or optionally 3365mm (120in or 132.4in) was much better suited to formal enclosed coachwork, but its 110km/h (68mph) top speed potential inevitably tempted some owners to order rakish open sporting bodies, sometimes from coachbuilders such as Papler in Cologne rather than from Untertürkheim's own workshops. As the example of the British imports makes clear, bare chassis were available for both 6/25 and 10/40 types.

Porsche's Targa Florio cars

Ferdinand Porsche had his own ambitions to design a supercharged racing car for Daimler, but there was not enough time to fulfil that ambition before the start of the 1924 racing season. As the management wanted another

One of the 1924 Targa Florio cars survives in the Daimler-Benz Museum. This picture shows that the spare wheel arrangements in the tail were quite different from those on the Indianapolis cars.

entry in the Targa Florio, which was to be run in April, Porsche reworked Paul Daimler's four-cylinder Indianapolis car. He modified the cylinder head and valve gear, and added mercury-filled exhaust valves for better cooling. With the blower engaged, the updated M 7294 engine was good for 150bhp at 4800rpm. The modified cars were known as PP types, and their first public appearance was at the 1924 Solitude Grand Prix near Stuttgart, when Otto Salzer drove one to victory and broke the lap record at 59.7mph.

Three cars were then entered for the Targa Florio. The drivers were Christian Lautenschlager, Alfred Neubauer and Hans Werner and, drawing on Count Giulio Masetti's experience in the 1922 event, the cars were painted red instead of the white that was the German international racing colour, in order to avoid delaying tactics from patriotic spectators. Werner's first place in car number 10 was a major event for the German public. He was the first non-Italian to win the Sicilian race since 1920, but perhaps of greater importance was that his triumph symbolised new hope on the international stage for a Germany so thoroughly crushed by the Great War and by the Treaty of Versailles which had followed it.

There were other triumphs during 1924 for the PP cars, which are often remembered these days as the Targa Florio types. Neubauer and Werner triumphed on the Semmering Pass hill-climb, and Otto Merz won the hill-climb at the Klausen Pass. The cars made a major contribu-

tion to Mercedes' impressive total of 98 victories in the 1½-litre and 2-litre classes during 1924, the others of course being achieved by the supercharged 1½-litre racers.

In this picture taken before the 1924 Targa Florio, driver Alfred Neubauer and riding mechanic Ernst Hemminger pose in one of the 2-litre PP racers used in the event. Neubauer would later become the legendary manager of the Silver Arrows racing team. Note that the bonnet panel differs from that on the Indianapolis car, and from the surviving Targa Florio car: the top panel finishes above the exhaust headers and not level with them. The unmatched front tyres are noticeable.

SPECIFICATIONS: SUPERCHARGED ROAD CARS

6/20PS (1921-23), 6/25PS AND 6/25/38PS (1924)

Engine:
1568cc 4-cylinder with
68mm bore and 108mm stroke
Overhead valves and overhead
camshaft
Compression ratio not known
Single Mercedes-Benz carburettor
Roots-type supercharger driven by
gear from crankshaft
20PS at 2800rpm (later 25PS)
38PS at 3200rpm with blower
engaged (6/25/38 only)
Torque not known

Gearbox:
Four-speed. Ratios not known.

Axle ratios:
Not known.

Chassis:
Channel-section steel
Wheelbase 2790mm
Track 1150mm

Weights and measures:
Overall dimensions
4050 x 1550 x 1550mm
Weight 1120kg with touring body
Maximum speed 100km/h (62mph)

6/40/65PS SPORT (1924)

Engine:
1499cc 4-cylinder with
65mm bore and 113mm stroke
Overhead valves and overhead
camshaft
Compression ratio not known
Single Mercedes-Benz carburettor
Roots-type supercharger driven by
gear from crankshaft
40PS
65PS with blower engaged
Torque not known

Gearbox:
Four-speed. Ratios not known

Axle ratios:
Not known.

Chassis:
Channel-section steel
Wheelbase 2650mm
Track 1320mm

Weights and measures:
Overall dimensions
4050 x 1550 x 1550mm
Weight 1050kg (estimated)
Maximum speed 120km/h (75mph)

10/40PS (1921-1924) AND 10/40/65PS (1924)

Engine:
2614cc 4-cylinder with
80mm bore and 130mm stroke
Overhead valves and overhead
camshaft
Compression ratio not known
Single Mercedes-Benz carburettor
Roots-type supercharger driven by
gear from crankshaft
40PS at 2400rpm
65PS at 2800rpm with blower
engaged (10/40/65 only)

Gearbox:
Four-speed. Ratios
4.25:1, 2.45:1, 1.50:1, 1.00:1

Axle ratios:
4.00:1, 4.20:1 or 4.30:1

Chassis:
Channel-section steel
Wheelbase 3050mm or 3365mm
Track 1340mm (front);
1300mm (rear)

Weights and measures:
Overall dimensions
4350 x 1700 x 2020mm
Weight 2150kg
(maximum permissible)
Maximum speed 110km/h (68mph)

KOMPRESSORS IN CONTEXT

The supercharged or Kompressor
models became an important part
of Mercedes car production in the
years leading up to the merger
with Benz in 1926. In these tables,
the Kompressor models are shown
in **bold.**

1923
6/25/38, 1568cc 4-cylinder
10/40/65, 2614cc 4-cylinder
16/45, 4080cc 4-cylinder
      Knight sleeve-valve
28/95, 7280cc 6-cylinder

1924
6/25/38, 1568cc 4-cylinder
6/40/65 Sport, 1499cc 4-cylinder
10/40/65, 2614cc 4-cylinder
15/70/100, 3920cc 6-cylinder
24/100/160, 6240cc 6-cylinder
28/95, 7280cc 6-cylinder

SPECIFICATIONS: SUPERCHARGED RACERS

6/40/65 1.5-LITRE CARS (1922)

Engine:
Type M 65134
1499cc 4-cylinder with 65mm bore and 113mm stroke
Single overhead camshaft
Compression ratio not known
Single Mercedes-Benz carburettor
Roots-type supercharger driven by gear from crankshaft
40PS at 4000rpm
65PS at 4000rpm with blower engaged
Torque not known

Gearbox:
Four-speed. Ratios not known

Axle ratios:
Not known

Chassis:
Channel-section steel
Wheelbase 2650mm
Track 1320mm

Weights and measures:
Overall dimensions
4050 x 1550 x 1550mm
Weight 1250kg
Maximum speed 135km/h (84mph)

TYPE 122 INDIANAPOLIS RACERS (1923)

Engine:
Type M 7294
1989cc 4-cylinder with 70mm bore and 129mm stroke
Twin overhead camshafts
Compression ratio not known
Single Mercedes-Benz carburettor
Roots-type supercharger driven by gear from crankshaft
150PS at 4800rpm with blower engaged
Torque not known

Gearbox:
Four-speed. Ratios
2.42:1, 1.30:1, 1.22:1, 1.00:1

Axle ratios:
Not known

Chassis:
Channel-section steel
Wheelbase 2700mm (106.3in)
Track 1340mm (front and rear)

Weights and measures:
Overall dimensions
3800 x 1700 x 1250mm
Weight 921kg (2030 lb)
Maximum speed 110km/h (68mph)

TYPE PP TARGA FLORIO RACERS (1924)

Engine:
Type M 7294
1989cc 4-cylinder with 70mm bore and 129mm stroke
Twin overhead camshafts
Compression ratio not known
Single Mercedes-Benz carburettor
Roots-type supercharger driven by gear from crankshaft
67.5PS unblown
126PS at 4500rpm with blower engaged
Torque not known

Gearbox:
Four-speed. Ratios
2.42:1, 1.30:1, 1.22:1, 1.00:1

Axle ratio:
Not known

Chassis:
Channel-section steel
Wheelbase 2700mm (106.3in)
Track 1340mm (front and rear)

Weights and measures:
Overall dimensions
3800 x 1700 x 1250mm
Weight 921kg (2030 lb)
Maximum speed 110km/h (68mph)

1925
6/25/38, 1568cc 4-cylinder
15/70/100, 3920cc 6-cylinder
24/100/160, 6240cc 6-cylinder

1926 (as Mercedes-Benz)
8/38, 1988cc 6-cylinder
300, 2968cc 6-cylinder
400, 3920cc 6-cylinder
630, 6240cc 6-cylinder
Model K, 6240cc 6-cylinder

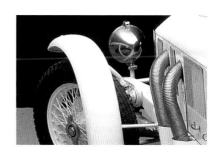

Chapter Three

BECOMING ESTABLISHED

The Porsche period

This is another pre-race posed picture, with Alfred Neubauer and riding mechanic Ernst Hemminger in the somewhat cramped cockpit of one of the supercharged 2-litre 8-cylinder racers prepared for the 1924 Monza Grand Prix.

When Paul Daimler left Daimler at the end of 1922, he left behind a wealth of experience with supercharged engines for road vehicles. The Mercedes board had every intention of capitalising on this, and in their new Chief Engineer Ferdinand Porsche they had found a man who was only too pleased to build on the foundations that Daimler had laid. However, Paul Daimler's policy of supercharging the small-capacity, cheaper cars was abruptly halted. The last of those models was available during 1925 and from then on, supercharged engines would be available only on racing, sports and expensive prestige chassis.

An early experiment

As explained in the last Chapter, Porsche set to work early on to improve the four-cylinder 2-litre cars that had made their appearance in 1922. As something of a sideline, he had one of them re-engined with a 1914 4.5-litre Grand Prix engine and fitted a supercharger to it. Though this seems to have been very much an experiment, the car did appear briefly in public. Mercedes decided to gain publicity by tackling the record for the hill-climb at the Semmering Pass, which had stood since 1909 at 7 minutes, 7 seconds. Otto Salzer was chosen to drive the blown 4.5-litre car, which gave trouble at the start when the supercharger failed. It was quickly replaced by one unbolted from a supercharged 28/95, and Salzer stormed up the hill-climb to break the record by two seconds. However, his triumph was short-lived. Hans Werner followed up with one of the 2-litre cars and clipped a further six seconds off Salzer's time. The record stayed with the Mercedes team, but most importantly the event had shown that the latest engine technology had now surpassed that of the legendary 1914 Grand Prix cars, even when assisted with a supercharger.

The 2-litre Grand Prix car

Paul Daimler's work on eight-cylinder engines at Stuttgart had included some studies for a supercharged 2-litre racing type, and when Porsche joined Daimler in 1923 he eagerly seized on these. He had management approval, too: the

Porsche's supercharged 8-cylinder racer is seen here without its bodywork. The fuel tank ran right under the rear half of the car, from the driver's seat to the tail.

One of the Monza racers survives today in the Daimler-Benz Museum.

Different thinking: all the supercharged Paul Daimler cars had the blower mounted on the nose of the crankshaft, but Porsche put his at the back of the engine. This is one of the 1924 Monza cars' engines, pictured out of the car in 1925.

Mercedes Board was only too aware of the publicity value inherent in racing success.

So Porsche developed the eight-cylinder car further, and had it ready in time for the Italian Grand Prix that was due to be run at Monza on 7 September 1924. The plan was to run in German racing white again, to avoid confusion with the red Italian cars. However, during the practice laps it became clear that the M218 engine had not been sufficiently developed: the bronze cylinder heads were porous and the cars lost their water in clouds of steam. So the cars were withdrawn. Other teams were also having trouble, notable among them Fiat, who withdrew all their entries. Fearing that the race would turn into a farce through too few entries, the Italian authorities decided to postpone it, setting a new date of 19 October.

Those five weeks of grace gave Porsche enough time to redesign the cylinder head of the 2-litre engine, and on 19 October there were four of the new models on the starting grid.

Their engines had the twin overhead camshafts and four valves per cylinder by then expected in a racing design, plus dry-sump lubrication to reduce height. The supercharger was mounted behind the engine, with its casing heavily finned to improve cooling, and the output was an astonishing 170bhp at 7000rpm. Car number 2 was driven by Hans Werner, number 6 by Alfred Neubauer (who would later become the legendary Mercedes-Benz racing chief), number 10 by Giulio Masetti, and number 12 by Count Louis Zborowski.

Right from the start the cars gave trouble. The Werner and Zborowski cars took two hours to start because of continuous spark plug problems. Once out on the track, the brakes and clutch were clearly not up to scratch, and the cars suffered from excessive oversteer. With the race under way Masetti was the first to retire, with a broken fuel pipe on the 43rd lap. One lap later, Zborowski's car tragically hit a tree at Lesmo, killing its driver. The Werner and Neubauer cars were then withdrawn, leaving the race to be dominated by the P2 Alfa Romeos and won by Alberto Ascari.

Back at Stuttgart, Porsche worked on another redesign, and the cars reappeared for the 1926 season. Now known as 130/150 models, they had redesigned tails which incorporated two extra seats and thus made them eligible for the 2-litre Sports category. In this form they were entered for the German Grand Prix at the Avus circuit on 11 July 1926, an event of particular importance in Germany because it was the first major international motor racing event to be held in the country since the end of the war. Yet the Mercedes works team shunned it, preferring to participate in a more high-profile event in Spain. So two of the 2-litre cars were lent to amateur drivers Alfred Rosenberger and Rudi Caracciola.

Rain made the track treacherous, and Rosenberger and his riding mechanic were severely injured when ether fumes from a leaking fuel tank overcame Rosenberger and their car skidded into a timing hut. Meanwhile, Caracciola demonstrated complete control of his car in the wet, and overtook the entire field of 43 other cars to assume the lead. Spark plug failure brought him into the pits and he dropped a long way back in the placings, but on returning to the track he once again threaded his way through the field and finished in first place. It

was a memorable achievement that kick-started his international racing career and earned him a place in the Mercedes works team. As for the cars, they went on to attain a formidable reputation, finishing the 1926 season with 21 placings out of 27 entries.

However, further development of Grand Prix cars was curtailed. The Mercedes-Benz Board believed that there was better publicity to be had from high-performance road cars which could be used in motorsport events both at home and abroad. The way forward was to ensure that these cars created an aura of glamour, gathering publicity from their association with celebrities of the time and from successes in hill-climb and track events. This line of cars had already been initiated before the end of 1926 with the legendary S model.

Production cars

The Mercedes production car range when Porsche joined the company was not a coherent one, and one of his earliest tasks was to give it the cohesion that it lacked. Picking up the reins in mid-1923, he was given just over a year to come up with a new range of cars. The Board wanted three of them: a 2-litre, a 4-litre, and a 6-litre. The German fiscal tax rating at the time was 4PS for every litre, so this meant that Porsche was aiming for new models with fiscal ratings of 8, 16 and 24PS. In practice, he brought the medium-sized car in at just under the 16PS barrier as a 15PS model.

Porsche embraced the existing Mercedes work on supercharged engines with enthusiasm, but he saw its production applications differently. The cost and complication of the supercharged engines was too great for the smaller models in the range, but the additional cost could be absorbed within the overall pricing of the larger and more prestigious models, and of course supercharging was invaluable for racing as well. As a result, he decided to develop technically advanced supercharged engines for the two larger cars but a simpler and more conventional naturally-aspirated type for the smallest 8PS type. He also decided that all the new engines should be six-cylinders, to give maximum refinement.

The 8PS car could safely be left until last, because the Daimler-designed 6/25 and 10/40 were scheduled to enter production in supercharged form in 1923 and would hold the fort for a few years. So Porsche focussed initially on the design of the larger models, drawing up a new supercharged overhead-camshaft engine that could be built in two different sizes.

He chose to use Elektron alloy for the cylinder blocks and aluminium for the crankcases in order to save weight. Only the detachable cylinder heads would be of cast iron. There would be an overhead camshaft operating valves in the vee formation that had proved so successful on the 1914 Grand Prix engines; there would be a single carburettor of Mercedes' own manufacture; and of course a Roots-type super-charger would be an integral part of the design. One of its key advantages was that it allowed an engine to develop peak power that was out of all proportion to its swept volume and therefore fiscal horsepower; this was value for money, 1920s style.

By contrast, the basic chassis design was no more than evolutionary. It was a ladder-frame of channel-section pressed steel, with semi-elliptic front springs and cantilever rear springs. There were brakes on all four wheels, and at the rear the handbrake had separate shoes. For the first time, these chassis would be available with the steering on the left as well as in its traditional position on the right, to suit those export territories which preferred it. On RHD chassis, the gear lever would be on the right, but on LHD models it would be located in the middle of the car. Wheels would be wooden-spoked artillery types when heavy coachwork was fitted, but for lighter cars there would be wire-spoked wheels.

The 15/70/100 and 24/100/140 models

The two larger Porsche models were introduced in 1924 as the 15/70/100 and the 24/100/140. The 15/70/100 (which had an engine small enough to rate at 15PS rather than the design

target of 16PS) replaced the old 16/45 that dated right back to 1910, but the 24/100/140 took Mercedes into a new sector of the market. In due course, the car would become the flagship, but the old 28/95 soldiered on for another year, perhaps largely as a safety precaution.

The 15/70/100 had an engine of 3920cc and sat on a wheelbase of 3630mm (142.9in). It was a large and heavy car, best suited to saloon or all-weather bodywork, and there were alternative axle ratios to suit the different weights of body that might be fitted. Mercedes themselves provided a good range from their own Sindelfingen plant. In the beginning, all of them had six seats; the staple model was an all-weather type, and for an extra charge this could be fitted with a removable panelled roof. Then there were a Pullman limousine, a coupé limousine, a landaulet and a Pullman-cabriolet. These five were joined in 1925 by a four-door, four-seater cabriolet.

All these bodies were heavy enough to need the wooden artillery wheels, but of course Mercedes also offered the 15/70/100 in chassis-only form so that buyers could take it to their

This open tourer body on a 1924 15/70/100 chassis is fairly typical of the bodies then in vogue. The chassis has the wooden artillery-type wheels that were an alternative to the wire spoked type.

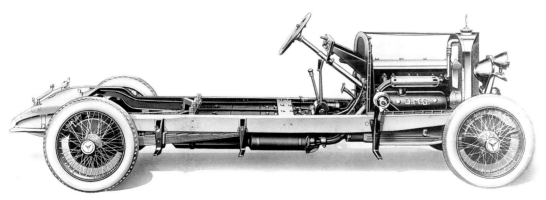

The 15/70/100 chassis had a sturdy channel-section frame with straight side members. This image, supposedly from 1924, has been extensively airbrushed, but the cantilevered half-elliptic rear springs are immediately obvious.

Richard Tauber was an Austrian tenor, widely regarded as one of the greatest singers of the 20th century, and his choice of a 15/70/100 as chauffeur-driven transport is an indication of the type of customer to whom the model appealed. The original of this photograph carries the singer's signature.

Can this really have been typical of the conditions at Daimler's Untertürkheim factory? The picture purports to show the test section in 1925, with 15/70/100 models on "slave" wheels queuing up for a shake-down in the hands of a test driver before being passed as fit for sale.

Despite the rakish two-seat sports bodywork, there is an air of solidity about this 24/100/140, an early example which dates from 1923. The exhaust pipes emerge from the bonnet side panel, although this was not a standard feature of the type.

favoured coachbuilder and have a body made to order. Some of the lighter bodies constructed outside Sindelfingen included open two-seaters, and wire wheels gave these a sporting appearance that their actual performance probably could not match. With lightweight bodywork and on the taller of the two axle ratios available, a 15/70/100 was capable of 112km/h (69mph), but with heavier bodywork and the lower axle ratio no more than 65mph was attainable.

Although the larger engine in the 24/100/140 shared the same basic architecture, its bore and stroke were both different from their equivalents in the 15/70/100. With a swept volume of 6240cc, it was intended for an altogether grander type of car, and the chassis was that much longer to suit: the wheelbase was a huge

The heavy 24/100/140 chassis still has artillery-type spoked wheels in this 1925 picture of a then-new open touring model. The young man at the wheel is Rudolf Caracciola, later Mercedes' star "works" driver, and on 22 August 1925 in this car he won the Klausen Hillclimb event run over a 14-mile course high in the Swiss mountains.

3750mm (147.6in). The bodies from Sindelfingen tended to be limousines, although there were also all-weathers and in fact the Reichswehr (German Army) took a number of these as staff cars. There were bare chassis, too, so that customers could indulge their whims and have bodywork built to order by an independent coachbuilder, and there was a choice of axle ratios to suit the body weight.

Needless to say, the big and powerful engine that had been designed to move heavy limousine bodies at respectable speeds also had a strong appeal to the sporting fraternity. With lighter bodywork, examples of the 24/100/140 claimed no fewer than 37 victories in long-distance events in Germany during 1925. The cars were exported, too, and in Britain were renamed 33/140 models to reflect their 33hp tax rating under the RAC classification scheme. With such an expensive rating (for comparison, the 1926 6½-litre Bentley was rated at 37.2hp and produced 147bhp), these cars were necessarily few and far between.

As far as the third model in the new Porsche range was concerned, that was announced as the 8/38 at the Berlin Exhibition in October 1926 and replaced the two small-capacity supercharged models, the 6/30 and the 10/40. Its engine was a simple 2-litre side-valve without a supercharger, and only its six cylinders marked it out from the ordinary. The car was actually beset with problems, did not enter production until March 1927, and had to be redesigned by Porsche's successor Hans Nibel in 1928.

Yet several histories of Mercedes-Benz mention a supercharged 2-litre model called the 200 that was introduced in 1924, and some even go so far as to add a short-chassis derivative called the 200K. No such models are recorded in the Mercedes-Benz archives at Stuttgart. It appears that confusion has arisen over the years from two factors. One is that the redesigned 8/38 of 1928 was indeed called a 200 (it was also known as the Stuttgart model), and the other is that there was indeed a super-

These pictures help to give an idea of the sheer size of the 24/100/140 chassis. This one was built up as a race-car transporter for the Monza Grand Prix in 1924. The idea came from DMG "works" drivers Christian Werner and Alfred Neubauer, and the car on the back is one of the supercharged eight-cylinder models designed by Ferdinand Porsche.

This Town Coupé on the 630 chassis again shows clearly where the model, originally a 24/100/140, was positioned in the market. At this level, the additional cost of the supercharger simply disappeared in the final bill.

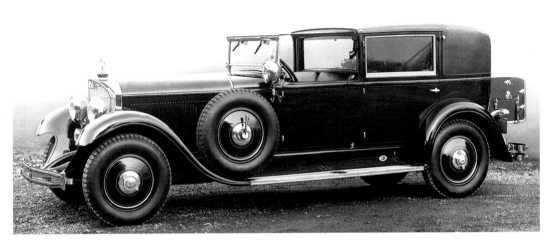

charged 2-litre engine in 1924 although that was an eight-cylinder used only in the works racing cars.

A source of considerable confusion to British enthusiasts of the supercharged Mercedes has been that the 15/70/100 model was renamed a 24/100 for UK consumption. It was not at all the same thing as the 24/100/140, of course; the different nomenclature came about because the British RAC horsepower rating was 24, while the 100 was the maximum output of the engine in brake horsepower with the blower engaged. *The Motor* tested an example in its issue of 23 March 1926. The car was fitted with a dignified and square-cut six-light saloon body built using the Weymann patents, although whether its construction had taken place in Britain or in Germany is not clear.

"Without the blower in action, the Mercedes saloon is capable of a performance comparable with that of any other high-grade touring car, its maximum being in the neighbourhood of 65mph on a 4.7:1 top gear. When the supercharger is working, the acceleration is vastly improved, and the all-out maximum speed is not far short of the 80 mile an hour mark on the same gear ratio." (In fact the quoted top speed on test was only 74.38mph.) The improvement in acceleration was graphically demonstrated by the figures: *The Motor* claimed a 10-60mph time of 44 seconds without using the supercharger, but a time of 22.4 seconds with the supercharger engaged. The car could also run at 4mph on top gear in traffic and then accelerate away smoothly.

"When bringing the blower into action the pedal is first depressed against the resistance of an extra strong spring, when a musical hum

The chassis of all the 24PS models was built to much the same formula as that of the 15/70/100, but with a slightly longer wheelbase as standard. This is almost certainly a short-wheelbase Model K: it has the underslung rear springs used on all the 630s from 1927, and those bright-metal exhaust downpipes are obviously intended to be seen when protruding through the bonnet side. The wire wheels also hint at the more sporting bodywork associated with the Model K.

warns the driver that the blower has started work. Immediately the sound is heard the pedal should be fully depressed and kept right down until the desired speed has been reached. When running at full speed the blower emits the shrill whine common to supercharged racing cars – a very stirring sound for those who have ever witnessed a Grand Prix race or some really fast events at Brooklands. We found that when wishing rapidly to overtake another car it was only necessary to depress the accelerator pedal to its limit, when the supercharger sang and we shot past the other vehicle."

Braking was less satisfactory, which was perhaps not very surprising on a car that weighed 2 tons 7cwt (5264lb, 2388kg) with two passengers aboard and could reach such high speeds. However, the importers, British Mercedes Ltd of Long Acre in London WC2, assured *The Motor* that all future models sold in the UK were to have servo-assisted brakes.

1926: the merger

The main German rival of the Daimler Motorengesellschaft had for many years been Benz & Cie, and as the German economic crisis worsened in the early 1920s the two companies had swiftly recognised that head-on competition was likely to lead to ruin for one of them. The key movers were the bankers on the supervisory boards of the two companies: Dr Emil Georg von Strauss was the Deutsche Bank man at Daimler, and Dr Karl Jahr was the Rheinische Credit-Bank representative on the Benz board. Jahr in particular had been in favour of a merger for many years, having first recommended such a move as long ago as 1916.

So on 1 May 1924 the two companies reached what they called an Agreement of Mutual Interest. In fact, a complete merger was the ultimate goal from the beginning, but for tax reasons was deferred. For the moment, the two companies would save costs though mutual co-operation in a number of areas, and a new brand name appeared at the end of May as Mercedes-Benz Automobil AG was established as a joint sales organisation.

A merger was formally agreed by the annual meeting of shareholders of the two companies on 28-29 June 1926. The two companies merged to become Daimler-Benz AG, and in future all products would be known by the Mercedes-Benz name. No chairman was appointed;

instead, equal numbers of appointees from the two merged companies ensured a fair hearing for both sides. Wilhelm Kissel from the Benz company became the new Managing Director.

Even so, cultural differences and geographical separation ensured that full integration would take many more years to achieve. There were no fewer than five separate factories to co-ordinate: Daimler had premises at Stuttgart-Untertürkheim, Stuttgart-Sindelfingen and Berlin-Marienfelde, while the Benz factories were at Mannheim (cars) and Gaggenau (buses and trucks). Many historians argue that full integration did not occur until after the end of the Second World War in 1945.

There were internal rivalries, too. The new Mercedes-Benz company now had joint Chief Engineers, as Ferdinand Porsche had been joined by his opposite number from the Benz company, Hans Nibel. Although Porsche retained overall responsibility, it cannot have been a comfortable situation. Worse, Porsche did not get on with Wilhelm Kissel, the Managing Director. Inevitably, Porsche's well-known temper got the better of him and the two clashed; the board resolved to replace Porsche with a more co-operative Technical Director at its meeting of 24 October 1928, and Hans Nibel took over on 1 January 1929.

In the meantime, Porsche continued to exert a powerful influence over the passenger car products of the merged companies. There were several other changes, one of note being that new Mercedes-Benz car designs acquired a project numbering system that started at 01 in 1926. The number was always preceded by W for Wagen, or car, and remains in use today. (In fact, Porsche had introduced W-prefix codes for new designs in 1923, but these had four-figure numbers in a different sequence.)

There was also a change in the use of model designations. Out went the over-complicated designations of 15/70/100 and 24/100/140, and in their place came simpler designations based on engine capacity. So the existing Porsche supercharged cars became Mercedes-Benz 400 and 630 models. Yet paradoxically, the 2-litre car that Porsche had been asked to design was released during 1926 with an old-style designation as an 8/38 model, and the Benz cars – the 4130cc DS and DSS types – went out of production because they were simply outclassed by their Mercedes rivals.

Italian coachbuilder Castagna produced some grand bodywork on the 630 chassis, and both of these were fitted with the K engine. The huge three-pointed star on the radiator of the saloon was a special feature, and the wheel discs would have been at the leading edge of design in the late 1920s. The Pullman cabriolet has no wheel discs, but it does have another ornate design on the grille and there appear to be curtains inside to screen the occupants from view. Both bodies betray American influence.

The Model K

All this changing of model designations has caused endless confusion for those interested in the supercharged Mercedes of the 1920s, and what happened next simply made things worse. So, before looking at the next development in detail, a brief overview of what happened will be helpful.

As already noted, when Daimler and Benz merged in 1926, the supercharged 24/100/140 model was renamed a Mercedes-Benz 630. At the same time, the company introduced a sporting short-chassis derivative known as the Model K and more often than not now called the 630K. Then from 1928 the engine of the Model K was uprated (to become a 24/110/160

type), and this was also made available as an option in the long-wheelbase 630 chassis. These more powerful 630s were known as 630 models with the K engine; they were never 630K types.

The 1926 Model K was destined to be very important in the overall story of the supercharged Mercedes. The big 6.3-litre six-cylinder engine had already attracted the sporting fraternity, who had ordered 24/100/140 chassis with lightweight bodywork and had campaigned the cars successfully in events. The market potential was not lost on Porsche and his team in Stuttgart, and by 1926 they had a new model ready to cater for that admittedly small sector of the market.

This was the Model K, and it married the 6.3-litre supercharged engine to a shorter, lighter chassis. It was this short chassis which gave the car its name: the K stood for "Kurz" or short. Specifically, the Model K's chassis had a wheelbase of 3400mm (133.8in) as against the

3750mm (147.6in) of the parent model. This made it much more nimble, although it was still a large car by later standards, and of course the loss of all that metal plus lighter bodywork made the Model K some 50kg (110lb) lighter than the flagship saloons. A bigger fuel tank was part of the standard chassis equipment, and a Model K was good for 145km/h (90mph) on the standard 3.28:1 rear axle ratio; alternative ratios of 3.5:1 and 3.00:1 were also available. Mercedes actually guaranteed that every Model K would achieve 145km/h.

Perhaps the most readily recognised characteristic of the Model K was the three bright-metal flexible exhaust pipes that emerged through the right-hand side of its bonnet. Their purpose was strictly functional, as they were intended to help dissipate under-bonnet heat. Nevertheless, buyers saw them as an attractive design feature, and from autumn 1927 Mercedes also adopted them for the 400 and 630 models. Subsequently, these outside exhausts became a symbol of the supercharged Mercedes in the popular imagination, although they were not in fact confined to supercharged models in later years.

The outside exhaust pipes had their effect on the design of the Model K's bonnet side panels, of course. Aiming to make the two sides as symmetrical as possible, Stuttgart's designers arranged the vertical cooling louvres in four groups, the front one being smaller than the others. The spaces in between them were used on the right-hand side for the exhaust pipes. The Model K's radiator was the same as on the long-chassis 630 and the older 24/100/140, with a three-pointed star on either side of the vee in the centre of its top frame. However, the very last examples – probably all long-chassis 630 types with the Model K's engine – had the different radiator associated with the Model SS cars, which had a single three-pointed star in the centre.

The Model K was specifically intended as a roadgoing sports model which could double as a weekend competition car, and its reputation was considerably enhanced during 1926 when Rudolf Caracciola drove it to successes at the internationally renowned Klausen and Semmering hill-climbs. On 12 September 1926, while Caracciola was driving at Semmering, Willy Walb took a Model K to first place in the class for sports cars over 5 litres at the Solitude event also famous for being the first occasion when Mercedes racing team manager Alfred Neubauer tried out his system for communicating with drivers by flags and sign boards from the pits.

On the road, it was generally considered to be quite a handful, with questionable roadholding

The Model K needed a sure hand on the wheel to get the most out of it in competition; the car was fast, but had not been designed to handle well. Nevertheless, works driver Willy Walb took this one to victory on 12 September 1926 at the Rund um die Solitude event.

Ornate but beautiful in its own way, and typical of the period, is this limousine by Saoutchik on a 630 chassis with the K engine. The interior trim would have been of the highest quality, even though the avant-garde patterns may have given onlookers eye-strain.

and poor brakes. British author "Bunty" Scott Moncrieff memorably described it as a death-trap in his writings. Nevertheless, it certainly had the performance. In 1926, the Earl of Cardigan wrote in *Car & Golf* magazine of the car's extreme flexibility on its top gear ratio. "All ordinary traffic conditions can be met by this gear ratio if desired", he noted, "and the engine will tick over at 10mph and accelerate from this speed without any apparent effort."

Inevitably, there were demands for more power and performance. So in 1928, the Model K's engine was uprated with bigger valves and a higher compression ratio. The result was an increase in power of some 10% before the supercharger was engaged and just over 14% with it engaged. Under the old Daimler nomenclature, the new model would have earned the name of 24/110/160 and indeed it was some-

This is Saoutchik again, with a torpedo cabriolet. The coachbuilder's taste for flamboyance is visible in the body mouldings and the curved door bottoms. The car was for another customer for whom only the K-engined 630 chassis would do.

times called that.

Meanwhile, there had also been demand for more power in the long-wheelbase 630 models, partly no doubt to offset the great weight of some of the luxury bodies with which they were being fitted. So Stuttgart used the new engine to kill two birds with one stone; it made the latest 110/160PS supercharged engine available as an option for the long-wheelbase chassis as well from 1928. The additional body weight and lower overall gearing of these cars ensured that they had nothing like the performance of the Model K and, of course, they were still known as 630 types. They actually outlasted the Model K in production, too. The short-chassis car was withdrawn in 1929 because by then the Model S offered a far better sporting chassis, and the standard 630 chassis went out of production at the same time. Nevertheless, there was a residual demand for the K-engined long-wheelbase 630, and another seven chassis were built, the last pair in 1932.

The Model K could be had with either left- or right-hand drive, and the standard comprehensive instrumentation could be arranged on the dashboard to suit the owner's wishes. By far the majority of Model K cars had open bodywork, not least because this was generally seen as more sporting in the late 1920s and the chassis was deliberately intended as a sports type. Indeed, the only bodies available from Sindelfingen appear to have been four-seat sports tourers, usually with four doors but sometimes with doors only for the rear compartment. The basic design could be varied in any one of a number of ways to produce something more individualistic for the customer.

Either 12-spoke wooden wheels or multi-spoke wire types could be had, and the wires could be covered by wheel discs as well. The twin spares were usually mounted one on either side of the bonnet, nestling in wells within the wings, but they could also be mounted at the rear. Some cars had louvred bonnet tops to add a more sporting air. The shapes of the wings themselves could be varied, and the shape and size of the trunk carried at the rear could also be adjusted to taste. Two-tone paintwork, with wheels painted in the main or contrasting colour, could make a big difference to the way the car looked, and so could the style of windscreen fitted. Front bumpers were an extra-cost option, and could again affect the car's appear-

K MODEL VARIANTS

The K Model was not an ordinary volume production car but a highly specialised and very expensive model. As a result, its specification was constantly evolving, and there were individual variations to meet specific customer demand. This has led to a great deal of confusion, and will no doubt continue to do so. Information is sometimes contradictory and some sub-variants may have been no more than experimental cars that were stages in the development of the later Type S. Many vital records of the period were destroyed during the Second World War, but Halwart Schrader identified the following in his 1979 book *The Supercharged Mercedes*. It demonstrates a progression in engine size from 630/630K (1926) to 660K (1927) and on to 680K (also 1927); the 6.8-litre engine would be adopted for the Model S that is covered in Chapter 4.

24/100/140 or 630 model
This was the standard car with the option of the K Model's engine.

24/100/160 or 630K model
Short-chassis model with works code W9456. This was the most widely sold variant.

24/110/160 or 620 and 620K models
Uprated engine in an even shorter wheelbase (50mm shorter than 630K). Open four-seat body with folding hood, separate folding windscreens for driver and passenger, upward slope to scuttle, louvred bonnet and rear-mounted spare wheel. Built in very small numbers, 1927-32.

25/130/220 or 660K model
Enlarged engine of 6559cc (98mm x 145mm) and underslung chassis to reduce height. Intended purely for competition work. Either 27 or 28 examples were built as development vehicles: 10 in 1927, 11 in 1928; 5 in 1929; 1 in 1930; and allegedly one more to special order in 1933. Maximum speed of 170km/h (105mph).

26/130/180 or 680K model
Lightened chassis and enlarged engine with 98mm bore to give the same 6.8 litres as the Type S. Competition model capable of over 100mph. Just 6 examples built as experimental and development models: 2 in 1927 and 4 in 1928 (Jürgen Lewandowski suggests that just one was built in 1928).

26/145/270 or 680K model
Six cars built as experimental development models, with 6830cc engine (100mm x 150mm), underslung chassis, two-seater body and overall weight of 1620kg. On a 2.4:1 final drive, it was capable of 177km/h (110mph).

Note also that the K Model was sold in the UK with the name of 33/180hp.

SPECIFICATIONS: PRODUCTION MODELS

15/70/100 (1924-1926)
AND 400 (1926-1929)
(TYPE W 836)

Engine:
3920cc 6-cylinder with 80mm bore
and 130mm stroke
Overhead valves and overhead
camshaft
Compression ratio 4.7:1
Single Mercedes (later Mercedes-
Benz) carburettor
Roots-type supercharger driven by
gear from crankshaft
70PS at 2800rpm
100PS at 3200rpm with blower
engaged
Torque not known

Gearbox:
Four-speed. Ratios 3.82:1, 2.25:1,
1.44:1, 1.00:1

Axle ratios:
4.88:1 or 5.33:1

Chassis:
Channel-section steel
Wheelbase 3630mm
Track 1430mm

Weights and measures:
Overall dimensions
5200 x 1800 x 1950mm
Weight 2400kg with saloon body
Maximum speed 112km/h (69mph)
on 4.88:1 axle ratio

24/100/140 (1924-1926)
AND 630 (1926-1929)
(TYPE W 9456)

Engine:
6240cc 6-cylinder with 94mm bore
and 150mm stroke
Overhead valves and overhead
camshaft
Four main bearings
Compression ratio 4.7:1
Single Mercedes (later Mercedes-
Benz) carburettor
Roots-type supercharger driven by
gear from crankshaft
100PS at 2800rpm
140PS at 3200rpm with blower
engaged

OPTIONAL K-MODEL ENGINE
(SEE RIGHT) FROM 1928.

Gearbox:
Four-speed. Ratios 3.82:1, 2.25:1,
1.44:1, 1.00:1

Axle ratios:
400:1 or 4.36:1

Chassis:
Channel-section steel
Wheelbase 3750mm
Track 1430mm

Weights and measures:
Overall dimensions
5320 x 1800 x 1950mm
Weight 2500kg with saloon body
Maximum speed 120km/h (74mph)
on 4.00:1 axle ratio

K MODEL (1926-1930)
(TYPE W 9456)

Engine:
6240cc 6-cylinder with 94mm bore
and 150mm stroke
Overhead valves and overhead
camshaft
Four main bearings
Compression ratio 5.0:1
Single Mercedes-Benz carburettor
Roots-type supercharger driven by
gear from crankshaft
110PS at 2800rpm
160PS at 3200rpm with blower
engaged
Torque 432Nm (318 lb ft) at
1400rpm

Gearbox:
Four-speed. Ratios 3.82:1, 2.25:1,
1.44:1, 1.00:1; reverse 3.2:1

Axle ratios:
3.10:1, 3.28:1 or 3.50:1

Chassis:
Channel-section steel
Wheelbase 3400mm
Track 1430mm

Weights and measures:
Overall dimensions
4735 x 1760 x 1850mm
Weight 2000kg with open touring
body
Maximum speed 145km/h (90mph)
on 3.28:1 axle ratio

ance quite dramatically.

Then, of course, there were the bodies built by outside concerns to special order. German coachbuilders known to have worked on the Model K or K-engined 630 were Balzar in Ludwigsburg, Papler in Cologne (including one car for the King of Albania) and Zschau in Leipzig. Joseph Neuss in Berlin built two cars for Von Hindenburg, the German Head of State; there was a cabriolet in 1929 and a Pullman limousine in 1931, both on long-wheelbase chassis with the Model K engine. From France came bodies by the Parisian coachbuilders Hibbard et Darrin (including a sedanca de ville on the long-wheelbase chassis), Million Guiet (a semi-formal saloon on the long chassis) and

SPECIFICATIONS: RACING MODELS

EIGHT-CYLINDER
MONZA RACERS (1924)

Engine:
Type M 218
1996cc 8-cylinder with 61.7mm bore and
82.8mm stroke
Twin overhead camshafts
Roots-type supercharger driven by gear
from crankshaft
170PS at 7000rpm with blower engaged

Gearbox:
Four-speed. Ratios 2.42:1, 1.30:1, 1.22:1,
1.00:1

Chassis:
Channel-section steel
Wheelbase 2700mm (106.3in)
Track 1340mm (front and rear)

Weights and measures:
Overall dimensions
3800 x 1700 x 1250mm
Weight 921kg (2030 lb)
Maximum speed 110km/h (68.3mph)

BUILD VOLUMES, MODEL K

Werner Oswald gives the following
breakdown of build volumes, year by
year:

1926	20
1927	74
1928	54
1929	2
(Total	150)

In addition, the long-chassis 630 model
was available from 1928 with the uprated
engine introduced that year for the
Model K. Oswald has these production
figures:

1928	24
1929	86
1930	5
1931	None
1932	2
(Total	117)

AND THE REST

It would be all too easy to run away with the idea that Stuttgart had gone over completely
to supercharged models in the 1920s. It had not. The economic circumstances of Germany
in the mid-1920s would not have permitted such a move.

So from 1926 there was the solid and conventional 300 model, slow enough to need an
increase in engine size in 1927 and to need uprating altogether to a 320 model in 1928.
That, too, was a Porsche design. From 1928, there was the eight-cylinder Nürburg model
which came initially as a 460 and later as a 500; and from 1929 the Mannheim 350 and 370
served customers lower down the market. None of these was exciting, but they provided
the solid sales foundation without which there could have been no supercharged Mercedes.

Saoutchik (several cabriolets). From Brussels
came bodywork by D'Ieteren Frères, and from
Vanden Plas in Holland a RHD formal limousine. From Italy there were bodies by Castagna
and Farina, and from the USA there were examples by Derham (in Rosemont, Pennsylvania),
Holbrook (Hudson, New York) and Rollston
(New York City).

All this high performance did the Mercedes
image a power of good, and the Model K in
particular established an expectation in the
marketplace. It was the fastest touring car of its
time, and became the first of a long line of
supercharged, big-engined sporting Mercedes
that would continue until broken by the Second
World War.

Fairly typical in style of late 1920s German bodywork is this Erdmann & Rossi open four-door on a 630 chassis fitted with the supercharged "K Motor". From the high stance of the car, it is immediately apparent that it was designed to go fast in a straight line, but that taking corners at speed might have been a little more tricky.

Quite understandably, the coachbuilder found more than one place to "sign" the bodywork.

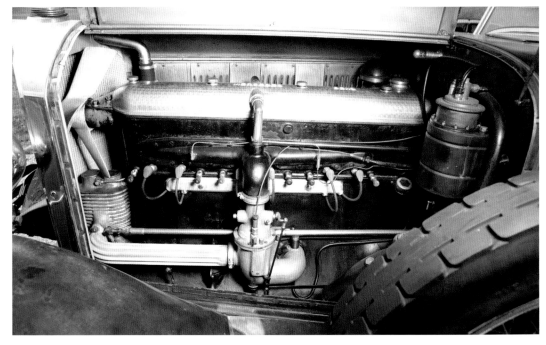

The triple outside exhausts, originally introduced to keep heat out of the engine bay, were much appreciated as a symbol of power and performance.

The finned supercharger was in front of the engine, and the pipe that led back to the carburettor is immediately obvious. So is the long rod that operated the supercharger through kickdown pressure. Even the cooling fan is an elegant work of art on this engine.

The identification plate of the car was prepared at the Untertürkheim plant, and was obviously not removed by the coachbuilder to have the total weight stamped into it. The 6202cc engine size shown is the German tax rating; the actual swept volume was 6240cc.

Though time has taken its toll on the upholstery of this 630, it is clear that the car was trimmed to a high standard of luxury.

The substantial steering wheel carried equally substantial levers for timing and mixture adjustment.

At this stage, the Mercedes-Benz radiator surround had a three-pointed star on either side of the vee at the top.

The rev counter on the right bears witness to the performance intent of this car.

Details mattered: note the three-pointed star on the pedals here.

Chapter Four

GLAMOUR AT SPEED

The S and SS

This car is supposedly one of the experimental models developed in the early days and classified as a 26/130/180 type. It was clearly on the drop-frame Type S chassis with the engine set well back.

The 630K left no doubt that Mercedes could deliver world-class performance, but the car was never very happy in its dual roles as luxury grand tourer and sports car. Its straight-frame chassis suited formal bodywork but its height from the ground meant that corners taken at speed could be something of a challenge, and the soft springing designed to bring comfort to saloon bodies was no help at all. Despite the bodywork that some of its wealthy buyers specified, the 680K was no sports car, and as a result there were calls for a more sporting chassis.

The job of creating one fell once again to Chief Engineer Ferdinand Porsche, and he started work on the new sports chassis in February 1927. Key among those working with him was chassis specialist Max Wagner, a former Benz engineer who had been involved with the design of the mid-engined "Tropfenwagen" and who would later go on to design the chassis for the Silver Arrows racing cars of the 1930s. Retaining the 3400mm wheelbase of the 680K, the two men dramatically improved the handling by lowering the frame and relocating the engine to improve weight distribution.

Central to the redesign was a drop-frame chassis, with the side members dipping gently downwards between the axles so that the bodywork could be mounted that much lower. At the

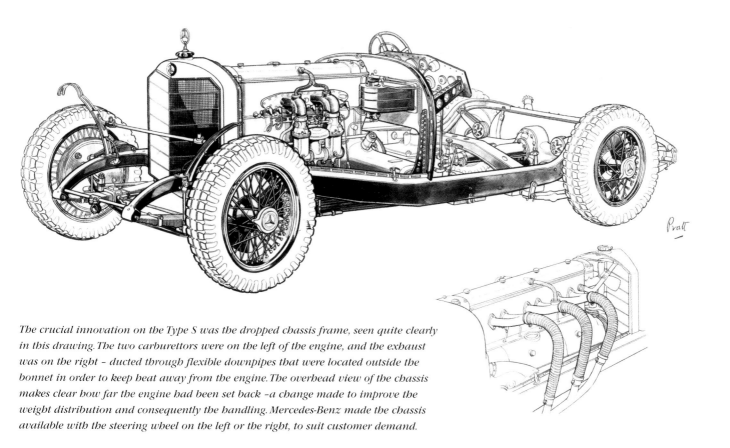

The crucial innovation on the Type S was the dropped chassis frame, seen quite clearly in this drawing. The two carburettors were on the left of the engine, and the exhaust was on the right – ducted through flexible downpipes that were located outside the bonnet in order to keep heat away from the engine. The overhead view of the chassis makes clear how far the engine had been set back –a change made to improve the weight distribution and consequently the handling. Mercedes-Benz made the chassis available with the steering wheel on the left or the right, to suit customer demand.

rear, the frame rose in an arch above the axle, which was now mounted with the springs underslung in order to keep overall height down. There were friction dampers at the rear and Houdaille hydraulic lever-arm types at the front, just as there had been since the 1908 Grand Prix Mercedes. On production cars, however, the position of the front dampers did vary: some were mounted inside the frame, and some outside. Competition cars often had twin dampers on each side at the front.

Meanwhile, the supercharged engine – further developed, as will be explained later – was set 355mm (14in) further back in the frame and mounted rather lower than before. This not only improved the weight distribution, but also gave a very long bonnet that completely changed the proportions of the car, adding to the impression of power and speed. Even the radiator was made shorter, and now had just seven horizontal bands instead of the eight of the 630K type. Nevertheless, it still retained the old Mercedes style of vee-front, with a three-pointed star on either side of the vee at the top. Engine and four-speed gearbox were mounted together as a unit, and suspended within the chassis on three mounting points.

These first examples of the new sports Mercedes were known internally by the same W9856 code as the 630K had been, with a distinguishing I (to make W 9856 I). For public consumption, however, they would be designated 680S , the S standing for Sport and the 680 revealing the size of their new engine. The 680 part of the name was probably dropped early on, and the cars have been universally known ever since as the Mercedes S type.

Sadly, we can only guess today at the exact sequence of events surrounding the creation of the new 6.8-litre engine, but it does look as if the new capacity was not achieved at a single stroke. There is a more detailed breakdown of the stages by which the engine was developed on page 41. Porsche and his team certainly tried out a 6.6-litre engine in 1927, derived from the production 6.3-litre type, and it seems to have been rather successful. Though probably intended initially only for development work, it actually entered limited production for competition use. There were no fewer than 27 cars fitted with it over a period of four years, and supposedly another one three years later.

This 6.6-litre engine (which created a car called the 660K) had a bigger bore than the production 6.3-litre type – 98mm instead of 94mm – but a shorter stroke, down to 145mm from the production 150mm. Quite possibly, that shorter stroke allowed the engine to rev more freely, which is why it was earmarked for competition use. With 130PS unblown and a massive 220PS with the blower engaged, this 6559cc engine supposedly gave the 660K a top speed of 170km/h (105mph), significantly better than the 145km/h (90mph) available from the production Model K.

There is, however, no documented evidence to show why the 6.6-litre engine was not adopted for the production cars. What does seem clear is that development work was going ahead on a second engine at the same time.

This one retained the 150mm stroke of the production 6.3-litre engine and combined it with the larger 98mm bore of the 6.6-litre type to give a swept volume of 6789cc, or very nearly 6.8 litres. It delivered the same 130PS as the 660K before the blower was engaged, but 180PS when fully extended, giving a top speed of 188km/h (117mph) on the tall-geared prototypes. That was certainly fast enough for road use. There seem to have been two prototypes in 1927 and either one or four more in 1928, depending on the source of information. These cars were known by a new works code of W9856 S, and led directly to the production models that became available in 1928.

There was more to the new 6.8-litre engine than a simple increase in the bore size, of course. In fact, Porsche had more or less redesigned everything except the basic configuration. The Elektron alloy block now incorporated wet liners, with bi-metallic pistons of iron and aluminium running on con-rods made of nickel chrome steel. The crankshaft was hollow-forged, ran in four bearings and had a vibration damper on the nose. The compression ratio was raised to 5:1, and instead of the earlier single carburettor there were two updraught carburettors. The gear-driven cooling fan was also mounted lower down to suit the lower radiator.

As Bentley had done in Britain, Mercedes went for reliability in their new engine by having each set of plugs fired by a different system. That way, if one electrical system failed, the engine would still continue to run. Bentley had used twin magnetos; Mercedes used a magneto to fire a set of plugs on the inlet side of the engine and a coil to fire those on the exhaust side, and Bentley would subsequently return the compliment by switching to such a system as well. The Mercedes system was complicated by the need to run different plugs on each side of the engine; the ones fired by the magneto on the inlet side were Bosch M180/7, while those fired by the coil on the exhaust side were Bosch DM220/5. However, customers of the production cars were advised that if they intended to run the car for long periods with the supercharger engaged (as they would, for example, in competition), they should fit specially hard heat-resistant spark plugs and run on a mixture of petrol and benzole.

Publicity through competition

Stuttgart made its initial statement of intent in public on 19 June 1927. That was the date on which Germany's new dedicated motor racing circuit, the Nürburgring set high in the Eifel Mountains, was officially opened. It was not an occasion that any major manufacturer could miss, and the Mercedes-Benz workshops supposedly prepared no fewer than eight cars to compete.

Two of the new 680S models were entered in the very first race, which involved 12 laps of the 15.5-mile circuit and was contested by a motley selection of German-manufactured cars that, in all honesty, never had a chance against the latest Mercedes. Car number 1 was driven by Rudolf Caracciola, and car number 2 by Adolf Rosenberger, while Rittmeister Von Mosch entered his own 630K as a privateer with number 3. All three cars ran in the German national racing colour of white. The result was a 1-2-3 finish in front of a crowd numbering some 500,000, with the two 680S models taking the first two places and Caracciola returning an average speed of 101.1km/h (63.5mph). As an initial public demonstration of the forthcoming Mercedes sports chassis, it could hardly have been better.

During the 1927 racing season, the 680S appeared on the circuits as a factory entrant in several important events. It was usually known by its rating; this was usually given as 26/120/180, but it would be risky to deduce from this that the engine had been detuned from the 130PS available from prototype examples. Those who recorded events at the time

Never a company to hide its light under a bushel, Daimler-Benz developed this advertisement to publicise its successes at the inaugural Nürburgring races.

The first public outing for the Type S was in front of a huge crowd at the opening race on the new Nürburgring in July 1927. The two cars nearer the camera are the new Type S models, with Caracciola at the wheel of number 1 and Rosenberger at the wheel of number 2. The third car is an earlier 630K type, driven by Von Mosch as a private entry. The difference in height is striking.

were probably just as confused by the multiple numbers in Mercedes designations as we are today, and the chances are that the cars had different states of tune at different events, anyway. The cars used must have been drawn from the first 10 examples built during 1927, all of them really factory experimental models.

On 17 July, just a month after the opening of the Nürburgring, the S claimed another three podium places in the German Grand Prix, driven (in order of finishing) by Otto Merz, Christian Werner and Willy Walb. Werner actually recorded the fastest lap in car number 7, but Merz finished three minutes ahead of him. Caracciola had also entered in an S, but his car broke down and he was forced to retire. It was at this event that the factory team cars were given a red stripe on the bonnet, contrasting starkly with the German racing white, in order to make them more readily identifiable to the watching crowds. Then during the speed events at the motor week in Baden Baden, Caracciola, Willy Walb and Rittmeister von Mosch all turned in sparkling results. There were hill-climb successes, too. It was in an S on 13 August 1927 that Rudi Caracciola famously broke the record for touring cars at the Klausen hill-climb with a time of 17 minutes 43.8secs and a speed of 72.3km/h (44.925mph), while on 18 September Georg Kimpel took an S to second place in the over-5-litre touring car class at the Solitude track near Stuttgart.

Six more cars built in early 1928 seem to have been retained as factory experimental models,

An S in racing trim: this is Otto Merz's car at the 1927 German Grand Prix where he was overall winner with an average speed of 102km/b, three minutes ahead of Christian Werner.

and must have been among the examples of the S that went on that year to notch up some more excellent results, setting 17 records and winning no fewer than 53 races. Over time, the S (and later SS) models became known as the White Elephants, a name which alluded both to their size and the German national racing white in which the "works" cars were painted.

On sale

Satisfied that they had a viable production specification, Stuttgart announced the public availability of the Type S for 1928; an example was at Olympia for the London Motor Show in October 1927, where it was described as a 36/220 model. The cost of the new car was simply staggering: in Germany a bare chassis

cost 26,000 Reichsmarks, while a complete car with Sindelfingen's own four-seat open sports body was 30,000 Reichsmarks. By way of comparison, a 1928 Mercedes-Benz 8/38 four-seat cabriolet with 2-litre engine cost just 9,500 Reichsmarks, and the cheapest two-seater sports variant was less than 7000 RM. Even a Model K chassis had cost a mere 20,000 RM. This was a formidably expensive machine, right at the top of the Mercedes-Benz range and built only to order for the super-rich. Owners tended to be wealthy businessmen and the celebrities of the day: German actor Willy Fritsch and film star Hertha von Walter were among the domestic owners, while Hollywood star Al Jolson owned a Mercedes Type S and US dance act The Rowe Sisters made sure of being photographed with one while in Germany.

Even though the car had made its public debut on the race tracks during 1927 and would continue to have an illustrious competition career, the very wealthy were generally more interested in luxury and comfort than in motor sport, and so the S was primarily intended as a grand touring machine and as a glamorous celebration of a wealthy lifestyle. Its sporting performance simply made it more fun to drive for those who enjoyed such things, and more interesting to brag about for those who were more concerned with the prestige of owning one. Rudge wire wheels, now universally fitted, ensured that the cars always had a sporting appearance at the very least.

In real terms, acceleration and maximum speed depended on which of the four optional

If there was such a thing as a "typical" Type S, this was it - with Sindelfingen's own two-door, four-seat tourer body.

American dance act The Rowe Sisters posed with a Type S when they visited Germany in 1927. The car is clearly one of the factory competition models, and interestingly has right-hand steering rather than the left-hand steering that was generally favoured.

axle ratios was chosen, as well as on the type of body fitted. The 2.5:1 ratio gave the highest top speed but slowest acceleration, the 2.76:1 ratio was the compromise option, and a 3.09:1 ratio was best suited to heavy bodywork. Other options of 2.48:1, 2.75:1 and 3:1 have been quoted, but may result from simple rounding of figures. Although the chassis was 200kg lighter than that of the old 630K, with a weight of just 1300kg, only the very skimpiest of bodies on the tallest gearing allowed an S to reach 190km/h (118mph). Altogether more typical was a maximum speed of 169km/h (105mph) with acceleration from 0-100km/h (0-62mph) in 14 seconds. Even so, this was undreamt-of performance in a road car at the time.

If there was such a thing as a typical S, it would have been one carrying the four-seater

From 1928, Daimler-Benz made a deliberate push to sell cars in the USA, promoting the Type S as both competition model and high-performance road car. US racing driver Ralph de Palma is seen with the S that he bought, and in which he won two races at the Atlantic City track in New Jersey on 30 May 1928.

touring body built at the Sindelfingen works, sleek and elegant enough not to look out of place in any gathering of expensive cars at the time. Daimler-Benz say that the vast majority of chassis carried this bodywork. Nevertheless, buyers could also choose a drophead coupé or a close-coupled open four-seater known as the "Spezial Sportwagen" (Special Sports, and not to

This is not an SS but a "Spezial Sportwagen" version of the Type S. The Sindelfingen-built bodywork is quite different from the standard tourer type, being more substantial-looking with a cross-brace behind the front seats and four doors instead of two. The twin spares are also carried at the rear rather than alongside the engine compartment.

Ordered by a New York buyer in 1928, this Type S was bodied as a two-seater sports model by Saoutchik in Paris. After 30 years in storage, it was extensively restored and was the overall winner at the August 2012 Pebble Beach concours event.

be confused with the later SS model even though it was sometimes called by that name). The set-back engine meant that there was now rather less room for the body than before, and Mercedes quoted a maximum body length within the chassis of 2300mm (90.5in), which was 250mm (9.8in) less than had been available on the 630K. That was quite a lot, but these cars

were large enough for the difference not to become a real problem in practice.

Many models had a louvred bonnet top, which added to the sporting appearance, and most cars had a flat radiator cap, but an attractive extra was a cap surmounted by the three-pointed star, with a water thermometer in the supporting stalk. The later Type S cars,

It is interesting to compare this roadgoing Type S, part of the Daimler-Benz Museum collection, with the competition models that were used at the inaugural Nürburgring event in 1927. Both date from the same year of 1927, but the wings and running-boards are altogether more substantial on the roadgoing car, where weight was less critical. The single spotlight and single windscreen wiper were typical of the period.

This is another Type S tourer from the Daimler-Benz Museum, this time featuring a different style of running-board and with the spare wheels mounted alongside the engine bay. The windscreen is a single-pane type, although two-pane screens were still quite common in 1927. The radiator surround is the later style, with a single central emblem.

probably from some time in 1928, took on the taller radiator of the bigger-engined Type SS models, complete with the single central wreathed star emblem.

The chassis was also available for bodying elsewhere, and both Erdmann & Rossi in Berlin and Papler in Cologne produced examples. In Switzerland, the Geneva company of Zietz built at least one tourer, and Gangloff built a roadster in 1927, while the Austrian firm of Armbruster also built a roadster. The French coachbuilder Saoutchik built an elegant Torpedo which was on the Mercedes stand at the 1928 New York Show (and took Best of Show honours at the 2012 Pebble Beach Concours d'Elegance), and also at least one cabriolet. A chassis was displayed at the Los Angeles Motor Show in 1928, in the hope of securing orders from the Hollywood set, and in due course some chassis found their way to the premises of the prestigious Murphy company of Pasadena. One survivor is a boat-tailed speedster. In Britain, examples were bodied by Cadogan, Freestone & Webb, Vanden Plas and Weymann.

Most Type S Mercedes were intended as elegant road cars, expressing the wealth and status of their owners, but some were bought for competition work, and these had an extra oil tank on the bulkhead to supplement the two gallons in the sump. The reason was simple: oil consumption of a hard-used engine was little short of appalling, and there was a serious risk that a hard-driven car would run out of oil altogether before the end of a long-distance race. A

disadvantage of the competition cars was said to be that their plugs tended to oil up if they were used in slow traffic. Some examples were also fitted with a vacuum brake servo made by Bosch.

Exactly how many Type S Mercedes were built is something we shall probably never know for sure. Most of the prototypes seem not to have been counted in the figures now quoted by the factory, and that could add more than 30 cars to the "official" grand total of 138 built between 1928 and 1930. The figure of 146 sometimes quoted includes eight very special stripped-out cars built during 1929 that were different enough to gain a special factory designation W06 II. They had a further increase in the compression ratio, this time to 6.5:1, and modified carburettors. These changes resulted in 190bhp at 3000rpm without the blower engaged, and a maximum output of a stupendous 250bhp with the supercharger in use. To Mercedes, they were therefore 26/190/250 models. A maximum speed of 195km/h (122mph) was obtainable with the right gearing and these cars were intended strictly for the race tracks.

At least one of the 1927 development cars which had been used in competition that year went on to become a demonstrator, and *Motor Sport* was able to test it for its April 1928 issue while the car was in Britain. Needless to say, the primary test venue was the Brooklands track, although the crew of four also found some good straight roads where they could try the car

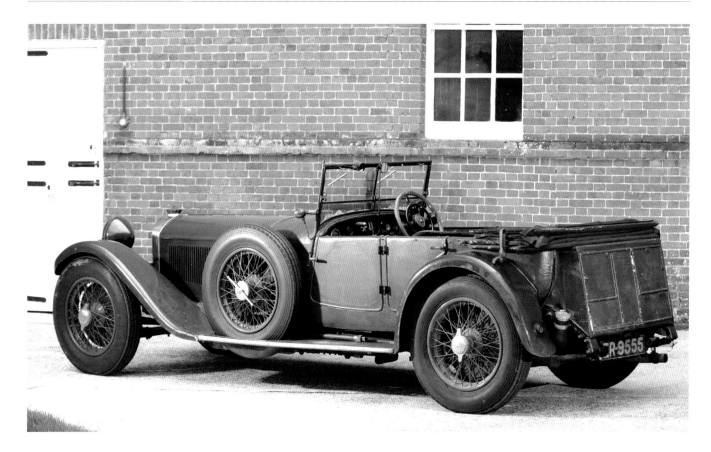

Barn finds are rarely more exciting than this. This 1928 Type S was put away in a lock-up during the 1950s and rediscovered in 2012. The sports tourer coachwork was by the London firm of Cadogan, and betrays typical British characteristics of the period.

This advertisement, featuring a Type S, appeared in Issue 18 of the fashion magazine Elegante Welt *("Elegant World") during 1928. The design was by the Offelsmeyer Cucuel agency.*

without fear of endangering other road users. Here, they noted, "seventy became a normal speed, ninety not uncommon, and on two separate occasions three figures were exceeded!" On one of those occasions, the car was climbing an appreciable hill.

In London traffic, the car proved much more tractable than the testers had expected. "The great car oozed through the densest tangle with a gentle persistence delightful to experience. Gear changing was definitely unnecessary, unless a dead stop were unavoidable, and it proved possible to trickle along on top gear without a sign of jerk or snatch. Given the chance of a gap in the traffic, using the gearbox... the car accelerated in a most satisfying manner, the upholstery simply hitting one in the back. As for refinement, "the exhaust note proved to be extremely quiet and unostentatious" and "the steering, at all speeds, was almost incredibly light and required little more than finger pressure". The gearbox was silent for the most part, and the testers liked its close ratios, but third gear whined noisily – perhaps, they thought, as a result of hard use. The major let-down, however, was the brakes. The maga-

zine concluded that they needed a servo.

At Brooklands, the car achieved 104mph on the Byfleet banking and then 110mph on the Railway straight, in each case with four passengers aboard. At 110mph, the writer noted that "the most outstanding feature was the extreme comfort of the front seats and the extreme discomfort of the rear ones". The track surface seems to have been a little broken, which cannot have helped the rear-seat ride, but the real problem was one of space. Although this car had the Sindelfingen-built four-seat touring body, the "rear seating accommodation... is really a dickey included in the bodywork". At the start of their journey, the two rear-seat passengers had uttered "many groans and cries of dismay, they being both over six feet in height."

Motor Sport also noted that the Type S Mercedes had "an entirely new found neatness, never previously associated with this marque". Overall, the testers concluded that the car could "beat anything, no matter what its power". At a time when motoring magazines not only tended to pull punches but also to favour the domestic product, that was praise indeed.

The Type S on the road.

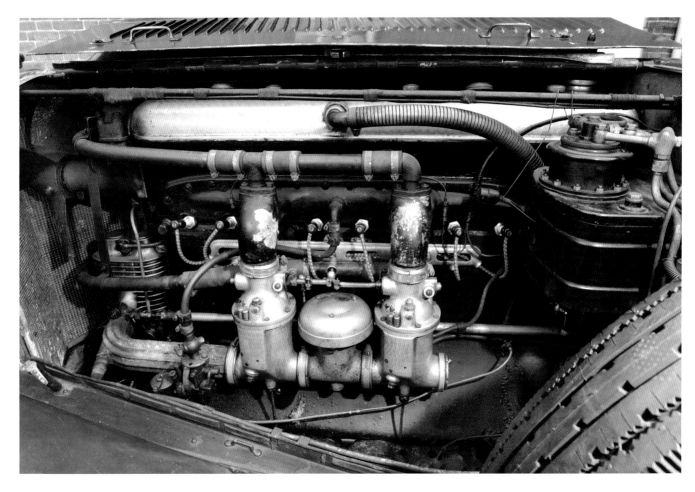

The finned supercharger was still located in front of
the engine on the Type S, but this time fed two
carburettors – each carrying a neat plate with its
maker's name. That forest of ignition leads was
necessary with the twin-plug engine.

The dashboard layout has a sporting air that befits the car's nature. That is a Tapley meter attached to the windscreen to the right of the steering wheel – a decelerometer used for testing brake efficiency. The switchbox is by Bosch and the speedometer with trip meter is by Veigel.

The arrangement of lockers set into the rear is interesting. The body was fabric-panelled, as is clear from the crazing on the section visible behind the mudguard.

Overhead view of the S chassis shows how far back the engine was set.

The M06 engine was essentially the same design as the older 6.8-litre, but now with enlarged cylinder bores. This view shows very clearly the cooling fins around the supercharger and its ducting, and the machine-turned finish of the Mercedes carburettors (which, incidentally, wear "Daimler Mercedes" badge plates).

Stage 2: the SS

On the race tracks, rivals force the pace of development. In the high-cost, limited-volume market inhabited by cars like the Type S, customers constantly demand more. So the Mercedes-Benz design office did not rest on its laurels once it had given the 6.8-litre engine a worthy home in the Type S chassis. Instead, it started work on a bigger and more powerful version of the supercharged engine.

Four experimental development cars were built in 1927-28, still numbered under the old pre-merger system as W1156 S types. They were essentially Type S models with the new engine. This had a bigger bore of 100mm and the same 150mm stroke as before, resulting in a swept volume of 7065cc. Some sources have wrongly quoted this figure as 7020cc, which was actually the size calculated to meet German tax regulations. The new engine had a new type code, too. It was known as the M 06 type. To keep operating temperatures at sensible levels, it was fitted with a larger radiator than the Type S; taller, to accommodate the extra cooling surface, this had a distinctive new configuration with a single, wreathed three-pointed star at the top in place of the twin stars on the Type S.

Modified horizontal twin carburettors and a modest compression ratio of just 5.0:1 delivered 140bhp unblown and 200bhp with the blower engaged. Weighing no more than 1680kg, these development cars had a maximum speed of 185km/h (115mph). For those whose interest lies in numbers, the cars were allegedly referred to internally as 700 models, after the size of their engines, and also as 27/140/200 types. That string of numbers reflected the increased annual tax liability of the larger engine (up to 27PS

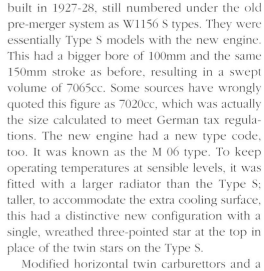

from the 26PS of the 6.8-litre), plus the unblown and blown power maxima. However, this system of numbering was already on the way out. It became meaningless as a way of identifying a car type from 1928, when Germany introduced a new motor vehicle taxation system. As far as the public was concerned, the car was never known as anything but a Type SS; the letters stood for Super Sport.

Testing revealed that the engine could handle a higher compression ratio, and with this now set at 5.2:1 the new chassis was ready for production. In-house, it became a 710 type to distinguish it from the lower-powered development cars; it was also a W1156 S II or a 27/160/200. To the relief of many a driver, it came with servo-assisted brakes as standard. Once the car entered production, it also took on a new internal designation. A different type coding system had somewhat belatedly been

Beautifully turned out, as only a Show chassis would be, this early SS chassis was photographed to show both sides of the 7.1-litre engine.

Stripped down, with only cycle wings to protect the occupants from flying stones and mud, this was the 1928 competition version of the SS, with its twin spares mounted at the rear.

The coachwork is by the English constructor Cadogan, the chassis is an SS from 1929. However, all is not quite as it seems. The body was built in 1930 and was originally on a Type S chassis; it was subsequently transferred to an un-numbered SS chassis (many original chassis frames were not numbered by Mercedes, although the reason is unclear). This car spent several years in the USA, returned briefly to the UK in the mid-1970s, then went to the Hayashi Collection in Japan. In 1996 it became part of the Bernie Ecclestone Collection, and was sold on again in 2007.

This car has been fitted with the anti-shimmy front suspension dampers, and also has a later type of hydraulic braking system with a Dewandre servo to give power assistance.

By this stage, the radiator surround carried a single circular Mercedes-Benz badge.

*There is something very English about the rear view.
The wheels are the correct 20-inch lock-ring types of
Mercedes manufacture. The paired stoplamps would
not have been original, and the left-hand one has
been added to meet modern regulations.*

Though the engine of this car may not be the original one, it is certainly of the correct type. The supercharger is the 15-finned item for a Type S.

The instruments are mainly British Jaeger units, which would not have been supplied by Mercedes-Benz but were probably fitted from new by Cadogan. The pair of dials behind the steering wheel are for the André Telecontrol dampers.

introduced in place of the old Daimler system, retaining the W (for Wagen, or car) but starting again numerically. So the Type SS was a W 06 model.

The first that the public got to see of the new bigger-engined Mercedes was at the Nürburgring, where the 1928 German Grand Prix was held on 15 July. Mercedes entered three cars: Rudi Caracciola had the first, Otto Merz had the second car, and Christian Werner crewed the third car with Willy Walb. These were really development cars, and are often described as having S chassis with SS engines, although that is to split hairs unnecessarily. It was a triumphant start to the career of the SS: Caracciola's car finished first with an average speed of 64.56mph and set the fastest lap time with 69.34mph, although Caracciola himself had collapsed with heat exhaustion and Christian Werner had switched cars to take Caracciola's mount over the finishing line.

Merz came second, winning the Ernes Merck prize for the fastest German sports machine, and Walb came third.

Even so, the SS only had a very short career as the ultimate derivative of Ferdinand Porsche's supercharged six-cylinder sports-racers. By September 1928, the basic design had been developed even further as the short-chassis SSK, which is described more fully in the next chapter. That month actually saw Mercedes

When Caracciola collapsed from heat exhaustion during the 1928 German GP at the Nürburgring, Werner took over at the wheel and piloted the SS to victory.

The crowd around the SS in the pits makes clear that this 1928 picture was taken during training for that year's German Sports Car Grand Prix.

With his SS garlanded with flowers on its triumphant return to the Untertürkheim works, Otto Merz basks in the glory of a win at the German Sports Car Grand Prix, held at the Nürburgring on 15 July 1928. With him in the car is his co-driver, Eugen Salzer. The bonnet carried a red stripe.

An SS in action in a German hillclimb event: the car is being driven by Ernst Günther von Wentzel-Mosau, the venue is the Semmering hillclimb, and the date is 16 September 1928. Von Wentzel won the 8-litre sports car class and set the fastest time in a sports car.

In the 1929 Gaisberg race, Manfred Von Brauchitsch drove an SS in full touring trim. Von Brauchitsch would later become a member of the all-conquering Silver Arrows racing team of the 1930s.

Manfred von Brauchitsch, photographed in 1937 at the wheel of a Silver Arrows Mercedes.

enter all three of the then-current derivatives in the Semmering hill-climb event. A sober-looking S won the under-8-litre class for touring cars in the hands of Franz Wenzler (a Daimler-Benz Director) with an average speed of 77.4km/h (48mph); the class for sports cars of under 8 litres was won by Ernst-Günther von Wentzel-Mosau with an SS at an average speed of 83.8km/h (52mph); and Rudolf Caracciola took the class for racing cars of up to 8 litres with an SSK averaging 89.9km/h (55.8mph) and claiming best time of day as well.

For the moment, of course, the SSK was simply not available as far as the buying public was concerned, and in wealthy circles the SS was now the car to have. Although the 6.8-litre Type S remained available, the new 7.1-litre SS

took over as the Mercedes flagship, becoming available through showrooms in November 1928 or thereabouts. Prices were once again far beyond the reach of all but the seriously rich. The bare chassis cost 31,000 Reichsmarks; with Sindelfingen's four-seater sports body an SS was 35,000 RM; a two-seater Cabriolet A was 42,000 RM and a four-seater Cabriolet C was 44,000 RM. Despite similarities, all these bodies were different from those seen on the Type S cars because the taller Type SS radiator also raised the line of the scuttle and therefore ultimately of the body's waistline.

Just 111 road versions of the SS were built between 1928 and 1933, plus a further four works competition specials with an even higher state of tune. From 1930, a raised compression

This is Sindelfingen's tourer body for the SS. It was elegant and imposing and, as the picture shows, actually managed to look quite rakish with the top up. Variations in colour scheme, the position of the spare wheels, and accessories such as the bumpers and stoneguards for radiator and headlights, make these two cars more different than they appear at first sight. The chassis could be had with either left-hand or right-hand steering.

ratio and different camshaft delivered a little more power, and under the old classification system the car became a 27/160/200. As on the Type S, there was a selection of final drive options to bias the car towards acceleration or maximum speed, or simply to compensate for heavier bodywork.

Not at all surprising was that development of the M06 engine continued after the production specification had been settled, and by the end of 1928 the works cars were delivering 170bhp unblown and 225bhp with the blower engaged. A bigger supercharger produced that last astounding figure, delivering 10psi of boost,

The basic tourer body could be finished to suit individual taste, and this 1928 example manages to look very different from the standard offering. The sweeping front wings have gone, to be replaced by helmet-type wings and built-in toolboxes, while the spare wheels seem to have been banished to the tail. Two-tone paint, front and rear bumpers, and a radiator stoneguard complete the transformation.

The long bonnet of the SS chassis helps give an impression of immense power in this side view of a roadster model. Just visible on the running-board is a Sindelfingen characteristic – a foot scraper on which passengers could wipe muddy boots before entering the expensively finished interior.

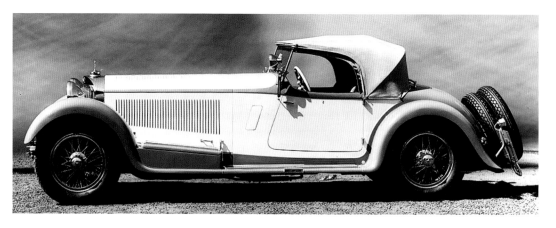

Expensive motor cars were fashionable among the Indian ruling classes in the first third of the 20th century, and wealthy rulers vied with one another for the most extravagant designs. The SS chassis was an obvious candidate for their interest, and that interest added to its kudos in Germany. The car pictured in this advertisement, which evokes the Maharajahs' taste for such machines, is nevertheless a standard Sindelfingen-built tourer – though somewhat lowered and elongated for effect.

In Britain, the SS was known as a 38/250 type, and this example was delivered to a British buyer in 1930. It then became very well-known while in the ownership of old-car specialist Bunty Scott-Moncrieff. The elegant shape of the doors is noteworthy, and must have made access for the front-seat occupants easier. The dashboard arrangement was fairly typical of the period, with the speedometer and rev counter mounted where they could most easily be seen and the minor instruments mounted where they could be made to fit.

Plenty of chrome contrasts with the dark-painted wire wheels on this SS cabriolet by the Italian coachbuilder Castagna.

The use of steps instead of running-boards gives an altogether more sporting air to this cabriolet by the Belgian coachbuilder D'Ieteren Frères. A tall driver would have had trouble seeing out of that letter-box windscreen.

This is Castagna again, although there are subtle differences on this SS cabriolet, which boasts a dickey seat and has its spare wheels carried at the rear while there are tool boxes on the front wings.

This was the Mercedes-Benz stand at the Paris Show in 1928, and the car in the foreground is an SS chassis bodied in typically dramatic fashion by Parisian coachbuilder Saoutchik. Oddly, the car seems to have the paired radiator stars associated with the early Type S rather than the single central star of the SS and later S.

There is an uncharacteristic awkwardness about this Vanden Plas body, which the coachbuilder's records show was supposed to be along the lines of one built on Bentley chassis. The outer panels were covered in fabric, and the body was completed in October 1929 for a cost of £429.

Actress Lilian Harvey was of mixed British and German descent, and became enormously popular in Germany in the 1930s as the era of the "talkies" began. She owned a special-bodied SS, which is pictured here in a signed photograph.

while a new camshaft was also in the specification. These cars were designated 27/170/225 types. Typically, they raced with either cycle wings or no wings at all to reduce weight and wind resistance.

The SS was built with both left- and right-hand drive for markets such as Britain, and like the Type S, it became a favourite of the rich and famous as well as a highly successful racing machine. Celebrity owners included British-born film star Lilian Harvey and German film star Willy Forst. In Germany, there were cabriolet bodies from Erdmann & Rossi, Papler, and the Stuttgart firm of Reutter. In Britain, Abbey, Barker, Curtis, Freestone & Webb, Harrington and Vanden Plas all built bodies on what was known in that country as the 38/250 chassis. From France came Kellner and Saoutchik creations, from Belgium a two-seater cabriolet by d'Ieteren Frères of Brussels, from Austria a four-seater cabriolet by Keibl in Vienna, and from Italy a cabriolet by Castagna. There were others,

The Vanden Plas coupé body on this SS chassis was built in Britain and looks it. The coachbuilder's records show that it was completed in May 1931 at a cost of £495.

The body on this 38/250, as the SS was known in Britain, was supposedly built by Harrington some time around 1930.

This car started life in 1928 as an SS, but in Britain it was rebodied by Abbey and acquired a 1936 registration number.

This 1929 SS was bodied as a fixed-head coupé by Curtis of London W1, its proportions emphasising the great length of the bonnet, which has been made to slope slightly upwards to the base of the windscreen.

Freestone & Webb bodied quite a number of Mercedes chassis between 1926 and the mid-1930s. Here we see a quite lofty four-door saloon, with incomplete coupé and tourer bodies alongside.

Another 1929 SS receiving a fabric-covered tourer body (or possibly a re-body) at the Folkestone workshops of Martin Walter.

Rudolf Caracciola's win in the 1929 International Tourist Trophy race with an SS was an indication that the Mercedes works team had international aspirations.

Caracciola with Christian Werner, who partnered him in the 1930 Le Mans.

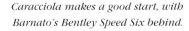

Carracciola with Otto Merz. They drove separate cars in the 1929 Tourist Trophy, which Caracciola won.

The Caracciola/Werner SS at Le Mans before the race.

Caracciola makes a good start, with Barnato's Bentley Speed Six behind.

too, not all of them firmly identified even now.

While these elegant bodies told of their owners' wealth and taste, "works" cars pounded the tracks. A particularly notable occasion was the Ulster TT in August 1929, when a team of two Mercedes contested the race. The drivers were Caracciola and Otto Merz. Merz, in car number 71, crashed but was so determined to continue that he ripped the damaged wing off his car with his bare hands and pressed on. The race nevertheless went to Caracciola.

The SS was meanwhile becoming the "works" team's choice for long-distance events, while the short-chassis SSK was reserved for hill-climbs and other carefully chosen outings. So it was with an SS that Mercedes tackled the Le Mans 24-hour race in July 1930, as their first entry in

Barnato closes on the Mercedes, Werner driving, on the Saturday evening at Le Mans. By 2.30am the white car was out of the race.

this now prestigious event. Arguably, the decision to enter just one car, crewed by Caracciola and his regular partner Christian Werner, was bordering on the arrogant. Nevertheless, the pair were fresh from their triumph at that year's Mille Miglia (where they had won in an SSK) and there was every reason to think that they would finish at the front of the front runners in the French event as well. With careful pre-event preparation, inspired by the example of the Bentley team, they were quietly confident.

However, the weakness of the SS as indeed of the other supercharged Mercedes was that the supercharger could not be used for long periods without risking damage to the engine. Knowing this, the five-car Bentley team worked out a race strategy which focused on harassing the Mercedes to force Caracciola and Werner to use the supercharger to excess. They must have been able to tell instantly how effective this was, too: as Cyril Posthumus sagely noted in *Motor* of 7 Jan 1978, "An unexpected snag [with the supercharger] in racing was that the opposition could always tell when the Mercedes were being hard pressed by the amount of blower scream". At Le Mans in 1930, the SS was formidably fast, as expected, but the Bentley tactics had the desired effect: the SS was obliged to retire on the 83rd lap with a blown head gasket (the Bentley team version of the story) or a

failed dynamo (the Mercedes version). It was Bentley's swan song. They won the event but retired from motor racing shortly afterwards.

Behind the wheel of an SS

Motor Sport managed to borrow Caracciola's Ulster TT-winning SS for a test drive while it was still in its German racing white and before its new owner, racing driver Earl Howe, had repainted it in his own colours of blue and silver, although it had acquired the UK number-plate of GW 302. Their impressions were published in the November 1929 issue, and once again the controllability of the car was impressive. "Although the Mercedes is a big car in actual size", they noted, "it handles in every way as well as the neatest little road-racer ever built...(and)... its extremely sober behaviour when once more back in the congestion which is London left nothing to be desired." The servo-assisted brakes had "astonishing power" too. However, "the acceleration using the gears is simply phenomenal... nothing but an actual run in the car can give any idea of the power developed by the latest 7-litre engine". The speedometer registered 114mph at the maximum engine speed of 3200rpm.

The Motor then managed to borrow a right-hand-drive 38/250 with the factory's own two-door, four-seat touring body and published

CHASSIS NUMBERS

No complete list of the chassis numbers for S and SS cars is known to exist, and current Daimler-Benz policy is "not to disclose or comment on ID numbers or number batches of our cars".

Engine and chassis numbers did not usually match on the six-cylinder cars, and it is worth noting the details of some surviving examples that are believed still to have their original engines.

Chassis no / Type / Year / Engine no / Commission no

35906 / S / 1928 / 68657
35947 / S / 1928 / 71819 / 40647
35964 / S / 1928 / 72166
36045 / SSK / 1929 / 77631 / 49748
40156 / S / 1928 / 72151

Nevertheless, the records of the UK sales company transcribed by Michael Frostick in *The Mighty Mercedes* give only the engine number (plus, occasionally, a Commission Number; see Chapter 1). This seems bizarre, but no doubt the company had its reasons.

HOW MANY WERE THERE?

In determining the build quantities of the Mercedes S and SS cars, we are dogged by the usual set of problems. First, many records have been lost. Second, the Mercedes-Benz "official" records appear to cover production cars only, and do not include development models. Third, there are many conflicting sets of figures that have been published over the years, and it is not always easy to discover what sources were used in compiling them. Fourth, the Daimler-Benz archives are no longer prepared to furnish sets of chassis numbers.

S

The "official" Mercedes-Benz production figure is 146 cars.

This is further broken down by Werner Oswald, in *Mercedes-Benz Personenwagen 1886-1984*, as follows:

1928	18
1929	123
1930	5

However, Oswald also includes a further 28 cars, of which 20 were built in 1927 and the remaining 8 in 1928. Other sources, as noted in the text, argue for 28 (or 27) 660K competition models built between 1927 and 1933. The similarity of the figures may be just coincidence, but it may be that these two groups of cars are one and the same.

SS

The "official" Mercedes-Benz production figure is 111 cars.
Of these, five were 27/170/225 types.
The others are all noted as 27/140/200 types, and in their total must be included the 27/160/200 models from 1930.

Werner Oswald gives a completely different set of figures, as follows:

27/160/200 model		27/170/225 model	
Total	32	Total	119
1927	3	1928	4
1928	13	1929	63
1929	14	1930	33
1930	2	1931	4
		1932	4
		1933	2
		1934	8
		1935	1

its evaluation in the issue dated 16 June 1931. Maximum speed, tested at the Brooklands track, of course, was 103.2mph on the standard axle ratio of 2.76:1, considerably lower than the 114mph of the racer that *Motor Sport* had tested but altogether more typical of a roadgoing SS. The zero to 60mph increment, not of great importance in 1931 but a yardstick in modern times, took a little under 20 seconds. Fuel consumption was quoted as 12-13mpg.

The Motor praised the car's "extraordinarily effortless" running, found its steering "somewhat heavy" and was not at all impressed with its brakes. Third gear in the close-ratio gearbox occasioned comment, being "so close to top that its use is mainly confined to securing even better acceleration at the higher speeds than is possible in top gear". Also interesting was that 'the blower makes but little difference below a speed of about 35mph, which represents an engine speed of only 1000rpm". This was, of course, a hugely expensive car with a price tag of £2350.

Delivered in the UK in 1930, this lovely SS tourer originally carried the registration number CJ 1490 and went to H Miles (Motors) Ltd.

The instrument dials visible here are all of UK manufacture, as are many of the switches.

Hood up, the rear interior is a luxurious cocoon – although that vertical backrest cushion might have been uncomfortable over long distances.

The kick-plates carry the Mercedes-Benz name.

SPECIFICATIONS

TYPE S
OR 26/120/180
(1928-30)

Engine:
6789cc 6-cylinder with 98mm bore
and 150mm stroke
Overhead valves and overhead
camshaft
Four main bearings
Compression ratio 4.7:1
Single Mercedes-Benz twin-choke
carburettor
Roots-type supercharger driven by
gear from crankshaft
120PS at 3000rpm
180PS at 3000rpm with blower
engaged
Torque 432Nm (318lb ft) at 1850rpm

Gearbox:
Four-speed; ratios 3.15:1, 1.81:1,
1.21:1, 1.00:1.

Axle ratio:
2.76:1 standard; 2.50:1 and 3.09:1
optional

Chassis:
Channel-section steel
Wheelbase 3400mm
Track 1425mm

Overall:
Overall dimensions
4700-5000 x 1700 x 1800mm
Weight 2000kg with cabriolet body
Maximum speed 170km/h (105mph)
on 2.76:1 axle ratio

TYPE SS
OR 27/140/200 (1928-1930)/
27/160/200 (1930-32)

Engine:
7065cc 6-cylinder with 100mm bore
and 150mm stroke
Overhead valves and overhead
camshaft
Four main bearings
Compression ratio 5.2:1
Single Mercedes-Benz twin-choke
carburettor
Roots-type supercharger driven by
gear from crankshaft
140PS (1928-1930);
160PS (1930-1932)
200PS at 3300rpm with blower
engaged
Torque 450Nm (332lb ft) at 1920rpm

Gearbox:
Four-speed; ratios 2.75:1, 1.55:1,
1.12:1, 1.100:1

Axle ratio:
2.76:1 standard; 2.50:1 and 3.09:1
optional

Chassis:
Channel-section steel
Wheelbase 3400mm
Track 1425mm

Overall:
Overall dimensions
4700-5000 x 1700 x 1750mm
Weight 2100kg with cabriolet body
Maximum speed 185km/h (115mph)
on 2.76:1 axle ratio

TYPE SS
OR 27/170/225
(1928-34)

Engine:
7065cc 6-cylinder with 100mm bore
and 150mm stroke
Overhead valves and overhead
camshaft
Four main bearings
Compression ratio 6.2:1
Single Mercedes-Benz twin-choke
carburettor
Roots-type supercharger driven by
gear from crankshaft
170PS
225PS at 3300rpm with blower
engaged
Torque 453Nm (334 lb ft) at
1900rpm

Gearbox:
Four-speed; ratios 2.75:1, 1.55:1,
1.12:1, 1.100:1

Axle ratio:
2.48:1 or 2.55:1

Chassis:
Channel-section steel
Wheelbase 3400mm
Track 1425mm

Overall:
Overall dimensions
4700-5000 x 1700 x 1750mm
Weight 2100kg with cabriolet body
Maximum speed 190km/h (118mph)
on 2.48:1 axle ratio

Restorers are not always as careful as they might be. This is a truly dreadful fake identification plate; it would not have taken much care at least to get the spelling of Untertürkheim right!

Although the engine top cover caries the Mercedes-Benz name, the lower casting on the exhaust side has the letters DMG, harking back to the pre-1926 days of the Daimler Motoren Gesellschaft.

Chapter Five

WHITE LIGHTNING

The SSK and SSKL

A short-chassis SSK stands next to a "standard" SS tourer and makes very clear the difference between the two sizes of chassis.

The story of what happened next is very well known – up to a point. In fact, the story of the short-chassis derivatives of the SS – the SSK and SSKL – is shrouded in half-truths, legends and supposition to such an extent that the word "probably" will occur with alarming frequency in the chapter that follows. Although the headline news is not in doubt, it is underpinned with uncertainties.

First of all, it is important to recognise that the short-chassis cars were not replacements for the S or SS but were derivatives of them that were built at more or less the same time and were intended primarily for competition use. What is indisputable is that the Mercedes engineers had realised at quite an early stage – in fact even before the SS had reached the marketplace in 1928 – that their new 7.1-litre car was too large to be competitive in the hill-climb events which were so much a part of the German motorsport scene in the late 1920s. What was needed was a more agile, manoeuvrable car.

So Ferdinand Porsche and his team set to work on the car that would be his last for Mercedes-Benz. Ever since the merger between

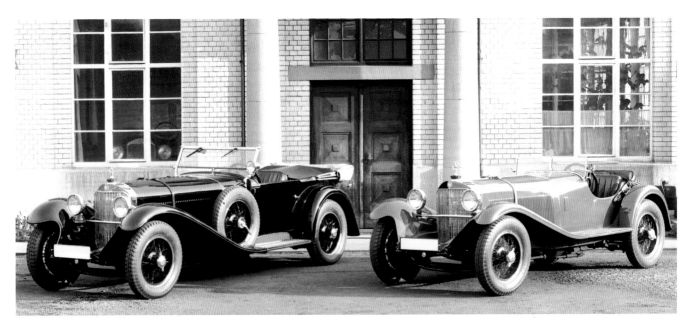

These two views of an SSK chassis, one taken from a sales catalogue and consequently somewhat cleaned up by an airbrush, show the single-minded determination behind its design. This was a hill-climb special, so it needed the shortest possible wheelbase to promote agility, plus the largest and most powerful engine to deliver performance. There was little room for anything else.

Daimler and Benz in 1926, there had been a somewhat uneasy truce in the engineering department, where the former Benz chief engineer, Hans Nibel, was obliged to work alongside Porsche as joint Chief Engineer. As already noted in Chapter 3, Porsche left at the end of 1928 and Nibel took over.

The new car was a formidable swansong for the great engineer. What Porsche did was simple and quite obvious: he shortened the wheelbase of the SS chassis by a massive 1450mm (17.7in), taking out weight in the process. Though the car was now realistically only a two-seater, that was of little consequence for competition. Besides, coachbuilders were adept at squeezing four seats into a short space to get around racing regulations if they really had to – although none would ever do that on this car. The short-chassis car was baptised an SSK ("Sport Special Kurz", or Short Special Sports) and took on the new works designation W06 II.

Even though the SSK was never intended as a volume-production road car, Daimler-Benz were certainly not averse to building a few to special

order for those with enough money and cheek to ask. Yet before the car was offered to the public, it had to prove that it was fit for the purpose for which it had been designed. So right from the start the SSK was pitched into hill-climb events with Mercedes' star driver Rudolf Caracciola at the wheel.

The new short-chassis car made its competition debut on 29 July 1928 at the Gabellach hill-climb event, and immediately demonstrated that it was indeed fit for purpose. Caracciola not only won the event but also set a new record for the Gabellach course. Further victories in the hill-climbs at the Semmering, the Schauinsland near Freiburg and at Mont Ventoux showed that the SSK was absolutely the right car for such events. At the final race on the Salzberg, a thrilling duel between between Caracciola's SSK and Hans Stuck's Austro-Daimler left the SSK in second place, but Caracciola was nevertheless rewarded with a special prize for outstanding sporting achievement.

Those first "works" SSKs were clothed in ultra-simple two-seat roadster bodywork, with a

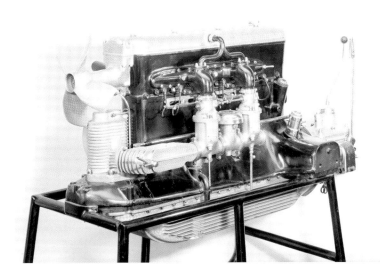

The "standard" SSK engine was of course essentially the same as that used in the SS. This one seems to have been finished to a high standard, perhaps for show purposes. A comparison with the SS engine pictured in Chapter 4 is interesting.

similarly simple folding hood that was more token than proper weather protection, and they had cycle-type wings that could be removed to reduce weight even further during competitive events. Indeed, the Mercedes crews regularly did remove them, and shed the headlamps and folding hoods as well. Nevertheless, the car that was offered to the public from November 1928 was a little more civilised. It came as standard with sweeping wings and running-boards which gave it more of a family resemblance to the S and SS models to which it was related.

The "works" SSKs were of course racing machines, and so the precise specification of their engines probably varied from one event to the next. Although it seems indisputable that they always had the same 7.1-litre swept volume, power outputs varied as the racing department's engineers tried new ideas. So

although the first production cars were described as 27/140/200 models, indicating that their engines delivered 140PS unblown and 200PS with the supercharger engaged, this was simply a convenient specification that was known to work and was not so extreme that the cars would be difficult or undriveable on the road. It would be completely reasonable to assume that the power outputs of the "works" engines rapidly exceeded these figures.

In fact, the SSK was only rarely described by this string of numbers, not least because its engines were identical to those in contemporary SS types, so that using the power designation would have been simply confusing. It was also true that these rating figures were no longer relevant to buyers of the cars after the German taxation system had changed in 1928; it was simpler just to call the cars SSKs unless there was a need to be technically precise.

It is worth being technically precise here, though, because it helps to understand the evolution of the SSK. As was only to be expected, engine development was more or less constant at Stuttgart, and the original 1928 specification was improved for 1929, with an extra 20PS available in the unblown state so that the specification of the later cars made them 27/160/200 types

The black-and-white picture shows very well how the SSK's engine and front end looked when new. However, various items are not present in order to show the engine more clearly. The colour picture shows the Daimler-Benz Museum's SSK, with the missing items – such as supports for the flexible downpipes – now in their correct places.

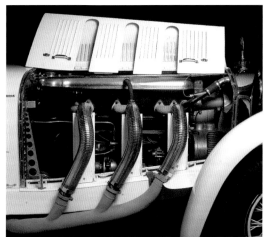

The SSK was offered as a roadgoing car as well, although relatively few were built. The minimalist bodywork was essentially the same as on the works competition cars, but the sweeping wings did make the car look more civilised. At the rear, there was just enough metal to cover the fuel tank and provide a mounting for the spare wheels. A fairly skimpy hood was standard equipment, as the catalogue illustration shows, but even that could be left off, as the picture of the two-tone car shows. The Mercedes name painted on the chassis side-member of that car is odd, and unexplained.

The "works" cars were nevertheless ahead of this. Using special fuel, their engines could tolerate a higher compression ratio and as early as 1928 were delivering 170PS unblown, with 225PS when the supercharger was engaged. These engines were still known as M06 types, although the cars that had them carried the W06 III designation. Then from 1929, some "works" SSKs were fitted with an even more powerful engine called the MS06; the S seems to have stood for "Spezial", and the cars also attracted the new designation of WS06. These engines had a bigger supercharger (known familiarly as the "elephant blower"), whose additional length of around half an inch forced air through the twin carburettors at pressures up to 12psi. With a different camshaft as well, the MS06 engine delivered 180bhp before the supercharger cut in and 250bhp once it was engaged. At least, those were the quoted figures, and the cars were

known as 27/180/250 types; some experts have claimed that the actual maximum output was as high as 275bhp, and that was certainly possible in view of later developments. A huge increase in maximum torque aided acceleration, too.

The SSK in production

Even to speak of a "production" SSK is potentially misleading because the word conjures up slow-moving assembly lines with workers toiling away at their repetitive tasks. It was quite simply not like that for the SSK, which was a hand-built car that was made only to order. The buyers to whom the model appealed were inevitably few and far between, and they had to be both wealthy and have more interest in the performance of their car than in its creature comforts. It would be reasonable to assume that many SSK buyers had at least one other, more practical car to use for everyday driving. The

Far too comfortable-looking to be a serious competition model, this SSK was bodied at Sindelfingen, presumably for a private customer. Note the rather awkward-looking rear end, which presumably contains luggage accommodation, and the relocation of the spare wheels to the sides of the bonnet.

Only seven SSKs were sold in Britain, where the car was known by the same 38/250 name as the SS; it was simply a short-chassis model. This one shows a number of variations from the standard specification, in the helmet-type wings and the tool box which doubles as a step. It was delivered new in 1929 and became well known after 1945 in VSCC circles when it was owned by George Milligen. The car, finished in red, sold for just under £4.2 million at auction in September 2004.

SSK was a machine for weekend fun.

Most of the competition cars sold to privateers probably had Sindelfingen's own simple two-seater body with cycle wings and the spare wheels mounted on the tail, above the fuel tank.

Modifications could be had to order, of course, and one car seems to have come from Sindelfingen with side-mounted spares and a slightly ungainly trunk at the rear – luggage space was never a feature of the standard SSK. Another body that Sindelfingen built to special order was one that featured teardrop wings and extra searchlights; it was delivered to the Maharaja of Bhopal in India as a tiger-hunting car.

Some outside coachbuilders were commissioned to do their best as well, and the German firm of Papler produced a neat cabriolet, while in Britain at least one was bodied by Corsica, famed for their lightweight coachwork. Carlton also bodied one, and Barker bodied a roadster for the Hon Dorothy Paget, who was using it at the time she was funding Tim Birkin's "blower" Bentley racing team. In 1932, a 1929 chassis

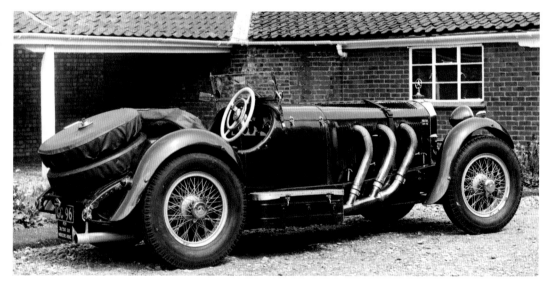

This SSK was built to special order for an Indian Maharajah as a tiger-hunting car. It was festooned with searchlights – one could be erected behind the driving compartment – and carried additional batteries to power them.

originally shipped to Japan was bought by Count Trossi and bodied in Britain with semi-streamlined coachwork by Willie White; that car has since become a well-known sight on the international concours scene.

Inevitably, the SSK was much less numerous than the S and SS types that had preceded it. No more than 38 (the exact figure is, of course, disputed) were built before production ended in June 1932, and about half of these were sold to members of the public, mainly for competition use. Some even had right-hand drive. They were attractively priced, if you were rich: a bare chassis cost 29,000 Reichsmarks and with Sindelfingen's own two-seater bodywork the complete car was 33,000 RM – figures somewhat cheaper than those asked for the slower and larger SS model.

Not every SSK was bodied as a roadster. These pictures show a very neat Cabriolet A body built by Papler in Cologne, whose logo is visible just in front of the door. The coachbuilder has managed the overall proportions very skilfully, to produce a car which at first sight looks no bigger than a British MG T series of the 1930s.

There was not much that could be taken off an SSK to reduce the weight further, but the Mercedes "works" team stripped the cars of wings and headlights for competition. This is Rudi Caracciola driving an SSK at the Semmering event in 1928, when he set a new record for the course.

The SSK in competition

Today, the SSK enjoys something that is more akin to a legend than a mere reputation, and it most certainly did become an extremely potent force in international motor sport events between 1928 and 1932, by which time it was being bested by the latest Alfa Romeo 8C 2300 models. But it is worth examining the SSK legend in a little more detail, to see what really lies behind it.

The fact is that the car did extremely well as a hill-climb special, fulfilling its design brief admirably. It was far less successful on the circuits and in long-distance races. After those initial successes in 1928, already recorded above, it continued to excel. One early 1929 result was Caracciola's win at the Zbraslav-Jiloviste hill-climb race in Prague, when he claimed best time for a racing machine at the event as well.

The year 1930 saw the publicity value of hill-climb events move up a notch, because this was the first year for the European Hillclimb Championship. There were rounds held in several different European countries, and this meant that the SSK could be used to publicise Mercedes excellence in a much wider area than the Swiss, German and Austrian mountain regions which had been its stamping-ground until now. Not that Caracciola would ever have done less than his best, but no doubt he entered every round of the new championship in 1930 with the exhortations of the Daimler-Benz management ringing in his ears.

He did not disappoint that management. Caracciola and the SSK won every round of the sports car hill-climb events for which they entered, with victories at Zbraslav-Jiloviste (Czechoslovakia), Cuneo (Italy), Shelsley Walsh (UK), Klausenpass (Switzerland), Schauinsland (Germany), Semmering (Austria) and Svábhegy (Hungary). This result saw Caracciola become the first-ever European Hillclimb Champion.

With the car once again stripped to its essentials, this is Caracciola with an SSK at Monaco in 1929.

Caracciola and an SSK in competition again, this time in 1930.

But the competition was now hotting up. Other manufacturers could also see that success in this championship would bring valuable publicity, and Stuttgart's engineers knew that they would have to keep on improving the performance of the SSK. So for 1931, they developed something new.

Despite these successes at hillclimb events, the SSK took some time to make its mark in circuit and long-distance racing. Its 1929 results on the tracks kicked off with a third place for Caracciola at the inaugural Monaco Grand Prix; he might have won but for a lengthy stop for fuel and tyres. In the Grand Prix des Nations for sports cars at the Nürburgring on 14 July, the SSK crewed by August Momberger and Max Arco-Zinneberg could manage no better than third place behind a pair of Bugattis. Momberger and the SSK achieved the same placing in that year's Italian Grand Prix. Mercedes clearly had reservations about the car's durability in long-distance races, too, because they declined to enter the Le Mans 24-hour race in June, leaving it to the big Bentleys to achieve their third successive Le Mans win against a field largely composed of American machinery.

In Argentina, Carlos Zatusek managed to get his hands on an SSK and campaigned it vigorously in his adopted country, claiming victories in the 500 Miles of Argentina race and in the Cordoba Grand Prix during 1929. Perhaps more impressive was Caracciola's heroic win in August at the International Tourist Trophy race in Ireland, where he battled through torrential rain to win at an average speed of 117.2km/h (72.8mph). Even so, this was more of a demonstration of Caracciola's skill at the wheel – not for nothing was he known as "der Regenmeister" (the rain master) – than of the car's inherent abilities.

The SSK remained unconvincing in long-distance events during 1930. Mercedes risked an entry in that year's Mille Miglia in April, with Caracciola partnered by Christian Werner, but their sixth place overall was a disappointment, despite the capital that was made out of it. The car finished more than an hour off the pace behind four Alfa Romeos and an OM, and a class win was no real compensation.

The story has been regularly repeated that Caracciola then drove an SSK at that year's Le Mans. However, the car most emphatically was not an SSK but an SS, as recounted in Chapter 4;

the short-chassis car was not right for the 24-hour race. Nevertheless it was an Irish event that was good for Caracciola and the SSK once again, when the pairing claimed victory in the Irish Grand Prix at Dublin's Phoenix Park circuit in July. In seven races, they won seven times and set seven new records. Caracciola had entered as part of a private team with British drivers Earl Howe and Malcolm Campbell, and the three were rewarded with the event's team prize. Howe is said to have been so impressed with his team-mate's performance that he immediately bought the winning car to go with the SS he already owned.

The SSK's successes continued into 1931, but the times were changing. First, the car was

The SSK made its last major appearances as a works racer during 1930, as the SSKL would take over for 1931. Here, Caracciola wins the Irish Grand Prix at Phoenix Park on 19 July 1930.

During the 1930 Irish GP, Caracciola is seen moving up on Earl Howe's Mercedes, itself an ex-works car.

Nearly a quarter of a century after it was built, this SSK waits in the paddock at a British race meeting in the 1950s.

rapidly supplanted that year by the new light-weight SSKL model as the flagship sports-racing Mercedes; and second, there was the minor inconvenience that for 1931 Mercedes-Benz no longer officially had a works racing team. Not that they allowed this to stop them.

Few all-original SSKs survive today, probably only four or five. There are, however, several impeccable replicas. Many of these have been built from components salvaged from original cars that were crashed during competition, and can thus be claimed to have some genuine Mercedes-Benz provenance. Cyril Posthumus listed no fewer than six surviving SSKs in 1978, and thought that at least four more existed, but he did not distinguish between the genuine SSKs and those created out of other cars. All of them rank among the most desirable cars for wealthy collectors, but auction prices of several million dollars inevitably restrict their ownership to a very small côterie of enthusiasts.

Behind the wheel of an SSK

Gordon Wilkins remembered his first drive in an SSK for *Car* magazine in March 1980. "I was careful to get it all together," he noted, referring to the need to remember that the accelerator pedal was in the centre and the brake on the right, "before pointing the SSK down a deserted straight and flooring the vital pedal. I felt like someone about to take a ride on a tiger, especially since the car had by then acquired a reputation for being unstoppable. As the blower engaged the noise was fantastic, but the acceleration was not. Mercedes-Benz talked of the S accelerating from walking pace to 103mph in a few seconds in top gear, but one press test quoted 0-60 in 18 sec for the SSK. Certainly the car did not display its best to 60, what with the blower cutting in and out and a difficult change from first to second. It was smoother and more flexible and generally more impressive at higher speeds. But one was not supposed to keep the blower engaged for more than 20 sec at a time, since there was always a risk of blowing a gasket.

"The SSK had a fine, relaxed feel cruising fast without the blower, the big engine working mostly below 3000rpm thanks to the high gearing which was ideal for fast, long trips. In spite of the kick-down clutch and all the plumbing, people at the time seemed to feel that throttle response compared well with that of the blower Bentley. The SSK's brakes were better than I had been led to expect; the problem seems to have been a need for frequent adjustment. All in all, the SSK was a tough, macho machine for rich extroverts."

This car from the Daimler-Benz Museum exemplifies the modern public perception of an SSK, but the cycle-winged cars such as this were of course intended specifically for competition use. The quick-release filler cap is also a competition item, and the dashboard is nothing if not businesslike.

Many surviving S, SS and SSK cars (and all the surviving SSKLs) are actually composed of parts of several different original cars. This car is on a genuine SSK chassis, although the body was probably built in Britain after the 1939-1945 war and subsequently modified to resemble more closely the classic Sindelfingen-built style. The car spent several years in the Bernie Ecclestone Collection.

The steering wheel and dash are correct on this car, but many of the instruments (here hidden from view) are British Jaeger units that would not have been original equipment.

The front axle has anti-shimmy dampers to prevent high-speed oscillations. The right-hand rear wheel is missing the centre of its eared hub spinner and the headlamps are slightly later Bosch units than would originally have been fitted.

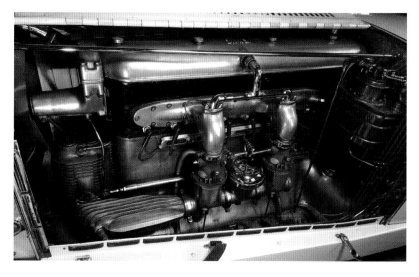

The three outside exhausts were characteristic of the supercharged models in the late 1920s.
The engine is a genuine original SSK unit, and incorporates a number of the magnesium components that were available from Mercedes-Benz to reduce weight for racing. They include the tops of the carburettors.

The radiator has a stone-guard of the type commonly specified for competition cars.

This is the classic SSKL, originally known simply as a 1931-model SSK. The drilling of the chassis frame is quite obvious here, and there are holes in the front of the side-members, too, although they are covered by light sheet metal to reduce the risk of flying stones hitting the underside of the engine.

SSKL: the ultimate lightweight

By the time the next iteration of the super-charged Porsche six-cylinder models appeared in public, Mercedes-Benz had officially withdrawn from motorsport. The Wall Street Crash of October 1929 had forced car makers all over the world to rein in their expenditure, and Mercedes-Benz, operating to a large extent at the more expensive end of the market, was particularly badly hit. During 1930 the company barely broke even; in 1931 it lost 7 million Reichsmarks; and it did not return to profit until 1933, when it began to make a strong recovery that would last for the rest of the decade. In the meantime, the Mannheim plant was mothballed and racing was identified as one very expensive activity that could reasonably be suspended, if only for the short term. So in November 1930, Mercedes-Benz announced that they would withdraw from competition.

However, Racing Department head Alfred Neubauer sensed that this withdrawal was likely to be only temporary, and he concocted a scheme to keep Mercedes-Benz cars in the public eye at motorsport events by means of a personal contract with the company's star driver, Caracciola. Wilhelm Kissel, the Managing Director, could see the sense in the plan, and approved it. The deal was that Daimler-Benz would provide equipment and support – a company car and a generous financial package as well – for Caracciola's racing in return for a percentage of all the prize money he earned. Neubauer assembled a small racing team around Caracciola, consisting of the latter's wife Charley (Charlotte), Willy Zimmer as mechanic and Wilhelm Sebastian as co-driver.

Those are not steps to help the crew get in, but shelves on which tools and jerry-cans could be stowed for long-distance races.

Besides, Mercedes had a formidable new car to use. Not only did this have the most potent version of the 7.1-litre engine yet developed, but it had also been through a radical weight-shedding programme. The car was initially known simply as the 1931-model SSK; only during 1932 did the name SSKL come into use,

Mudguards and headlamps were removed to shed weight for track events. This was Caracciola in an SSKL after winning the Avus race in Berlin in 1931 at an average speed of 185.7km/h (115 mph).

Another race, another garland of flowers for the winning SSKL. Here, the plates protecting the drillings in the frame sides have been extended further rearwards.

those initials standing for "Super Sport Kurz Leicht", or Lightweight short-chassis Super Sports. The SSK was very much a "works" special, and it took on the works build code of W06 RS, the RS probably standing for "Rennsport Spezial" or Racing Special.

The racing department had been gradually developing the supercharged engine to coax more and more power from it, and this development programme was guided by Albert Heess. The enlarged or so-called "elephant" supercharger had already been seen in the works SSK racers, and by 1931 the engine was able to deliver 240bhp before the blower was engaged, and a stupendous 300bhp at full stretch. For the SSKL, this ultimate version of the supercharged Porsche six-cylinder engine was known as an M06RS type. Its very high compression ratio (for the time) demanded the use of special racing fuels, and the torque that delivered its stupendous acceleration was simply massive.

Meanwhile, Max Wagner had overseen the

weight-saving programme. The bodywork of the SSK was already so skimpy that there was no substantial saving in weight to be made there. The engine was already as light as it could reasonably be, as it made extensive use of aluminium alloys such as Elektron and in any case needed all the strength it could find in its construction to withstand the additional strains being put on it by constant demands for more power. So Wagner shed weight from the chassis. He began with thinner-section steel for the frame, and drilled large holes in the side members, a series of smaller holes in the bulkhead support frame, and yet more holes in such items as the clutch and accelerator pedals. The result was a colossal saving of 125kg (275lb). With the same minimal two-seater bodywork as the SSK, and stripped of the cycle wings and headlamps needed for road use, the racing SSKL was claimed to have a maximum speed of 235km/h (146mph).

So this was the car that made its public debut in April 1931 in the hands of Caracciola and Werner at the Mille Miglia event. Mercedes were understandably keen to improve on their sixth place at the 1930 event, and they knew that it had been largely bad luck that had robbed them

Caracciola's victory in the 1931 Mille Miglia was a huge triumph for Mercedes-Benz, even though the SSKL was supposedly a private entry. This is car number 87 awaiting the starting flag; co-driver Wilhelm Sebastian is holding his hand up to wave as Caracciola talks to his wife, Charley. The lamps are all protected against flying stones by fabric covers, the radiator has a stoneguard, and the drilled chassis also has protective sheets right back to the front of the back wheel. There is no stowage shelf on this side; as the picture above shows, tools and jerrycans were stowed on the co-driver's side only.

Though this car looks the part, it is not a genuine SSKL. No genuine cars are known to survive. This one was constructed in the USA in the 1960s for General Motors design chief Bill Mitchell on the basis of a 1928 Type S, and uses parts from a number of different cars. It is generally considered one of the finest replicas to exist. In these views, the non-original windscreen is clear, and the headlights are of an earlier Bosch pattern than was used on the genuine SSKLs. After passing through the hands of other US collectors, it became part of the Hayashi Collection in Japan, and then in 1996 joined the Bernie Ecclestone Collection. It was sold on again in 2007

of a win. Even so, the choice of an unproven short-chassis car for a long-distance event was a big risk.

Although the SSKL was not officially a works entry, it is doubtful whether many onlookers noticed, or even cared. This was a Mercedes-Benz, and just as there was no real doubt about its provenance, so there was never any doubt about Mercedes' intentions. The Caracciola/Sebastian SSKL tackled the Italian classic with determination, and that determination was rewarded with victory. The SSKL

finished in first place overall with an average speed of 101.1km/h (62.8mph) over the thousand miles, marking the first Mille Miglia win by a non-Italian in a foreign car and the first time the average speed had exceeded 100km/h. For much of the race, Caracciola had simply no idea of how well or otherwise he was doing: the support provided by Mercedes did not run to the wayside spares dumps and other support that the Italian manufacturers provided for their teams. His time of 16 hours, 10 minutes and 10 seconds was just under 11 minutes ahead of the

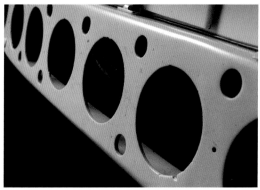

The chassis frame of this car is an original Type S that has been shortened just ahead of where it sweeps up over the rear axle – the only place where the chassis can in fact be shortened successfully. The drilling to lighten it was carried out according to original Mercedes-Benz specifications.

Gordon Crosby captured the drama of the 1931 German Grand Prix, where for lap after lap Caracciola in an SSKL fought for the lead against Chiron and Varzi in Bugattis, and Nuvolari's Alfa Romeo. The cars were still in sight of each other as they went into the final lap, but Caracciola, exhausted, hung on to win.

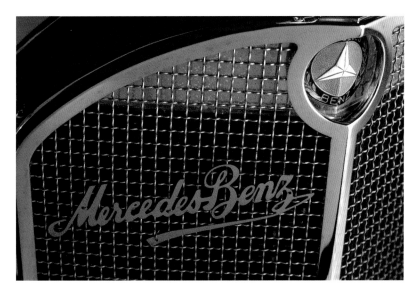

The stone-guard is to original specification, although it is questionable whether Mercedes-Benz would have allowed one of their cars to leave the factory with the company name attached like this!

second-placed Alfa Romeo of Campari.

It was a huge triumph at a time when Mercedes' racing fortunes seemed otherwise at a low ebb, and Caracciola went on to uphold the German maker's reputation with the SSKL at many other events that year, winning the Avus Grand Prix, the Eifelrennen and the German hill-climb title as well, not to mention the German Grand Prix for good measure, against opposition from Alfa Romeo, Bugatti and Maserati. However, the SSKL was not quite all-

conquering that year; a supercharger failure put it out of contention after 39 laps at Monthléry in the French Grand Prix, when Otto Merz was Caracciola's co-driver.

For the 1932 racing season, Caracciola was tempted away to drive for Alfa Romeo; Mercedes mostly stayed away from racing that

The engine of this car is in fact from a Type S, but has been fitted with the correct SSKL-type pressurised fuel system, which was needed for sustained high-speed driving. It also has the split cam cover that is today considered more desirable than the single-piece type.

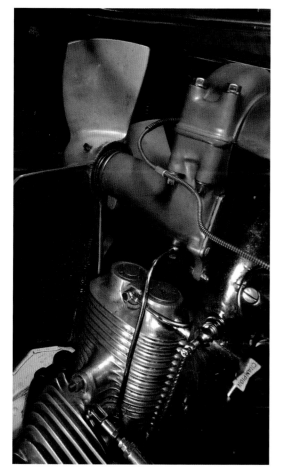

year, and although Hans Stuck was entered for the German Grand Prix in July, his SSKL failed to start the race. It was Stuck who dominated the sports car class in the hill-climb events during 1932, and finished the year as European Champion. Caracciola, meanwhile, demonstrated that his successes had not been completely down to the excellence of the Mercedes-Benz machinery he had been given to drive when he took the equivalent racing car title for his new employers in Italy.

This SSKL was bodied experimentally by Vetter in Cannstatt for Otto Merz to drive at the May 1932 Avus race in Berlin. Merz, seen here at the wheel, was tragically killed when the car left the track during practice.

The SSKL streamliners

However, Daimler-Benz did make a limited return to the tracks in 1933 with the specific aim of winning the Avus race on 21 May. The event was to be attended by government VIPs and Mercedes was keen to attract sponsorship. So two special versions of the SSKL were built with streamlined bodywork; whether they were specially built new chassis or used the chassis of older works racers is not clear. Their shape earned them the German nickname of Gurke (gherkin or cucumber).

The basic design of the streamlined body was by the aerodynamicist Reinhard von König-Fachsenfeld, and the two cars were constructed by the Vetter company in Cannstatt, better known for its commercial vehicle bodies but also involved with Paul Jaray and his researches into streamlining. The two streamlined SSK bodies differed slightly one from another. One car had a high tail, and the other had a tail with a downward curve, apparently modified to Vetter's own design to tackle the 9km-long straights of the Berlin track. Caracciola had re-signed for the Mercedes team but was unable to race because he was convalescing after an accident in a privately-entered Alfa Romeo. So the seat in the number one (low-tailed) car went to Otto Merz, while the number two car was allocated to Manfred von Brauchitsch.

Sadly, tragedy struck during practice at the Avus track on 18 May. Heavy rain had soaked the track, but the Mercedes drivers decided to see how the cars would behave under those conditions. On one of the long straight sections, Merz's car appears to have become airborne, coming down some 36 metres further on where it hit a cement milestone, somersaulted and rolled several times. Merz was thrown out and later died in hospital. Von Brauchitsch, driving as a privateer and on trial for a place in the Mercedes team, decided to go ahead with his entry – a brave decision even in those circumstances. His car eventually placed no better than fifth, behind two Alfa Romeos and two Bugattis, although it did achieve an astonishing top speed of 143mph and an average of 194.4km/h (120.7mph) over a distance of 183 miles. It also took a class world record over the 200km distance. Von Brauchitsch secured his place in the team, and went on to race for Mercedes from 1934 to 1939.

Numbers

Nobody, of course, should be under any illusion that the SSKL was ever intended for series production. It was a hand-built racing special, based on a car that was itself individually assembled by hand. In consequence, very few indeed were made. The totals are in dispute, like so many other things about the SSK and SSKL cars.

The best figures suggest that there were 12 altogether. Breaking this figure down, the works might have needed three in the beginning, and perhaps another two for the later streamliners if these were not built on the chassis of older works cars. That leaves seven more, which would have been sold to very deserving (and persistent) privateers for competition use.

Also bodied by Vetter, by with a different rear end design, this was the second of the experimental streamliners entered for the race at the Avus track on 22 May 1932. Manfred von Brauchitsch was on trial for the Mercedes "works" team, and went ahead despite the unexplained accident with Merz's car during practice. He won the 1.5-litre class and took a class world record over 200km.

SPECIFICATIONS – SSK MODELS

(1) "PRODUCTION" MODELS (1928-30); TYPE W06 II

Engine:
7065cc 6-cylinder with 100mm bore and 150mm stroke
Overhead valves and overhead camshaft
Four main bearings
5.2:1 compression ratio
Single Mercedes-Benz twin-choke carburettor with annular float chamber
Roots-type supercharger driven by gear from crankshaft
140PS (1928-29) or 160PS (1929-30) at 3300rpm
200PS at 3300rpm with blower engaged
Torque 450Nm (332lb ft) at 1920rpm

Gearbox:
Four-speed; ratios 2.75:1, 1.55:1, 1.12:1, 1.00:1

Axle ratio:
2.76:1 standard; 2.50:1 and 3.09:1 optional

Chassis:
Channel-section steel
Wheelbase 2950mm (116.1in)
Track 1425mm

Overall:
Overall dimensions
4250-5000 x 1700 x 1725mm
Weight 2000kg
Maximum speed 185km/h (115mph) on 2.50:1 axle ratio

(2) "WORKS" CARS (1928-30); TYPE W06 III

Engine:
7065cc 6-cylinder with 100mm bore and 150mm stroke
Overhead valves and overhead camshaft
Four main bearings
6.2:1 compression ratio
Single Mercedes-Benz twin-choke carburettor with annular float chamber
Roots-type supercharger driven by gear from crankshaft
170PS at 3300rpm
225PS at 3300rpm with blower engaged
Torque 458Nm (337lb ft) at 1900rpm

Gearbox:
Four-speed; ratios 2.75:1, 1.55:1, 1.12:1, 1.00:1

Axle ratio:
2.76:1 standard; 2.50:1 and 3.09:1 optional

Chassis:
Channel-section steel
Wheelbase 2950mm
Track 1425mm

Overall:
Overall dimensions
4250-5000 x 1700 x 1725mm
Weight 2000kg
Maximum speed 192km/h (119mph) on 2.50:1 axle ratio

(3) "WORKS" CARS (1929-30); TYPE WS06

Engine:
7065cc 6-cylinder with 100mm bore and 150mm stroke
Overhead valves and overhead camshaft
6.2:1 compression ratio
Single Mercedes-Benz twin-choke carburettor with annular float chamber
Roots-type supercharger (enlarged "elephant blower") driven by gear from crankshaft
180PS at 3300rpm
250PS at 3300rpm with blower engaged
Torque 562Nm (414lb ft) at 1900rpm

Gearbox:
Four-speed; ratios 2.75:1, 1.55:1, 1.12:1, 1.00:1

Axle ratio:
2.76:1 standard; 2.50:1 and 3.09:1 optional

Chassis:
Channel-section steel
Wheelbase 2950mm
Track 1425mm

Overall:
Overall dimensions
4250-5000 x 1700 x 1725mm
Weight 2000kg
Maximum speed 192km/h (119mph) on 2.50:1 axle ratio

Perhaps Stuttgart could have sold more, but not every would-be owner would have been able to persuade Daimler-Benz to part with such an exotic piece of machinery; the company would have vetted order applications very carefully to make sure that only drivers with impeccable credentials got their hands on an SSKL. They did not want the bad publicity that would result from repeated failures in competition. The entry price of 40,000 Reichsmarks for the cycle-winged two-seater that was Sindelfingen's only offering must also have worked as a major deterrent to buyers. So a number of SSK owners had their cars modified to SSKL standard, or to as close to it as they could get. Stories that the drilled SSKL chassis was prone to breakage may have originated here,

SPECIFICATIONS – SSKL MODELS

"WORKS" CARS ONLY, 1931

Engine:
7065cc 6-cylinder with 100mm bore and 150mm stroke
Overhead valves and overhead camshaft
7.0:1 compression ratio
Single Mercedes-Benz twin-choke carburettor with annular float chamber
Roots-type supercharger driven by gear from crankshaft and permanently engaged
240PS at 3400rpm
300PS at 3400rpm with blower engaged
Torque 688Nm (507lb ft) at 2000rpm

Gearbox:
Four-speed; various ratio combinations to suit the event

Axle ratio:
Various, chosen to suit the event

Chassis:
Channel-section steel
Wheelbase 2950mm
Track 1425mm

Overall:
Overall dimensions
4250-5000 x 1700 x 1250mm
Weight 1750kg
Maximum speed 235km/h (145mph)

HOW MANY WERE THERE?

Determining build quantities for the SSK and SSKL cars is problematic. The official Mercedes-Benz line is that there were 33 short-chassis cars in total, and the company does not attempt to differentiate between the two types. Nevertheless, figures quoted by Werner Oswald in his book *Mercedes-Benz Personenwagen 1886-1984* appear to have been taken from factory documents and suggest a figure of 54 cars; of these, 42 were supposedly SSKs and 12 were SSKL types.

Discrepancies in the build figures might result from the factory practice of updating cars to the latest specification. Thus, a 1928 SSK built with the the 225PS specification might have been updated with the 250PS specification in 1929 and then converted to an SSKL in 1931. It would then appear three times in the record, and would appear to be three separate cars when it was in fact just one.

That the Oswald figures (whatever their provenance) are inaccurate seems indisputable, not least because they suggest a start to SSKL production in 1929. The SSKL is generally considered to have been built for one year only (1931), although of course it remains possible that two more chassis were constructed later for the streamlined cars. Nevertheless, for the sake of completeness, the doubtful figures that Oswald quotes are given below.

SSK 27/170/225 model		SSK 27/180/250 model		SSKL 27/240/300 model	
Total:	32	Total	10	Total	12
1928	3	1928	1	1929	2
1929	18	1929	6	1930	1
1930	4	1930	2	1931	2
1931	4	1933	1	1932	5
1935	2			1933	1
1933	0			1934	1
1934	1				

when chassis that had been drilled with rather less accuracy than the task demanded simply gave up under the strain.

The official line from Mercedes-Benz Classic is that there was a combined total of 33 SSK and SSKL models; the individual totals have not been divulged separately, and it may indeed be impossible to calculate them for certain.

Chapter Six

GRAND DESIGNS

The 770, 1930-1938

*The 770 was more
usually known as "Der
Grosse Mercedes" (the
word becomes Grosser
when the "der" (the) is
omitted). This early
advertisement notes that
the car was "created for
a circle of lucky people,
who wish to set no limit
on the fulfilment of their
wishes".*

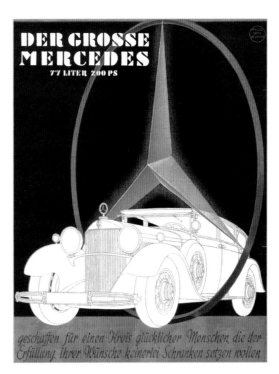

By the end of the 1920s, Mercedes-Benz had built up a full range of cars that covered the requirements of every likely customer in Germany. For the family buyer (and of course they would have had to be well-to-do families in 1920s Germany) there was the new 200 range; for the wealthy businessman, there was the Nürburg range, newly topped out from 1928 by the addition of the model 460 with its 4.6-litre eight-cylinder engine; for the very wealthy, there were Porsche's supercharged six-cylinders. Yet there was still something missing, right at the top of the range.

Even royalty needed cars and, even though there was no longer a royal family in Germany, there were plenty of royal families around the world for whom other makers were already building exclusive and expensive cars. In Britain, there were Rolls-Royce and Bentley, still separate companies at this stage; in the USA, there was Duesenberg; and in France Bugatti had made a determined (but ultimately unsuccessful) pitch at that market with their Type 41 or Royale model. Worse, as far as Stuttgart was concerned, was that rival German manufacturer Maybach seemed to be heading in that direction with their DS7 model of 1929.

The Maybach challenge must have been felt keenly at Stuttgart. Wilhelm Maybach had been Technical Director of Daimler in its early days, but in 1909 he had set up an aero-engine factory with finance from Graf Ferdinand von Zeppelin, and in due course his son Karl joined him there, after benefitting from engineering experience at Daimler. The Maybach Motor Works, banned from making aircraft engines by the 1919 Treaty of Versailles, had turned to making engines for cars, trucks and railway locomotives, and in the mid-1920s diversified into building complete cars as well. Mercedes-Benz decided that they would have to go one better than Maybach, if only to retain their prestige within the automotive industry.

These are two early examples of the Pullman Limousine, whose six-window body reflected American designs of the time. The rear-view mirror on the back of the spotlamp was a characteristic of Mercedes models in the 1930s.

So Wilhelm Kissel approved the idea of building a hugely expensive flagship model that would be aimed not at the celebrities who were buying the supercharged Porsche sports-racers but rather at the very top of society. The new Mercedes was to be a car for kings and emperors, a car for state occasions, and a symbol of real power rather than merely wealth. Success with such a car would be a powerful statement of Mercedes' own superiority within the automotive world, and it would also ensure that the name was associated with high-quality cars in every country where it found buyers. In crude terms, a "royal" Mercedes would provide a massive boost for exports.

The job of designing the new car fell of course to Chief Engineer Hans Nibel, and in practice it appears that the work was guided by him with the able assistance of his young deputy, Fritz Nallinger. Nibel's strength lay in his elegant engineering solutions for much smaller cars, and it may be that he was uncomfortable with working on the new flagship car. That could explain why the new model, coded W07, ended up as a relatively unadventurous design – and was sometimes criticised for that very characteristic. An equally plausible explanation could be that Nibel simply was not given enough time to develop anything less conventional, and that all he could do was to deliver current Mercedes-Benz engineering scaled up to suit a bigger car. One way or the other, there is no doubt that the car introduced as the 770 at

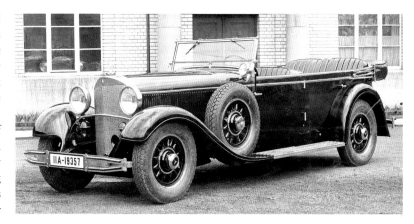

the Paris Motor Show in autumn 1930 was a convincing statement of Mercedes-Benz engineering abilities.

The chassis

From the start, the 770 was always going to be a very large car. Size suggests power and size brings the space for luxury, but it also adds weight. No car with the pretensions of the new Mercedes could afford not to offer superlative performance as well, and that was going to

The open tourer was built as a seven-seater and was deliberately intended as a car to be seen in.

This seems to be one of the very early chassis, although it cannot be dated very accurately. All the early cars had wooden spoked wheels because these were trusted to support the huge weight of a completed 770. The loops of wire at the ends of the front wing support brackets are for the sidelights, and the projection alongside the bulkhead is the spare wheel support arm.

Both left-hand and right-hand steering were available. This early dashboard shows the neat and comprehensive instrumentation.

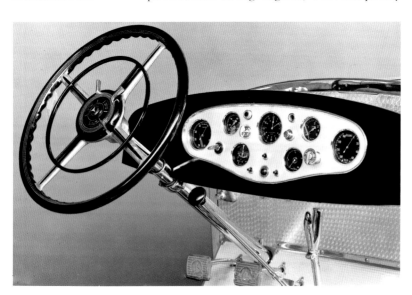

demand the most powerful and refined engine that Stuttgart could provide. Despite the impressive performance of the existing 7.1-litre supercharged six-cylinders, these engines were not going to be suitable: they were high-performance racing engines, with completely the wrong power delivery characteristics for a grand limousine.

Besides, they had only six cylinders. Even the latest Nürburg 460 saloon had an eight-cylinder engine, and so the new flagship model could not possibly have fewer than that. Multi-cylinder engines were beginning to appear at the very top of the market, too: Maybach had a V12, so did Voisin in France, while Duesenberg had a straight-eight. To develop a completely new vee-type engine would take a long time, and Nibel was probably under pressure to deliver the new flagship Mercedes quickly. So he settled for a compromise in the shape of a straight-eight engine that could be supplied with or without the Mercedes trademark supercharger. The additional length that such an engine would demand had its own impact on the dimensions of the new chassis.

The overall dimensions of that chassis must have been one of the first things to be established, and its length was very probably deliberately set at 5600mm in order to make six metres the size of the typical production example. Within that length, the wheelbase was settled at 3750mm (147.6in). These dimensions made the new chassis far and away the largest Mercedes of its time. Indeed, few cars anywhere were larger; only the long-wheelbase versions of the Rolls-Royce Phantom, Bentley 8-litre, Bugatti Royale and Duesenberg Model J could lay claim to greater size – a pantheon of names that is a clear reminder of the pretensions of the new Mercedes.

With such a large chassis, Nibel must have been unwilling to risk anything too adventurous, and indeed the chassis frame of the 770

was one of its more conventional elements. It was a steel channel-frame type, built with a nod towards the advances made by Porsche on the S, SS and SSK because its massive side-members dipped slightly behind the front axle and rose sharply over the rear axle in order to give a lower build and the best handling possible from what would inevitably be a tall car with a fairly high centre of gravity.

Beam axles were only to be expected, and for the front Nibel chose a sturdy H-beam forging of chrome-nickel steel. At the rear, he specified a banjo axle made from pressed sheet steel with a cast alloy differential case. Both axles were suspended on conventional semi-elliptic leaf springs with double-acting hydraulic lever-arm dampers. Heavy cars of the time were still commonly fitted with wooden spoked wheels, and most examples of the new large Mercedes would have these, right through until 1938. However, Nibel's team came up with an alternative wire-spoked type that was strong enough to take the weight of some bodies, and this was used for some Cabriolet derivatives. Both wooden and metal-spoked wheels were attached to the hubs by centre locks with eared metal spinners. Big and heavy wheels that are not mounted rigidly tend to wobble at speed, and so the front spring shackles were fitted with anti-shimmy blocks.

The brakes, too, were conventional in concept, but inevitably huge in order to give this big car reasonable stopping power. The drums had longitudinal cooling ribs and the foot pedal operated a mechanical linkage through the medium of a vacuum servo. The steering was by worm and screw in order to give a good feel of the road but, in a car of this weight, it was of course rather heavy at lower speeds. Nibel also specified a fully automatic central chassis lubrication system, which used engine oil at operating temperature.

The engine

The new engine was going to be absolutely critical to the success of the new car, and here Nibel took no chances. Although he stayed with an in-line configuration because Mercedes had no experience of car engines with a vee configuration, he realised that there was nothing to be gained from simply enlarging existing designs. So neither bore nor stroke was inherited from any previous Mercedes engine. The eight cylinders of the M07 design were housed in a block of chrome-nickel alloyed cast iron, and the bottom half of the crankcase was heavily ribbed,

with a detachable sump cast from Elektron alloy. The crankshaft was made of chrome-nickel steel and incorporated solid-forged counterweights; it ran in no fewer than nine bearings and had a progressive vibration damper at its front end. With a 95mm bore and truly massive 135mm stroke, the swept volume worked out at 7655cc, a figure which lay behind the 770 designation. Nibel chose to use aluminium pistons, and set the compression ratio at a conservative 4.7:1.

Even the top end of the engine dispensed with proven Mercedes practice. The camshaft was mounted at the side of the block, running in nine bearings, and operated overhead valves through roller tappets, pushrods and rocker arms. The cylinder head was made of cast iron and did follow earlier practice in its use of two spark plugs for each cylinder, those on one side fired by a coil and those on the other by a magneto. There was a single dual-choke updraught carburettor with an accelerator pump and cold starting aid, mounted on a light alloy inlet manifold that was heated by exhaust gas and through thermostatically controlled hot air flaps.

The new eight-cylinder was beautifully finished, too, with machine-turned metal surfaces for the inlet manifold and top cover, and an enamel finish elsewhere. There were two brightly-finished exhaust pipes on the right of the engine, as often as not concealed under the bonnet on completed cars but sometimes allowed to protrude through the bonnet side in the manner of the pipes associated with the sports-racers of the late 1920s. Those, of course, had three pipes, with two cylinders discharging into each; the eight-cylinder engine had an interesting eight-into-three-into-two system, which must have caused some difficulties in development. The three cylinders at each end of the block discharged into one three-branch pipe each, and the middle pair into the third pipe. From there, the spent gases were fed into a collector box that exhausted through the two chromed downpipes.

The new 7.7-litre was not at all the same kind of engine as the Porsche-designed six-cylinders. The purpose of the extra cylinders – prestige reasons aside – was to make the engine run more smoothly. Extra power was not really an issue, and in fact the M07 engine's maximum power output of 150PS was only just on a par with that of the smaller-capacity, 7.1-litre, six-cylinder engine in the SS. Much more important was what happened at the lower end of the rev range, where a huge 392Nm of torque were generated at just 1200rpm. The engine did not have to reach high revs to give of its best, and in fact its peak power came at 2800rpm, about 6.5% lower down the rev range than the 3000rpm at which the six-cylinders delivered their maximum.

But that was just the start. For those who wanted more performance, there was of course an alternative supercharged version. Here, too, the M07 engine differed from earlier practice. The Roots-type supercharger was mounted not in front of the engine but alongside its front end on the right-hand side. Perhaps the thinking here was to reduce the overall length of the power unit. Engagement was achieved in the way associated with earlier engines, and when the driver pressed against the spring at the end of the accelerator's travel, the linkage went over-centre and engaged the supercharger through a multi-plate clutch and a gear train. However, great care was taken to reduce the characteristic mechanical whine that had proved so enthralling on the supercharged sports-racers; this was, after all, to be a luxury car. So, although the supercharger could certainly be heard working, it was very much quieter than on an S, SS or SSK.

It delivered the goods, too. With the supercharger engaged, maximum power jumped to 200bhp at the 2800rpm power peak. Torque was even more impressively increased, to an astounding 535.8Nm at the slightly raised engine speed of 1500rpm. It all made a difference of 10km/h (6.2mph) to the top speed of a typical production car, raising it from 150km/h (93.2mph) to 160km/h (99.4mph). As things were to turn out, only 13 770s would be delivered without the supercharger – which added 3000 RM (or the price of a small family car) to the cost of the vehicle.

With either version of the engine, the drive was transmitted through a twin dry-plate clutch to a three-speed gearbox. This had a light alloy housing containing helical spur gears, and was harnessed to an overdrive unit that worked on all three gears. Alternative overdrive ratios were available (one overdrive unit was made by Mercedes, the other bought in from Maybach), and there was the usual choice of axle ratios to suit bodies of different weights and customers with more interest in acceleration than top speed or vice versa.

What Mercedes saw as the chassis was completed in the traditional way with a bulkhead behind the engine, and an instrument board. There were outriggers bolted alongside the engine to carry a spare wheel on either side, where it would be let into the wings that were also usually supplied by the chassis department. Then there was the imperious Mercedes vee-radiator, chromed and frequently protected by a herringbone-pattern stone guard. Between the wings, a chromed cross-brace supported massive free-standing headlamps, and there were double bumpers of spring steel at each end, complete with thick rubber facings to absorb minor knocks.

Bodies

Traditionally, the grandest luxury cars (and many of those several rungs further down the ladder) had been supplied as chassis only, and buyers turned to a specialist coachbuilder for custom-built bodywork. But with the 770 Mercedes broke the mould. From the start, they intended to offer a range of bodies designed and constructed at Sindelfingen. This inevitably reduced the problems caused when outside coachwork did not quite live up to customer expectations, it allowed Stuttgart to exercise greater control over the build quality and aesthetics of the finished product, and above all it ensured that more of the profit ended up in

the Mercedes-Benz coffers – a not insignificant consideration for a low-volume flagship model. Of course, chassis would also be available without bodywork for those who insisted, but....

In practice, the Sindelfingen body plant did its best to cover all the angles by introducing a range of six different bodies for the 770. It was

Although the seven-seat tourer body was built to a standard design, there was room for some detail variation. This later car has a two-pane windscreen and shows that colour schemes could make a lot of difference. The two chromed arms above and behind the rear number-plate could swing out to make a luggage grid, and the chromed strips above protected the paint on the back of the body from damage when a trunk was being carried

This was the Cabriolet B design from Sindelfingen. The downward curve at the top of the body behind the seats allowed the folded hood – always a large and ungainly mass, however neatly concealed in its fabric cover – to sit a little lower down.

four windows; the Cabriolet C had two doors and two windows, the Cabriolet D had four doors, and the Cabriolet F had six seats, achieved by fitting the rearmost seat right at the back of the car where there might otherwise have been an outside trunk or enclosed boot.

Interiors were one area where customers were offered a wide choice of options. They could choose from leather or velvet upholstery, and some chose other more exotic materials. Wood trim was expected, but the nature of that wood could be specified. Ash trays and oddments boxes were more or less standard equipment; some cars were fitted with drinks cabinets. More or less standard was a forced-air heater for the rear compartment, from which the occupants could contact the chauffeur by means of an intercom system. Even the driver had an electric screen heater to reduce misting, and when the Autosuper radio was fitted, he had speakers to his left and right, just the same as those fitted in the rear compartment.

Generally speaking, dashboards followed a common layout, although customers who asked for something different could be accommodated. Standard features were a 160km/h speedometer with trip and mileage recorders, a rev counter, a clock, and gauges for coolant temperature, fuel and oil pressure, plus a combined ammeter and voltmeter. The steering wheel had its usual

also as accommodating as possible when customers asked for special features, so that the bespoke touches traditionally associated with specialist coachbuilders remained available – at a cost, of course. The six bodies included just one closed type, which was the rather grand and grandly-named six-light Pullman saloon; Stuttgart had acquired rights to use the Pullman name, otherwise associated with luxurious railway carriages, and was already using it on luxury versions of its 5-litre Nurburg saloon.

There was a six-seat open tourer, and the other four bodies were cabriolets. These were given identifying letters, in the German fashion of the time. The Cabriolet B had two doors and

This is the Cabriolet C design, broadly similar to the Cabriolet B but of course with a longer body behind the doors to accommodate a bench seat in the rear. Both these examples have wire spoked wheels.

This tourer must be one of the 19 chassis that were supplied to independent coachbuilders, and that curved front door window strongly suggests the style of the coachbuilder Papler. Although the basic body shape seems to conform to the Sindelfingen norm, the front door hinges on the bulkhead rather than the centre pillar and the door handles are more curvaceous than the standard type. The windscreen for the rear-seat passengers was not standard equipment, either.

The more curvaceous lines of the 1934 facelift are evident in the shape of the windscreen frame on this Cabriolet F. Note also the coachbuilt trunk at the rear.

complement of levers sprouting from the hub and governing mixture and ignition timing, with a third lever to operate the overdrive. The horn was, as usual, operated by a ring.

Just four cars were built in 1930, the year the new 770 was launched, but 1931 would be the model's best year, with a total of 31 cars sold. Orders thinned out in 1932 and 1933, probably not for any economic reasons but more because the car was no longer the latest must-have sensation among the ultra-rich.

Facelifts

So Stuttgart made some subtle modifications to keep it fresh. The first set arrived in 1934, and a second in 1936. Sales were rejuvenated to an extent, although never again approached their 1931 peak. The 1934 changes banished the rigidly geometric look to the bodywork which had been inspired by American designs of the late 1920s and was by now looking decided outdated. A rake to the windscreen, initially determinedly vertical, helped to modernise the appearance, along with rounder roof contours. The front wings were reshaped with softer lines and deeper valances, and blended more smoothly into the running-boards. The headlamp support bar disappeared and the lamps were now mounted directly to the wings, while

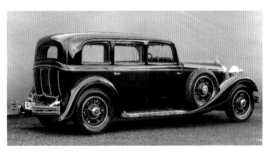

This Pullman Limousine from the mid-1930s shows how the body design was updated with new wing shapes and with more curves in the roof and window pillars. The famous Sindelfingen boot-scrapers are in evidence on the running-boards, too. This was the style current from 1934 to 1936, still with horizontal bonnet louvres.

The second facelift in 1936 saw the wings redesigned again, smaller sidelamps, and rubber-faced single-bar bumpers. The headlamps, too, have changed. This tourer has a few extra features: three extra driving lamps and no fewer than four horns. The windscreen seems to have an anti-mist panel and the windscreen wipers pivot from the bottom of the frame rather than the top.

This Cabriolet F shows the features of the 1936 facelift cars, with reshaped wings, horizontal bonnet louvres, and a built-in luggage boot. The rear roof portion looks so solid that it is hard to imagine it being made of fabric; there is even a glass division behind the chauffeur.

the fuel filler was concealed behind a flap in the rear wing. It all produced a majestic-looking car with enough conservatism in its appearance to appeal to its target audience, although there was no doubt that some features were already anachronistic, notable among them being the wooden-spoked wheels.

The 1936 redesign retained those wooden wheels, which really did look out of place by this time. Otherwise, even deeper wing valances

This late-model Cabriolet D has a few special touches of its own. Note the chrome strip along the bottom of the body, and the rear wheel spats, which were fashionable in 1937-38.

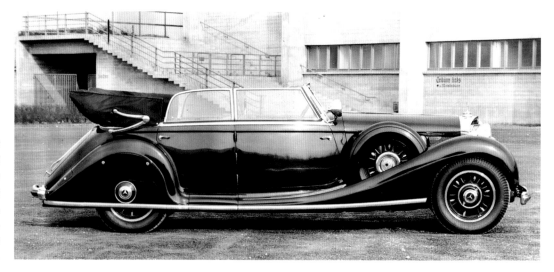

gave the car a more modern air, along with new sidelights in streamlined housings, single-bar bumpers (again rubber-faced) and horizontal louvres in the bonnet sides, which helped the car look longer and slightly sleeker. The more formal designs now had a built-in boot instead of a folding luggage rack, but this did nothing for the lines of the cars and always looked like an unhappy afterthought. It almost went without saying that customers could order a set of hand-made leather cases to fit the boot of their 770s as an optional extra. Some late cars were fitted with wheel spats to meet the current fashion – and of course the 770's spats always carried a three-pointed star emblem on the outside, supposedly over the axle end but in practice just slightly to its rear.

Build volumes in this second phase of the 770's production remained fairly consistent at about one car a month, although it was interesting that 1937 brought a massive drop in price for the bare-chassis 770, perhaps in an attempt to attract more orders and clear stocks of parts before the replacement-model 770 came on-stream.

Buyers

When the 770 was introduced in 1930, Mercedes-Benz had hoped that it would appeal to international royalty, and no doubt expected a few sales to be made to the very wealthy in Germany as well. Sadly, the car could hardly have been introduced at a worse time because the world-wide effects of the 1929 Wall Street Crash caused even those who could afford the car to restrain their enthusiasm: in a time of economic depression, they did not want to be picked on as targets of envy by those who were struggling financially.

Nevertheless, some cars did reach royal owners. Notable among them was the Emperor Hirohito of Japan, who bought no fewer than seven examples; there were right-hand-drive cars for use in Japan and left-hand-drive examples for use when abroad in countries that drove on the right. Another royal user was the exiled German Kaiser, Wilhelm II, who was then living in the Netherlands. He took delivery of a Cabriolet F model that was one of the small number of 770s built without a supercharger. The Kaiser was so fond of the car that he gave instructions

In Japan, Emperor Hirohito had a whole fleet of Grosser Mercedes. Some had left-hand drive and some, like this one, had right-hand drive. Note the Imperial emblem ahead of the radiator stoneguard and on the door. The picture with two of the Emperor's staff shows one of the cars still in service in 1952, by which time it was around 30 years old.

One of Hirohito's cars is today preserved in the Mercedes-Benz Museum. This was a left-hand-drive example.

This early tourer was used as a parade car by the German government, and is seen here in September 1935 with Adolf Hitler aboard at Nürnberg.

for it to be used as his funeral carriage, and it was duly modified for that task when he died in 1941. Today, returned to its original condition, the car belongs to the Mercedes-Benz Museum.

Other head-of-state owners included Archduke Josef in Budapest; Admiral Miklós Horthy, the Hungarian Regent; Antonio Salazar, the Portuguese Prime Minister; King Farouk of Egypt; and King Faisal of Iraq, whose special Cabriolet D carried a body by Voll & Ruhrbeck in Berlin. Closer to home, owners of the W07 770 included the Lord Mayor of Munich, Karl Fiehler; Otto Wolff, a Cologne industrialist who sat on the supervisory board of Daimler-Benz AG; Federico J. Vollmer, a Hamburg merchant; and Axel Tidstrand, an industrialist from Sågmyra in Sweden.

Many cars were also delivered to the Reich Chancellery in Berlin for use by the German government. Some were saloons, but the majority seem to have been open tourers, which became favourites as parade cars of the Nazi regime. Adolf Hitler began to use a 770 parade car as early as 1933, and there seem to have been regular government purchases of new models right through until the replacement model became available in 1938. One consequence of this was that Stuttgart received orders

This beautiful grey Cabriolet F was built for the exiled Kaiser Wilhelm II and since 1950 has belonged to the Mercedes-Benz Museum collection. The picture with the top up shows the Kaiser's chauffeur at the wheel. The wheel discs seem to have been a special order.

THE KAISER'S 770

The 770 owned by Germany's exiled Kaiser Wilhelm II has belonged to the Mercedes-Benz vehicle collection since 1950. It is a Cabriolet F, one of only eight W07 models built with this type of bodywork, and was ordered by the former Kaiser's chamberlain on 8 September 1931. It was handed over to the former Kaiser on 22 January 1932, and cost 44,500 RM plus 1400 RM for the overdrive gearbox.

The car was a great favourite of the Kaiser's during his exile at House Doorn in Utrecht, Holland. It was also specially finished to meet his wishes, its grey paint exactly matching the colour used on warships of the old Imperial German Navy. The car had wooden spoked wheels with metal disc covers painted to match the

Mounted on the left of the dashboard in the Kaiser's car is the "ship's telegraph" by which he communicated his wishes to the chauffeur.

Daimler-Benz is normally very protective of its trademarks, but it granted permission for the radiator cap to carry the former Kaiser's coat of arms instead of the three-pointed star

bodywork. It was one of only 13 W07s ordered without a supercharger, and had several special features to suit its owner. Instead of the three-pointed star on the radiator cap, there was the Hohenzollern arms. Inside, the Kaiser himself had designed the signalling system – not unlike that in a naval vessel – by which he could instruct his chauffeur while on the move. He invariably sat on the right of the middle row of seats, and just in front of him in the division was a control panel with seven buttons. Each button lit a light segment in a circular panel to the left of the instrument panel, so that Wilhelm's aide-de-camp could relay the Kaiser's wishes to his driver. A map case and a net for the Kaiser's marshal's baton had also been installed at his request.

When Kaiser Wilhelm died at Doorn on 4 June 1941, his body was laid to rest in a chapel next to the gatehouse before being transferred to a mausoleum built in the grounds. In accordance with his wishes, the funeral procession to the chapel was led by the 770, which had been fitted with a platform behind the front seats to carry the coffin. After that, the car was returned to its original condition and never used again until handed over to the Mercedes-Benz collection.

As late as 1 June 1939, when the Prince Regent of Yugoslavia came to Berlin and this picture was taken, examples of the first-generation 770 were still in use as ceremonial vehicles for state occasions in Germany.

for several armour-plated cars.

Not all the armoured bodies were for Nazi officials, however. Two, for example, went to Portugal. One was the car for Antonio Salazar, and the other was delivered to the chief of his repressive secret police, the PVDE (Polícia de Vigilância e de Defesa do Estado). The Salazar car, a six-window Pullman saloon, still survives.

BODY TYPES, W 07 MODELS

The Daimler-Benz Media website gives the following figures for the Sindelfingen-built body types fitted to the W07 770 cars. These figures agree completely with the ones Jan Melin established during his researches at the Daimler-Benz archives.

Cabriolet B	2
Cabriolet C	4
Cabriolet D	18
Cabriolet F	8
Tourer	26
Pullman Limousine	42

In addition, there were 19 chassis supplied to independent coachbuilders.

BUILD VOLUMES

Mercedes-Benz state that a grand total of 119 W07 770 chassis was built between September 1930 and June 1938.

Werner Oswald gives the following breakdown of build volumes, year by year:

1930	4
1931	42
1932	9
1933	4
1934	11
1935	11
1936	10
1937	13
1938	13

BODIES BY INDEPENDENT COACHBUILDERS
A total of 19 bare chassis were supplied to independent coach-builders. The full details of coachbuilders are not available, but the following information has been established.

The known bodies were:
Auer (Cannstatt) Two-seater cabriolet, 1931
Castagna (Milan) Four-door Cabriolet
Erdmann & Rossi (Berlin) Four chassis; no details available
Josef Neuss (Berlin) Sedan de Ville, 1932
Papler (Cologne) No details available
Reutter (Stuttgart) No details available
Voll & Ruhrbeck (Berlin) Cabriolet D
    built for King Faisal II of Iraq.

PRICES

Chassis	Standard	Supercharged
	29,500 RM	32,500 RM
	24,000 RM from 1937	
Open tourer (6 seats)	39,000 RM	42,000 RM
Pullman limousine	38,000 RM	41,000 RM
Cabriolet B (4 windows)	44,500 RM	47,500 RM
Cabriolet C (2 windows)	41,500 RM	44,500 RM
Cabriolet D (4 doors)	44,500 RM	47,500 RM
Cabriolet F (6 seats)	44,500 RM	47,500 RM

IDENTIFICATION NUMBERS, W07 MODELS
Generally speaking, chassis and engine numbers for these cars matched. A replacement engine would have its number prefixed by A (for "Austausch", "exchange")
These figures were established by Jan Melin and are taken from his book, *Mercedes-Benz, The Supercharged 8-cylinder Cars of the 1930s, Volume 1*.

Number(s)	Total	Remarks
77653-77655	3	Pilot-production run
83801-83825	25	
83840	1	
85201-85275	75	
182061-182075	15	
	119	

Jan Melin has also identified the numbers allocated to 34 cars subsequently cancelled and therefore not built. These were 84814 (1 car), 85276-85300 (25 cars), and 189465-189472 (8 cars). He also notes that an engine numbered 89146 was built, but was used in a bus.

SPECIFICATIONS, 770 (W07)

1930-38

Engine:
7655cc 8-cylinder with 95mm bore and 135mm stroke
Overhead valves and side camshaft
Nine main bearings
Twin-plug cylinder head with dual ignition by coil and magneto
Compression ratio 4.7:1
Single Mercedes-Benz twin-choke carburettor with accelerator pump and cold starting device
Roots-type supercharger driven by gear from crankshaft (fitted to most cars)
150PS at 2800rpm, 200PS at 2800rpm with supercharger engaged
392.5Nm (289lb ft) at 1200rpm
535.8Nm (394.5lb ft) at 1500rpm with supercharger engaged

Gearbox:
Three-speed with overdrive. Ratios 2.73:1, 1.52:1, 1.00:1; overdrive 0.71:1 or 0.76:1; reverse 3.3:1

Axle ratios:
4.50:1, 4.88:1 or 4.30:1

Chassis and suspension:
Channel-section steel chassis frame
Semi-elliptic springs on front axle
Underslung semi-elliptic springs on rear axle

Brakes:
Mechanical operation on all four wheels, with Bosch-Dewandre vacuum servo

Weights and measures:
Overall dimensions
5600 x 1840 x 1830mm
Wheelbase 3750mm, Track 1500mm
Weight 3500kg (maximum permissible)
Maximum speed 150km/h (93mph) unsupercharged; 160 km/h (99mph) supercharged
Fuel consumption 29-30 litres per 100km (9.5-9.7mpg)

Chapter Seven

AN OVERLOOKED PIONEER

The 380, 1933-1934

The front view of the 380's chassis offers no surprises, although it is perhaps worth noting that the bumper blade is entirely chrome and does not have the rubber facing seen on the more expensive Mercedes models of the time.

The 380 model that came from Stuttgart for 1933 and 1934 has the questionable distinction of being the forgotten supercharged model of the 1930s. There are several reasons why this perfectly good car – and one which introduced important chassis innovations – tends to be left out of the conversation when supercharged cars are mentioned.

One reason is that the 380 initiated a new line of refined sports models which were quite different in character from the hairy-chested sports-racers of the late 1920s, and is therefore seen in some quarters as a betrayal of what the supercharged Mercedes had once represented. Another is that its performance was certainly disappointing; Mercedes recognised that quickly enough and replaced it after a short production life – this small production run being yet another reason why the car is often forgotten. Finally, many motoring enthusiasts today cannot get around the idea that the supercharged models always had a K after their engine-size designator; as the 380 did not, the idea persists that it was not a supercharged car – and that idea is only reinforced by the fact that Mercedes offered it both with and without a supercharger, in exactly the same way as they had with the Grosser 770.

The economic depression that followed the Wall Street Crash of 1929 was the critical factor that made the 380 so different from the Porsche-designed S, SS, SSK and SSKL. It had a big effect on Mercedes-Benz, diminishing customer demand for the supercharged Porsche six-cylinders and obliging the company to withdraw from motor sport at the end of 1930. Bugatti, Maserati and Alfa Romeo stepped into the performance breach with lighter, faster cars, and by 1932 the heyday of the supercharged Mercedes-Benz sports racer was over. For a time, it must have looked as if supercharging would be relegated to the function of adding performance to gentle behemoths like the 770 Grosser Mercedes.

Besides, German society was changing as well. The decade-long party of the 1920s died

with the depression, even if the decline in living standards was not so marked among the wealthy. Attitudes changed, and there was a new seriousness of purpose afoot. The Weimar Republic lived out its final years under President Von Hindenburg at the start of the 1930s, giving way to the start of a new era in 1933 when Von Hindenburg was obliged – much against his better judgement – to appoint Adolf Hitler as Chancellor.

For Hans Nibel, Chief Engineer of the Car Division at Stuttgart as the 1930s opened, it must have been very tricky to decide on a future product policy. One of the big questions was whether the market for high-performance cars would ever return. So Nibel proceeded with great caution, drawing up a product strategy that provided a range of solid saloon models which could be further developed as high-performance models if the market wanted them. The market did indeed want them; the taste for rapid travel on Europe's rapidly expanding road network did not go away, and for the wealthy, a fast and stylish touring car remained among the essential purchases.

So it was that Stuttgart's next supercharged model was announced as early as February 1933, at the Berlin Motor Show. Known to the public as a 380 model, and to Stuttgart as a W22 type, it promised plenty of performance and plenty of the glamour for which German customers still had a strong predilection.

However, this 380 model (never known as a 380K, despite what some writers have suggested) certainly did not spring forth fully formed. Nibel had arrived at it by a series of cautious engineering steps, perhaps always having his ultimate goal in mind but being obliged by the economic uncertainty of the time to move towards the W22 stage by stage. Before the 380 itself was introduced, he brought to market two other models that bore the name 380S (with works codes W10 and W19) and can be seen as precursors of the supercharged car. Looking back on model development in that period can be confusing, and it is important to explain here exactly what happened before looking at the supercharged cars themselves.

Working up to the 380

The development story really goes back to 1929, when the Nibel-designed 350 and 370 Mannheim saloons (with 3.5-litre and big-bore

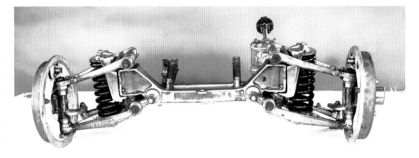

3.7-litre engines respectively) were introduced as fairly routine replacements for older designs. These models were supplemented a year later by a short-chassis 370K (K for "Kurz", or short), available only with cabriolet bodywork, and a short-wheelbase 370S (S for Sport) which was a more sporty model that came as a Roadster or a Sport Cabriolet. Though even the 370S was no sports-racer in the SS or SSK mould, the stylish Sindelfingen-built bodies it carried pointed the way forwards; the customers liked what they saw and so, encouraged, Nibel planned more of the same.

The plan was to replace the Mannheim

Although the 380's independent front suspension also offers no surprises from today's perspective, Stuttgart's engineers were clearly proud of it and the Daimler-Benz archives contain pictures taken from every conceivable angle. Quite clear here is the way it was mounted to a removable cross-member that was bolted to the main chassis frame.

models progressively from 1933, and Nibel now drew up the new designs he needed. In place of the 370 saloons there would be a smaller-engined 290 (the 350 had lasted only one year, to 1930), but in place of the 370S and 370K there would be a bigger-engined, more powerful car. The two new models would use a common engine design, with six cylinders for the 290 but eight cylinders for the more powerful 380. The basic design was to have the same conventional architecture as the Mannheim models' engines, with side valves and a side camshaft, but would also have new bore and stroke dimensions of 78mm and 100mm. The new six-cylinder became an M18 and the eight-cylinder engine was an M19.

It is the eight-cylinder cars that are of interest in the story of the supercharged Mercedes. They were introduced in 1932, a year before the six-cylinder 290 saloons, and carried the name of 380S. They carried the same W10 works code as had been used for the Mannheim models, and to all intents and purposes their chassis was that of the older cars, with the same beam axles, leaf springs and mechanically-operated brakes. That is confusing enough; today, Mercedes-Benz regularly calls these models 370S types despite

the bigger eight-cylinder engine, and that only adds to the confusion. Just 94 examples were built, 38 in 1932 and a further 56 in 1933.

While this W10 380S was still attracting customers, Nibel completely redesigned its chassis and introduced the new model alongside it. The new car was known to Mercedes as a W19 but was still marketed as a 380S and had a slightly more powerful version of the same eight-cylinder engine. Its new chassis was essentially that designed for the forthcoming 290 (W18) models, which would appear in February 1933 at the Berlin Motor Show. It had box-section instead of channel-section side members, a transverse leaf spring for the front beam axle, and swing-axles at the rear with double concentric coil springs; there were hydraulic brakes all round. Eighteen were built in 1932 and a further two in 1933 before the car was redesigned for the second time.

Like the first-stage or W10 380S, this second-stage W19 model came only with two-door cabriolet bodywork – a Cabriolet A with two seats and two windows, a Cabriolet B with four windows and an extra pair of cramped rear seats, and a Cabriolet C with just two windows and the extra pair of cramped rear seats. Again

The Cabriolet A body from Sindelfingen's own coachworks presaged the glamorous lines of the later eight-cylinder cars. The shutters in the bonnet side suggest that this is a 1934 model of the 380.

like the earlier 380S, all versions of the car cost the same 16,500 RM. This pricing policy seems bizarre today, but probably made sense at a time when there were severe uncertainties in the market.

W22 380: a vision realised

None of these early eight-cylinder cars was supercharged. Nibel seems to have kept that option on hold until the 380S cars had proved that a market for such cars still existed. The supercharged model was then released as a third stage in the process, arriving alongside the 290 at the Berlin Show in February 1933. To add to the confusion for anyone trying to understand the Mercedes model ranges of the early 1930s, it was now a plain 380; there was neither S for Sport nor K for Kompressor. It had also been redesigned yet again, and could be had with four different versions of the eight-cylinder engine.

This was the W22 model. It had a box-section steel chassis with a slightly shorter wheelbase

than the 380S types (3140mm instead of 3200mm). Most important was that this new frame provided the necessary torsional rigidity for an all-independent suspension system. Such systems were one of Hans Nibel's key interests, and for the W22 380 he specified coil springs on all four wheels, with swing-axles at the rear and unequal-length top and bottom wishbones at the front. The wheels were now 17-inch types rather than the 18-inch size of the 380S, and

This was the Cabriolet B body from Sindelfingen. The car is thought to have been a pilot production model.

The front end design on this 1933 380 Cabriolet B is very similar to that found on the 770 Grosser models. This seems to have been the standard production design, with a larger boot than was envisaged on the pilot-production car pictured overleaf, and a different side trim strip which helped make the car look longer and better balanced.

brought with them wider tracks – very much wider at the rear. There was a three-speed plus overdrive gearbox, a choice of two axle ratios, and the hydraulic brakes had Bosch-Dewandre vacuum servo assistance. The imposing vee-fronted radiator associated with the sports-racers and the Grosser Mercedes was chosen in preference to the flat-fronted type used on the Mannheim models.

The least powerful engine variant was the M22, which was unsupercharged and delivered 90PS at 3200rpm for a top speed of 120km/h. This could be had at no extra cost with a supercharger, mounted in the traditional Mercedes manner out in front of the crankcase. The blown

engines had a slightly lower compression ratio but would deliver 120PS at 3400rpm with the supercharger engaged, and their top speed was a claimed 130km/h.

Next came an engine called the M22K. This was again supercharged, but this time the supercharger was not mounted out in front like an afterthought but was integral with the crankcase. Without the supercharger engaged, the output was 90PS at 3200rpm; with the blower working, there were 140PS to be had at 3600rpm, although the top speed was quoted as 130km/h – no higher than the 120PS engine with its separate supercharger.

By 1934, customer opinion that the 380 was underpowered had registered firmly at Stuttgart, and it looks as if Nibel was instructed to deliver a more powerful engine for the car to keep sales alive until the 500K replacement model reached the showrooms. Undoubtedly pressed for time, Nibel's solution was a big-bore version of the existing engine that gave a 140km/h top speed, coupled to a modified gearbox with lower first and second ratios that improved low-speed acceleration. As Halwart Schrader says, in *The Supercharged Mercedes*, these cars were built as a batch in 1934.

This final version of the 380's engine was called the M22 I (that is a Roman "I", indicating a new mark or version), and displaced 4019cc as against the 3820cc of the others. Like the M22K, its supercharger was built into the crankcase. Unblown, it was claimed to deliver the same 90PS at 3200rpm as the two earlier versions of the engine, but there were now 144PS at 3600rpm when the supercharger was engaged.

In production
Like the 380S types, the W22 380 models were all priced the same (although a bare chassis was cheaper). The price was 19,500 RM, regardless of engine choice or bodywork choice. This naturally tended to drive buyers towards the cars that represented the best value for money, and as a result it is doubtful whether any of the unsupercharged 380 were made.

Most 380s had Sindelfingen's own bodywork, of course, and there was a choice from the same three cabriolet types as before, plus a two-seat Sport Roadster, a two-door Tourer, and a four-light, four-door saloon. Body styles did not change fundamentally in the two seasons of the

380's production, although the Cabriolet A models did switch from a front-hinged door to a rear-hinged "suicide" type for 1934. Among the 19 cars thought to have been bodied by outside coachbuilders were a six-light four-door saloon by Baur in 1933, a Cabriolet C by Autenrieth in 1934 and a cabriolet by Hornig of Meerane, of unknown date. Erdmann & Rossi also took 8 chassis, according to Jan Melin's researches.

None of the 380s, supercharged or not, had exhaust pipes protruding through the bonnet sides in the fashion characteristic of the Porsche supercharged sports-racers and some of the big 770s. This was presumably because there was no need for the feature: it had been introduced to improve underbonnet cooling, and perhaps that was simply not an issue on the 380. The 1933 cars had a series of louvres in both sides of the bonnet, and the 1934 models had six individually openable vent panels per side instead; the earlier 380S models seem to have had two rows of vertical louvres, one above the other. Front bumpers generally had plain facings,

although some pictures from the 1930s show cars with the rubber facings used on the later 500K models. It is obviously possible that these had been fitted retrospectively to update a car's appearance. Early cars had circular sidelights perched on the wings, but the last ones seem to have had the low-profile lights more associated with the mid-1930s.

The Cabriolet C design is seen here on a 1933 car with the horizontal bonnet louvres.

These two pictures show Sindelfingen's four-door saloon body, but the two cars have some noticeable differences. The earlier example, shown in dead side view, has two boot-scrapers on the running-board and a spotlight on the windscreen pillar. The other car has a different style of running-board, no spotlight, a bright highlight line on wings and running-board and a later, more compact style of sidelight on its front wings. The attitude of the rear wheel on the later car is a reminder that it has independent suspension at the rear as well as the front.

One car built in early 1934 had a particularly interesting history. Supplied to the Racing Department at Stuttgart, it may well have become the personal transport of racing driver Rudi Caracciola, who was certainly photogaphed with it. Still owned by Mercedes in 1937, it was then rebodied in a style developed for the contemporary 540K models that Sindelfingen called a "Kombinationswagen". The basic body, wooden-framed with aluminium panels in the usual way, was a two-seat roadster. To this could be bolted a convertible top (which made it into a Cabriolet A) or a steel hardtop (which made it into a Coupé). The special body was presumably a special order for the Berlin businessman who eventually bought the car. This 380 survives, however, and was painstakingly restored in the early 2000s by Kienle Automobiltechnik in Germany.

The 380's failing was that its new chassis with all-independent suspension could handle far more power than was available from even the final 4.0-litre supercharged engine. Its buyers did not take long to work this out or to pass on their thoughts to Stuttgart. So 380 production was brought to an end in mid-1934, and the model was replaced by the new and much more powerful 500K. As Jan Melin has pointed out, some customers who had ordered 380 models actually took delivery of their successor 500Ks instead. It seems unlikely that they would have been disappointed.

BUILD VOLUMES

Mercedes-Benz quote a total of 154 W22 models of all types. Jan Melin claims a total of 157.

Werner Oswald agrees with the Mercedes-Benz overall total of 154, and gives the following breakdown of build volumes, year by year:

1933   93
1934   61

BODY TYPES

Jan Melin's researches uncovered the following data concerning the body types fitted to the 380.

Cabriolet A	16
Cabriolet B	54
Cabriolet C	44
Tourer	11
Roadster	7
Saloon	6
Chassis only	19

PRICES

As noted in the main text, all the Sindelfingen-bodied 380 models were priced at 16,500 RM – although no doubt Mercedes-Benz charged extra for special features demanded by individual customers.

The bare chassis for all varieties of 380, regardless of engine type, was priced at 13,000 RM.

IDENTIFICATION NUMBERS

Generally speaking, chassis and engine numbers for these cars matched. A replacement engine would have its number prefixed by A (for "Austausch", exchange)

The chassis identification numbers and production figures that follow were established by Jan Melin and are taken from his book, *Mercedes-Benz, The Supercharged 8-cylinder Cars of the 1930s, Volume 1.*

Number(s)	Total	Remarks
89141-89145	5	Pilot production cars
95271-95370	100	
103321-103371	51	Some documents state that 103371 was not a W22; this would reduce the total in this group to 50
105410	1	
	157	Possibly 156; see note above

There was also an engine number 89148 that was presumably built as a spare.

**SPECIFICATIONS, 380 (W22)
1933-34**

Engine (1):
3820cc 8-cylinder with 78mm bore and
100mm stroke, type M22
Side valves and side camshaft
Five main bearings
Compression ratio 6.0:1
Single Mercedes-Benz twin-choke
updraught carburettor
90PS at 3200rpm
Torque figure not available

Engine (2):
As for engine (1) but with add-on Roots-
type supercharger
Compression ratio 5.54:1
120PS at 3400rpm with supercharger
engaged
Torque figure not available

Engine (3):
3820cc 8-cylinder with 78mm bore and
100mm stroke, type M22K
Side valves and side camshaft
Five main bearings
Compression ratio 5.54:1
Single Mercedes-Benz twin-choke
updraught carburettor
Roots-type supercharger integral with
crankcase
90PS at 3200rpm
140PS at 3600rpm with supercharger
engaged
Torque figure not available

Engine (4):
4019cc 8-cylinder with 80mm bore and
100mm stroke, type M22I
Side valves and side camshaft
Five main bearings
Compression ratio 5.54:1
Single Mercedes-Benz twin-choke
updraught carburettor
Roots-type supercharger integral with
crankcase
90PS at 3200rpm
144PS at 3600rpm with supercharger
engaged
Torque figure not available

Gearbox:
Three-speed with overdrive.

Ratios with 3.8-litre engines
2.86:1, 1.80:1, 1.00:1; overdrive 0.70:1;
reverse 3.55:1

Ratios with 4.0-litre engines
3.41:1, 1.60:1, 1.00:1; overdrive 0.70:1;
reverse 4.30:1

Axle ratios:
5.11:1 or 4.70:1

Chassis and suspension:
Oval-section steel tube chassis frame
Independent front suspension with twin
wishbones, coil springs and lever-arm
dampers
Swing-axle rear suspension with double
(concentric) coil springs and lever-arm
dampers

Brakes:
Hydraulic operation on all four wheels, with
Bosch-Dewandre vacuum servo

Weights and measures:
Overall dimensions
4690 x 1730 x 1620mm
Wheelbase 3140mm
Track 1435mm (front), 1480mm (rear)
Weight 2420kg (maximum permissible)

Maximum speed
120km/h (74mph) unsupercharged;
130km/h (81mph)
with supercharged 3.8-litre engines;
140km/h (87mph)
with supercharged 4.0-litre engine

Fuel consumption 21 litres per 100km
(13.5mpg)

Chapter Eight

THE 500K

1934-1936

Mercedes car production hit its lowest point in 1930, when only 3635 chassis were produced. But sales began to pick up thereafter and production rose to 6057 in 1931, 8282 in 1932 and 11,640 in 1933. The 1935 figure of 15,579 was very nearly twice the number achieved in 1926 when Daimler and Benz had amalgamated, and production reached even higher levels for the rest of the decade.

Most of these sales, of course, were of dependable but unexciting middle-class saloons, and the design and development of these were the primary tasks of the car engineering teams. However, Mercedes had long since recognised the value of flagship models – cars which may not have sold in large numbers or brought in huge profits, but which served to remind potential buyers of the company's engineering abilities and to reinforce an image of prestige and desirability. A special section of the engineering division looked after these, designing and building limited-production bodies for the most expensive chassis. This was the "Sonderwagen" (special car) section, and from September 1932 it was headed by Hermann Ahrens, who joined Mercedes from rival maker Horch.

The forward thinkers at Stuttgart already knew that there was no more to be had from brutal sports racers like the SS and SSK. At the top end of the market, the future lay in high-performance touring cars, combining the latest technology, more creature comforts and a dash

1935 Special Roadster on the 500K chassis.

of glamour. The 380S and later supercharged 380 models described in Chapter 7 were first steps in that direction, but their final derivatives provided roadholding and handling that simply cried out for more powerful engines. So Hans Nibel's engineers set to work on a new supercharged straight-eight to provide that power. At about the same time, the Sonderwagen section began to look at more glamorous bodywork to complement the expected higher performance.

Engine and chassis

The new engine that was fundamental to the concept of the new car must have come together during 1933. It was coded M24 (later M24 I, when further developments created an M24 II type). The design target seems to have been 100PS without the supercharger engaged, which inevitably meant that the engine would have a capacity somewhere between the 3.8-litre M22 that delivered 90PS and the 7.7-litre M06 that delivered 150PS. In the event, a swept volume of just of 5 litres (5018cc) delivered what was required.

In most respects, the new 5.0-litre engine was really a scaled-down version of the 7.7-litre eight-cylinder used in the Grosser Mercedes, with the same nine main bearings and the same pushrod overhead-valve architecture. Nevertheless, its 86mm bore and 108mm stroke were entirely unrelated to the 95mm and 135mm dimensions of the 7.7-litre engine. Its supercharger also followed the latest thinking in

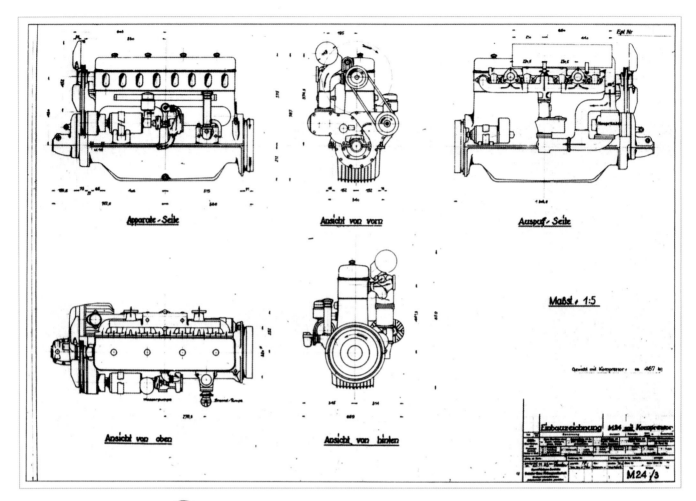

The eight-cylinder engine was designed specially for the new 500K models. This 1/5 scale general arrangement drawing dates from 25 November 1933.

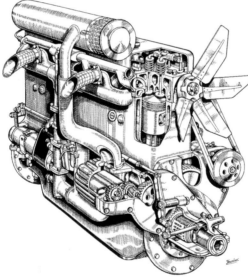

This cutaway drawing illustrates the layout of the M24 engine and, in particular, the arrangement of the supercharger, which is alongside the block as it had been on the engine of the 7.7-litre Grosser models. The drive for the cooling fan is offset to make room for the supercharger drive from the crankshaft.

being located alongside the cylinder block to reduce the length of the engine, as had been done for the later 380 models.

With a 5.5:1 compression ratio and a single updraught carburetor whose double chokes each fed four cylinders, the desired 100PS were achieved at a 3400rpm. With the blower engaged, 160PS at the same engine speed guaranteed markedly better performance than the 380's best of 140PS. As usual, the owner's manual recommended never using the supercharger for more than a minute at a time, but a minute is a very long time for an overtaking manoeuvre on the road and these cars were fast enough not to need extending very frequently.

In production, higher compression ratios were also made available so that customers could take advantage of higher-octane fuel where it was available (in practice, this would most often have been racing-type mixtures which added benzole to standard pump fuel). As in the 380, a gearbox with three speeds plus an overdrive was thought to be enough, but driving ease was improved by adding synchromesh between second and third speeds; the ratios were the same as had been used on the special batch of 4.0-litre 380s, but the overdrive ratio was even higher to reduce engine revs at speed.

As for the chassis, the box-section type developed for the later 380 models was just the starting point. The wishbone-and-coil independent front suspension was retained more or less unchanged, but on late 500s (probably only the 1936 cars) the swing-axle rear end was improved by fitting horizontal compensating springs that stiffened the suspension in roll but did not adversely affect the soft ride. The car was lowered slightly, too, by using 17-inch wheels in place of the older model's standard 18-inch size. A favourite option on production models was to have the spokes of these wheels blacked out, leaving only the elegant bolt-on balance weights as highlights around the rim. The 380s had all shared the same 3140mm wheelbase, but the designers seem to have felt that this demanded too many compromises and also limited the variety of bodies that could be offered. So the chassis for the new 5.0-litre car was drawn up with alternative wheelbase lengths. The standard size would be 3290mm – a little longer than on the 380 – but there would also be an optional short wheelbase of 2980mm. For these cars, the radiator grille was moved forwards over the axle, in order to leave enough room for the passenger cabin on the shortened chassis. Very few of these cars were built, although the precise number is not known.

Developing the bodies

Meanwhile, work was under way on the bodies for the new car. There had been six standard types for the 380 it was to replace, but for the new one there would be no fewer than ten – eight on the standard wheelbase and two more on the short chassis. It looks as if not all of them were planned from the beginning, however, because a special streamlined coupé type called the "Autobahnkurier" went from drawing-board to completion in just 10 weeks prior to the new car's public announcement in February 1934.

These bodies were not simply evolutions of those that had been seen on the 380, although inevitably there were some similarities. They

Normal-Roadster
2 Türen — 2 Sitze — 2 Notsitze .... RM 22000.—

Spezial-Roadster
2 Türen — 2 Sitze — 2 Notsitze .... RM 28000.—

Cabriolet „B"
2 Türen — 4 Fenster — 4 bis 5 Sitze .... RM 22000.—

Offener Tourenwagen
2 Türen — 4 bis 5 Sitze .... RM 22000.—

This illustration from a 1936 sales brochure shows four members of that year's 500K family. From the top, they are the Standard Roadster, the Special Roadster, the Cabriolet B and the Open Tourer.

took the sweeping wing lines that had been so successful on those cars and added to them new valances, while harmonious curves and the new lower stance made the cars look longer and sleeker and, above all, more glamorous. Longitudinal vents on the bonnet sides added to the impression of length, replacing the vertical louvres of the 380. There were even new bumpers, faced with twin strips of rubber. Much of the credit for the transformation must go to Friedrich Geiger, who had joined the Sonder-

The Autobahnkurier was a nod towards contemporary interest in streamlining. This was the 1934 show car, which was certainly an attractive design if not altogether practical. A handful of other examples was built, though as hand-built, special-order models they all differed from one another to a greater or lesser degree.

wagen section in April 1933 as his first job after training as a design engineer. Though Geiger would go on to become Mercedes' chief styling engineer in the 1950s, at this stage he was still a new boy in his mid-20s and was of course working to Hermann Ahrens.

The new car was developed with the works code of W29, and for public consumption became a 500K. The 500 of course reflected its engine capacity and the K stood for "Kompressor", or supercharger. It was introduced at the Berlin Motor Show in February 1934, but there were no customer deliveries until the summer of that year. Three different body styles, all on the standard wheelbase, introduced the 500K. The cabriolet was perhaps expected, but the other two were breathtaking. One was the rather self-consciously streamlined Autobahnkurier coupé. The other was the design that made Friedrich Geiger's reputation – the gorgeous Special Roadster.

The Special Roadster was on the Mercedes show stand again at the Paris and London Motor Shows that autumn. In Britain, where a bare chassis was also shown at Olympia, the importers chose not to encumber it with a complicated number designation (it would have

been a 37/160 if they had) but instead to keep things simple. They called it the Type 500 – Supercharged. Using the sales ledgers from the London importers, Michael Frostick identified 65 500K models sold in Great Britain between October 1934 and January 1938 in his 1971 book *The Mighty Mercedes*; not all, however, were registered on British plates.

In the meantime, more new bodies and the short-wheelbase chassis became available. The number of cabriolet styles was increased to three (Types A, B and C according to their configuration), while a two-door Tourer, a Roadster and a more conventional coupé were added to the other styles on the standard wheelbase chassis. On the short chassis, Sport-Roadster and Sport-Coupé designs were introduced, early examples (including an experimental streamlined coupé with faired-in rear wings and vee screen) making their appearance as works entries in the Round Germany Run from Baden-Baden during July 1934. Then, of course, bare chassis of both lengths were made available for custom builders.

The Round Germany Run, or "Deutschland Fahrt" as it was known in its home country, was a 2000km endurance run over German roads. Speed limits were waived for the occasion, and cars had to maintain a minimum average speed. It had first been held in July 1933, and on that occasion Mercedes-Benz had entered no fewer than 14 cars, from a 2-litre to an SSK, with five of them in Class 1. This was for cars with engines of more than 4 litres, and their required average was 88km/h (54.7mph). The event started in Baden-Baden and took in Stuttgart, Munich, Nuremberg, Dresden, Berlin (the Avus race-track), Magdeburg, Cologne, the Nürburgring and Mannheim before finishing back in Baden-Baden. Clearly, it was an ideal way of demonstrating cars on public roads, and so the Stuttgart factory seized on the 1934 event to display its latest 500K models.

Again held in July, the 1934 event had its route altered to include Leipzig and Dortmund, making the overall distance 2195.8km (1364.4 miles). Mercedes again entered several cars, including a 380 that won a gold medal in Class 2 in the hands of Prince Max zu Schaumburg-Lippe. This was an excellent result, but much more important from the factory's point of view were the 500Ks. They did not disappoint. A red roadster, wearing number 13 and driven by

The two-tone colour scheme sets off the lines of this Cabriolet A body to perfection. It is of course essentially the same body as had earlier been offered on the 380 chassis. The tall side-lights on this car hark back to earlier times, and suggest it may have been a very early example or possibly a prototype.

Rudolf Uhlenhaut with Wemmer as his co-driver, won a gold medal in Class 1. So, too, did a rather special 500K with streamlined coupé bodywork, wearing number 10 and driven by Bernet. Although the streamlined coupé body did not enter production (and the car is said to have been rebodied later), its unusual and purposeful appearance must have helped to attract attention to the latest supercharged Mercedes.

The Sindelfingen bodies

That the 500K was a hand-built car for the fabulously wealthy is key to understanding it. Its customers were certainly hugely impressed by the attractive bodies available direct from Sindelfingen, but many of them were used to ordering bespoke designs and expected the same sort of choice when they ordered a 500K. So there was plenty of choice on offer, and of course even choosing between a single or two colours for the coachwork could make a huge difference to the appearance of a car. Decorative body mouldings could be varied; spare wheels could be moved from the tail to the wings or vice versa; and it appears that the cabriolets did not have to have external hood-irons. On top of that, Sindelfingen introduced design variations periodically, to keep the 500K fresh.

Some things did remain constant. All models from the beginning had safety glass windscreens, which was very advanced at the time and did not become a German legal requirement until 1938. All bodies had either a drop-down rear luggage grid or fitted suitcases. All cars except Special Roadsters built before the

middle of 1935 had vertical bonnet slats; the Special Roadster always had horizontal louvres, and these became standard on the late 1935 and 1936 models with other bodywork as well. Most 1934 and early 1935 cars had twin bumpers, with two rubber protective strips; some designs were more ornate than others. The later cars had single-blade bumpers, with a single rubber strip on most designs but none on the Special Roadster. The 1934 cars, Special Roadsters excepted, also had tall round side-lights mounted on the wings; Special Roadsters and all the later examples with other bodies had squatter, streamlined side-lights.

In the popular imagination, every 500K built between 1934 and 1936 was a Special Roadster, but that is very far from the truth. By far the most popular bodywork on the 500K was actually the Cabriolet B – a two-door, four-window design on which the folded hood sat in a huge and ungainly package behind the rear bench seat. There was no doubting its elegance, or that the sweeping wing lines lifted it above similar designs on earlier Mercedes, but it was essentially a conservative style. This was a car for the rich to be seen in when the top was down, but that heavy top with its standard external hood irons made it a quiet and weatherproof high-speed tourer when required. Like all the open 500Ks built by the Sindelfingen body works, the Cabriolet B had leather upholstery, and it also came with a set of fitted suitcases as standard.

Reflecting the continued popularity of open cars at the top end of the market (as long as they were equipped with a weatherproof hood), the next most popular bodies were the Cabriolet C and Cabriolet A. The Cabriolet C, with two

The most popular of Sindelfingen's own bodies was the Cabriolet B, seen here with its top open (on an early car) and closed (on a later example). It was certainly more practical than the Cabriolet A, but the additional seats in the rear compromised the design of the hood, which looked awkward and inelegant when erect and blocked the driver's view to the rear when folded.

doors but no side windows behind them, was inevitably more useful for those who occasionally wanted to carry friends or family in the rear seats (from which they could barely see out) but who were more likely to use the car solo or as a couple. Like the Cabriolet B, it carried its spare wheels mounted alongside the bonnet. Of the 90 Cabriolet C models that surviving records show to have been built, just four were on right-hand-drive chassis for Britain.

The Cabriolet A presented a considerably sleeker profile. With only luggage space behind the front seat, it did not need the tall convertible top of the other two cabriolets and was also able to carry its twin spare wheels mounted at the tail. This helped the bonnet look longer, again adding to the sleekness of line and, perhaps most important, the impression of power.

Still on the standard-wheelbase chassis, the open Tourer body provided room for five passengers but had a lower windscreen than the Cabriolet B, which looked quite frumpy beside it. As befitted the Tourer definition, its side windows did not wind down into the doors and body sides but were removable. In typical Mercedes fashion these were not the flimsy canvas screens associated with British tourers of the time; instead, they had real glass in solid chromed metal frames.

Then, of course, there was the Roadster, introduced in autumn 1934 as a less glamorous alternative to the Special Roadster. Though sharing its basic shape with the more expensive car, it had plainer wings and a straightforward single-piece windscreen. There was room for two in the cockpit and two more in a dickey seat behind, and the car had no weather protection worthy of the name. The Standard Roadster was for buyers who wanted to look the part of the sporting motorist but were not serious enough about performance and handling to go for the rather more cramped Sport Roadster on the short-wheelbase chassis. Jan Melin has discovered that a single Roadster was built at the Mannheim factory rather than at Sindelfingen. He notes that this was a stripped-down car and guesses that it was intended for rally use.

The Special Roadster promised all the disadvantages of the ordinary Roadster, but it was incomparably more glamorous and customers had to pay extra for it. The passenger compartment with its cutaway door tops on the first cars seemed tiny sandwiched between the long

The Cabriolet C hood design still looked heavy, but was much less awkward than the Cabriolet B type. The penalty, as always, was reduced vision for the rear-seat passengers. Cars were supplied with a neat hood bag to cover the folded top; it is absent in this picture.

bonnet and curvaceous tail, rather like the cockpit of a single-seat racing aircraft – and it resembled that even more when the simple hood was erected to meet the low windscreen which was split into two by a chromed spike. The two spare wheels were of course carried on the tail, perched outside the bodywork on the first cars, and customers could order a dickey seat in the tail in place of the integral boot. The long, sweeping wings had valances – a piece of design for design's sake that worked exceptionally well. Chromed body side and wing mouldings emphasised the flowing lines, and

The first versions of the Special Roadster had a rounded tail with the spare wheels carried externally. Nevertheless, the rear wings already had that characteristically beautiful sweep. Special Roadsters always had horizontal bonnet louvres and this one, as an early car, has the twin bumpers with rubber protective strips. Note also the ornate arm supporting the rear light cluster.

More elaborate wing valances and chromed finishers helped to mark out the 1935 Special Roadster on the 500K chassis. There are split-level bumpers with black rubber facings, and entrance to the dickey seat is now by a single step outside the body. There are two spare wheels on the tail here, and the rear has those strikingly ornate tail lamps carried on swan-like chromed mountings.

As always, the eight-cylinder engine was beautifully finished. The earlier six-cylinder cars had three external exhausts; these eight-cylinder engines had just two. The supercharger arrangement was quite different from earlier engines, with the "blower" being mounted alongside the engine rather than in front. That canister-like filter at the front of the engine is the air intake for the supercharger.

White steering wheels were not compulsory, and this car has a black-rimmed wheel to go with its grey upholstery. The instruments are set in a panel with a mother-of-pearl finish, and there are twin wiper motors and no grab handle for the passenger.

The wraparound style of the upper trim sections helped to make the early Special Roadster's cabin a welcoming and cosy place to be. Later models lost this feature.

BODY TYPES

Jan Melin's researches uncovered the following data concerning the body types fitted to the 500K.

Cabriolet A	33
Cabriolet B	106
Cabriolet C	90
Tourer	16
Roadster (all types)	29
Coupé	3
Autobahnkurier	4
Saloon	20
Chassis only	41

from the beginning in 1934 the bonnet sides had horizontal air vents instead of the louvres that featured on all the other 500K models. These further emphasized the car's length. A very special feature was the twin spotlights mounted alongside the windscreen pillars, which carried rear-view mirrors on their backs as well as adding to the chrome embellishment on the car.

As the flagship model of the 500K range, and the fashion leader as well, the Special Roadster was modified more often than the other models. So the original design with twin spares on the tail, chrome moulding all round the wings, and cutaway door tops lasted only until mid-1935. The body was then changed, taking on taller doors with straight tops that gave an even more aircraft-like silhouette, while the tail was elongated so that the twin spares could be recessed into the bodywork (although when both were carried, the outer one still stood clear of the panels). At the same time, the chrome beading running all round the wing valance was deleted and replaced by chrome "flashes" on the sides of those valances.

Exactly how many Special Roadsters were built on the 500K chassis is not clear. The figure of 29 that is regularly quoted is actually for Standard and Special Roadsters combined, so the total must have been rather fewer; at a guess, then, there were between 15 and 20. Jan Melin's researches uncovered that the most popular colours were Chestnut Brown, Gunmetal,

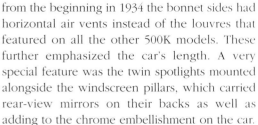

The bumpers on this 500K have no rubber facings at all. The twin flagpoles are surmounted by the eagle and swastika symbol, which indicate that it was owned by a member of the German government. The number-plate was later used on Hermann Göring's 540K, the "Blue Goose", and this car may also have belonged to Göring, though it is not the "Blue Goose". This is the rear view of the same car, showing the elongated tail introduced during 1935. Note the step on the wing, to assist passengers climbing into the rear dickey seats.

Yellow and Yellow-Green; there is an early Chestnut Brown Special Roadster in the Mercedes-Benz Museum but the later (and extremely impressive) bright red car in the collection is not really representative of the way they were.

Of the closed cars, the most numerous were the saloons. In the beginning, these had a four-door body that was very similar to the one used on the 380 models, with a rather formal and upright passenger cabin making a marked contrast with the flowing wing lines. However, from some time in 1934 – perhaps beginning in the autumn – this was replaced by a two-door design with rather more harmonious proportions. All saloons came with a roller blind for the rear window, with a cord that enabled it to be operated from the driver's seat.

There were just three coupés, all with a shorter roofline than the saloons, a single window on each side, and the spare wheels banished from wings to tail in order to make the car look longer. These seem to have been individually constructed, and perhaps there was no "standard" design. One was built in 1935 for works driver Rudolf Caracciola, with a special windscreen that was deeper than the side windows and reached up to the roof. There was a 1935 car described by Mercedes simply as a Sports type but realistically a coupé as well. Then in 1936 came a more streamlined-looking car, with the spare wheel sunk into the tail and covered by a metal panel, plus spats over the rear wheels in the very latest fashion.

Finally, the Autobahnkurier was a nod towards the contemporary interest in streamlining and aerodynamics, which were still

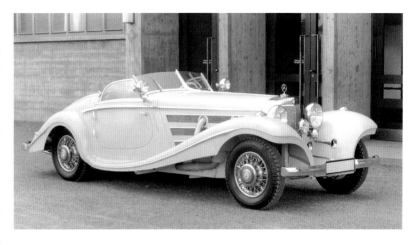

The Coupé seems to have been an under-appreciated design at the time, and only three were built. This car was specially built in 1935 for Mercedes "works" driver Rudolf Caracciola, and has a taller windscreen than standard. It is a strikingly attractive car.

imperfectly understood. It was built on the sports version of the 500K chassis, with the engine set back 185mm (7.3in), and was described at the 1934 Berlin show as "a special one-off version built for high speed". In place of the flowing wing lines of the other models, it had pontoon-type wings with spats on the rear pair, and the wheels had steel discs over their wire spokes to act as fairings. Even the front bumper was faired in, although the standard grille and headlamps can have done nothing for the airflow. This was the only closed 500K to share the chromed spike of the Special Roadster's windscreen, a feature that was probably for effect more than anything else. The sharply sloping tail with its tiny rear window meant that

Another late example of the 500K, showing to good advantage the flowing wing lines that were so much a part of the car's elegance.

This is a late Coupé - possibly the last on 500K chassis - with horizontal bonnet louvres, a single rubber strip on the bumpers, and the wheel spats that were becoming fashionable just as 500K production was drawing to an end. In this form, the lines are beautifully balanced.

The interior of this 1936 car now in the Mercedes-Benz Museum reveals the neat design and exquisite detail that made these Sindelfingen bodies the equal of those by the established independent coachbuilders. Clearly visible are the rear-view mirrors on the backs of the pillar-mounted spot lamps. It is interesting to compare this interior with that of the earlier Special Roadster pictured on page 130 and page 132.

there was room for only one passenger in the rear, who sat sideways, while the spare wheel was hidden out of sight.

Though the show car may have been described as a one-off, the Autobahnkurier design was listed for sale at 24,000 RM, some 9% more than the standard cars but still less than a Special Roadster. It is worth noting that similar streamlined, sloping-tail designs were also built on other Mercedes chassis at the time, including the 290. The 500K model was therefore perhaps not quite as special as it sometimes appears.

Mercedes-Benz records show that another three Autobahnkurier bodies were built on the 500K chassis, making four in all. The Berlin show car went to a customer in Brussels; another car went to the Paris banker Comte de Rivaud in 1934, and the last car was built in spring 1935 and delivered to a Chinese businessman, Tan Tjoan Keng, who lived in Batavia (now Jakarta), Indonesia. Each one had individual features, the French car

sporting a streamlined radiator fairing that hinted at some contemporary French designs and concealed the Mercedes grille, and the Indonesian car seeming to have a higher build as well as a special raked radiator. The fourth car is sometimes described as a 540K, although in fact it was a very late model 500K fitted with the 5.4-litre supercharged engine; the distinction is a fine one. Built on chassis number 130898, it was presented by the German government to Mohammed Reza, the Shah of Iran. It seems to have been painted two-tone green, and is thought still to survive in Iran at the time of writing.

One other car has sometimes been counted as an Autobahnkurier, but actually had a very different style of body. This was the special streamlined coupé that was driven by Bernet in the 1934 Round Germany Run. It was quite unlike the other three, with a very different style of body with curved windscreens and cycle wings; the outer panels were supposedly made of leather stretched over a wooden frame to save weight. Although it may have been part of the same line of aerodynamic development as the Autobahnkurier, it is misleading to describe it as one. Its original body was later removed and the car was rebodied, although the style of this second body is not clear.

There were of course two bodies specially designed for the short-chassis 500K as well. However, no reliable figures are available to indicate how many short-chassis cars were actually built. The bodies on offer were a Sport-Roadster, which was somewhat predictable in appearance. It looked rather stripped down with its cycle-type wings and louvred chassis valances, but it gained distinction from a split windscreen as used on the Special Roadster. The Sport-Coupé on the short-wheelbase car was altogether more elegant, with its twin spares mounted on the tail and very pleasing proportions. However, few seem to have been made.

The coachbuilt bodies

It was no great surprise that the Sindelfingen-built bodies satisfied most customers, but the very wealthy were accustomed to making their own decisions and not all of the 500K's buyers were prepared to be told by Stuttgart what they could and could not have. So a number of 500Ks were sold as bare chassis.

The number has been calculated as 41, which represented quite a high proportion of the total 500K chassis built (although that figure is in dispute, as the sidebars show). It means that there were more coachbuilt 500Ks than there were of any Sindelfingen body types except the Cabriolets B and C. However, the identities of all those who constructed bespoke bodies on the 500K chassis have not been established.

In Germany, the most prolific coachbuilder on the 500K chassis was Erdmann & Rossi, who were in Berlin. Jan Melin's researches revealed that 18 of the 500K chassis went to this coachbuilder – a little under half of the total bare chassis sold. The 1935 cars included a four-door Tourer for a businessman from Danzig, and a Sport-Cabriolet with a body that is thought to have been intended originally for a Horch

Though the 500K would give way to the 540K later in the year, Mercedes still proudly displayed a 500K Special Roadster at the 1936 Berlin Show.

Not many cars were built with right-hand drive, but this one was. It was delivered to a British owner in May 1936.

This very special Roadster was bodied by Erdmann & Rossi for the King of Iraq in 1935. The car still exists.

Erdmann & Rossi were again responsible for this unique car, built in 1936 for a leading German industrialist.

Mounted on a 500K chassis for the 1934 Round Germany Run, this lightweight coupé body had aerodynamic styling and its outer panelling was said to be made of leather, stretched over a wooden frame.

chassis. At the end of that year, a very special streamlined roadster was constructed for the King of Iraq; inspired by an Erdmann & Rossi design on a 290 chassis at the Berlin Motor Show in February, it had all four wheels concealed by spats. The car survives and has been displayed at the Speyer Museum near Heidelberg in southern Germany.

A spatted Roadster was shown at Berlin in 1936, and in February that year Erdmann & Rossi built a very interesting streamlined two-door saloon with aluminium panels and a plexiglass roof. This car was built for Friedrich von Siemens, a politician and member of the family that founded the Siemens electrical company. It was painted in silver-blue, with leather upholstery in a colour described as light grey-beige.

Around eight 500K chassis were bodied in Britain. Two of the bodies were built by Windover, one – a flamboyant roadster – by Mayfair, and others by Vanden Plas and Freestone & Webb. Chassis number 113622 was given a three-position drophead coupé body by Corsica in 1936. There may have been others.

The 5.4-litre 500Ks

As so often happens with low-volume, special-production cars, the last examples of the 500K seem to have been transitional types, with a specification half-way towards that of the 540K that replaced them in 1936 after just over two years in production. Some sources claim that the final cars inherited the modified swing-axle rear suspension designed for the 540K. Certainly, a number of 1936 cars were built with the new 5.4-litre engine, and probably these were reserved for very special customers. There can be little doubt that senior members of the Nazi Party would have been among them.

Jan Melin's researches showed that a total of 13 500K chassis were actually fitted with 540K engines. Twelve of these were built in 1936, and of course the new 540K had been previewed at the Berlin Show early that year. However, the thirteenth car was one of the pilot-production batch built in 1934. If that 5.4-litre engine was fitted to the car when it was new, it suggests that Stuttgart was already planning the larger and more powerful engine before the first customers had even taken delivery of their 500Ks.

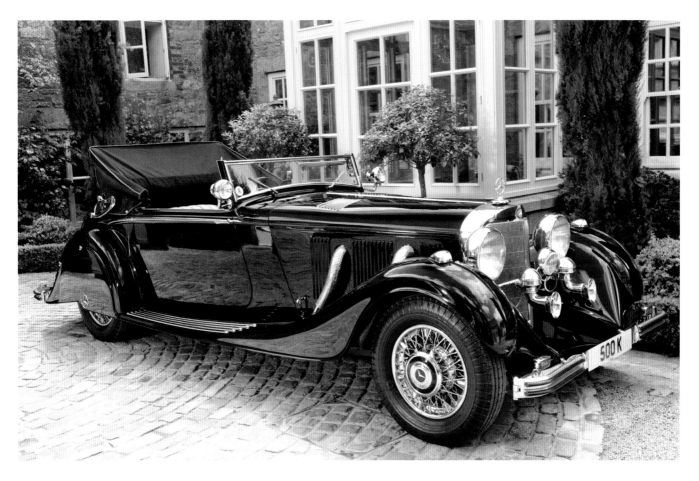

A Mr James ordered this magnificent 500K in the UK for July 1935 delivery. The cabriolet bodywork was by HJ Mulliner, but retained the typically German style of folded hood at the rear and also borrowed the latest style of spatted rear wheels. It had enormous presence.

*Just visible here are
the additional
ventilation louvres
in the bonnet top.*

*The identification
plate of the car
carries the German
taxation figure for
the engine capacity;
though it read
"4984cc", the actual
size was 5018cc.*

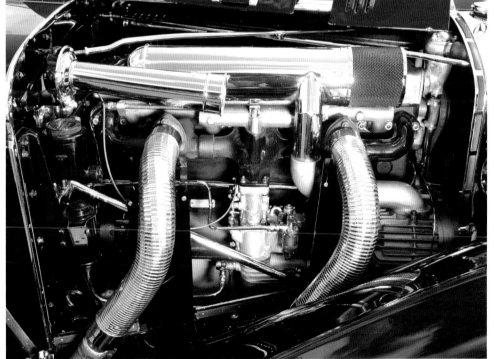

Despite those twin horns ahead of the radiator, there is still a horn trumpet under the bonnet! Very clear here is the top-mounted air intake filter of the 500K engine's supercharger.

The standard W29 instrument panel is here set within a typically British figured wood dashboard.

As so often, it was the details that made the luxury car: the roller sunblind for the passenger, and the set of fitted suitcases behind the seats. HJ Mulliner "signed" the car in the usual way.

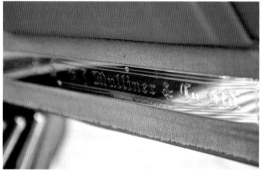

*There was a certain
amount of swagger
about the style of
these external horns.*

Behind the wheel of a 500K

Stuttgart appears to have been reluctant to allow road-testers to get their hands on the 500K when it was first released. Halwart Schrader reports in his book, *The Supercharged Mercedes*, that the journalist from the *Allgemeine Automobil-Zeitung* had to gain his impressions from the passenger seat while a factory representative drove the car. By the autumn, however, the company seems to have become less precious, and through the intermediary of the British importers a representative of *Motor Sport* magazine was able to try a left-hand-drive 500K Roadster (though not the Special Roadster) that had been used by the Racing Department as a support vehicle at that year's Spanish Grand Prix.

The report appeared in the November 1934 issue of the magazine, and the writer was clearly impressed. "Here is a massive 'unbreakable' car," he wrote, "capable of travelling indefinitely at high speed and yet not difficult to handle, a man's car in a period when chromium plate and snow-plough radiators are making ever-increasing inroads into the ranks of the thoroughbred sporting vehicle."

Flexibility was clearly a characteristic: the car would normally pull away from rest in second gear, and would "crawl along at walking pace in third if required". The 500K was fast, easy to drive and comfortable, too: "instead of being a full sports model [like the older 38/250 or SS] requiring continual use of the gear box and having rather harsh suspension, the five-litre is practically a two-gear car, and is as comfortably suspended as one could wish for, while still capable of exceeding 100mph." High speeds were maintained effortlessly: "at 75 to 80mph... the Mercedes sweeps along silently on two-thirds throttle". However, the usual Achilles heel of these cars was only too apparent, and "the brakes unfortunately did not come up to the standard of the rest of the chassis."

Just under a year later, *The Autocar* published impressions of a 500K Cabriolet B, tastefully finished in Linden green with dark mole wings and body flashes, that they had been able to sample on German roads and at the Nürburging race track. In the issue dated 16 August 1935, they admitted that the 500K was "a dream car possible only for the wealthy", but that had not stopped them enjoying it. The car achieved an indicated 160km/h (100mph) on the Autobahn with four up, and during a stint in Belgium demonstrated the comfort of its all-independent suspension by "travelling at a steady 75-80mph... even on the worst pavé, without the occupants of either front or rear seats feeling any harshness at all. This was really amazing, as any who know the Belgian roads will agree."

BUILD VOLUMES

Mercedes-Benz quote a total of 342 500K models of all types. This figure is contradicted by Jan Melin's researches, which uncovered only 305 cars recorded by Daimler-Benz as 500K types. Of those, 13 (see separate table) were fitted with 5.4-litre engines, which reduces the "true" 500K count to just 292 examples.

Werner Oswald gives the total as 354, with the following breakdown of build volumes, year by year:

1934	105
1935	190
1936	59

IDENTIFICATION NUMBERS

Generally speaking, chassis and engine numbers for these cars matched. A replacement engine would have its number prefixed by A (for "Austausch", exchange)

The chassis numbers and production figures in these tables were established by Jan Melin and are taken from his book, *Mercedes-Benz, The Supercharged 8-cylinder Cars of the 1930s, Volume 1*.

Number(s)	Total	Remarks
98453-98457	5	Pilot production cars; one car with 5.4-litre engine
105131-105180	50	
105351-105400	50	
113621-113270	50	
123681-123780	100	Two cars with 5.4-litre engines
130851-130900	50	Ten cars with 5.4-litre engines
	305	The 13 cars with 5.4-litre engines were recorded by Daimler-Benz as 500K types, although some authorities (including Jan Melin) count them with the 540K cars

Although the Sindelfingen coachworks offered a comprehensive range of coachwork, there was nothing to prevent wealthy buyers ordering something bespoke. This car was a special order dating from 1935 and delivered to Arturo Lopez in Paris in March 1936. It combines the centre body section of a Cabriolet A with some of the design elements associated with the Special Roadster - the front wings, scuttle, vee-screen and elegant long tail with its inset spare wheel.

The car's performance even surprised the Mercedes representative who accompanied it, when he was persuaded to attack a steep hill at the Nürbrurging. That same representative also assured *The Autocar* reporter that it was possible to keep the supercharger engaged for up to about five minutes and to speeds of 170-175km/h (105-108mph). However, the maximum indicated speed during the continental trip was 102mph, and the writer found that "one could maintain about 85mph without using the supercharger... Without the supercharger... one would call the machine merely a pleasant and reasonably fast touring car, but in no wise an exciting sports car."

The Autocar also managed to secure a right-

The long rear-hinged doors are from a Cabriolet B or C, and allow good access to the rear seats.

hand-drive, British specification 500K Cabriolet B for one of its proper road tests in 1936. This was published in its issue of 12 June, by which time the car was already being replaced in its native country by the 540K model. "The design and construction throughout are typically thorough and well executed," they reported. In character, the 500K was a very fast touring car, "with the considerable extra power provided by the supercharger held in reserve for occasions when the utmost acceleration is wanted".

Without the supercharger in use, they found it "quiet, easily handled, even docile", but "the result of blowing is terrific. One's foot goes hard down, and an almost demoniacal howl comes in... The rev counter and speedometer needles leap round their dials." Acceleration through the gears produced a 0-60mph time of 16.5 seconds, which was very quick for 1936.

The magazine concluded that "this is a master car, for the very few. The sheer insolence of its great power affords an experience on its own."

The tail cleverly combines the essentials of the long Special Roadster design with the needs of the cabriolet body. The tail lights seen here appear not to be original items.

XSY 440

Under the bonnet, everything is as expected with the 500K engine.

The cooling louvres in the bonnet sides were a work of art in themselves.

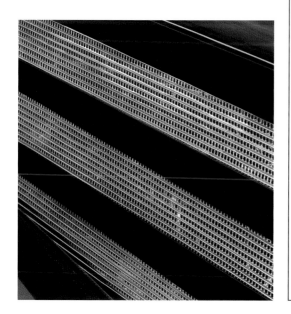

PRICES

The prices of 500K models were inevitably affected by the amount of custom-finishing required. Nevertheless, catalogue prices were quoted, as below. Mercedes quoted a single price for most variants, but the special bodies on the standard chassis cost extra.

	Standard	Short-chassis
Chassis	15,500 RM	15,500 RM
Roadster		22,000 RM
Sport-Roadster		22,000 RM
Coupé	22,000 RM	
Sport-Coupé		22,000 RM
Cabriolet A		22,000 RM
Cabriolet B (4 windows)	22,000 RM	
Cabriolet C (2 windows)	22,000 RM	
Saloon (four-door)	22,000 RM	
Tourer (two-door)	22,000 RM	
Autobahnkurier	24,000 RM	
Special Roadster (1935)	26,000 RM	
(1936)	28,000 RM	

The central body section provides room for four passengers; in a Special Roadster, the rear two were banished to a dickey seat. The wide wheelarches nevertheless make the rear seat quite narrow.

SPECIFICATIONS, 500K (W29)
1934

Engine:
5018cc 8-cylinder with 86mm bore and
108mm stroke, type M24 I
Single camshaft acting through pushrods on
overhead valves
Nine main bearings
Compression ratio 5.5:1 or 6.5:1
Single Mercedes-Benz twin-choke
updraught carburettor
Roots-type supercharger integral with
crankcase
100PS at 3400rpm
160PS at 3400rpm with supercharger
engaged
Torque figure not available

Gearbox:
Three-speed with overdrive; synchromesh
on second and third. Ratios 3.42:1, 1.60:1,
1.00:1; overdrive 0.62:1; reverse 4.30:1

Axle ratios:
4.88:1 (standard); 5.11:1, 4.46:1 and 4.18:1
optional

Chassis and suspension:
Box-section steel chassis frame
Independent front suspension with twin
wishbones, coil springs and lever-arm
dampers
Swing-axle rear suspension with horizontal
compensating spring, double (concentric)
coil springs and lever-arm dampers

Brakes:
Hydraulic operation on all four wheels, with
Bosch-Dewandre vacuum servo

Weights and measures:
Overall dimensions
(standard wheelbase models):
Roadster 5000 x1880 x 1330mm
Cabriolet B and C 5200 x 1800 x 1630mm
Saloon 5100-5200 x 1820 x 1650mm
Autobahnkurier 5170 x 1820 x 1520mm

Overall dimensions
(short wheelbase models):
Roadster 4880 x 1900 x 1500mm
Coupé 4880 x 1900 x 1480mm
Wheelbase 3290mm (standard)
or 2980mm (short chassis)
Track 1512mm (front), 1502mm (rear);
short-chassis cars and optional on standard
wheelbase 1535mm (front) and 1547mm
(rear)

Weight 2700kg
(maximum permissible, standard wheelbase)

Maximum speed 160km/h (100mph)

Fuel consumption 27 litres per 100km
(10.5mpg);
British magazines recorded 11-12mpg on
road test

The downside, as so often, was the brakes. *The Autocar* tortured the English language to take the edge off its criticism, but reported that "they are not over-sensitive brakes that can be too easily applied with extreme results." That translates roughly as "the brakes need a firm shove and need some time to stop the car."

The Motor got its hands on a similar car, quite probably the very same one, in time to publish a road test in its issue dated 7 July 1936. "Chassis and coachwork are so robust as to suggest that this car could be driven hard for years without suffering mechanical depreciation," the testers reported. On the road, they discovered that there was no value in engaging the supercharger below 1500rpm (which corresponded to 30mph in direct top and 48mph in overdrive). Above those speeds, however, "the blower makes a big difference to the acceleration available." The car reached 102mph on the Brooklands track in overdrive with the supercharger engaged, and 85mph without. "The riding and handling on the banking were exceptionally good," but *The Motor* criticised the gearchange as "not quick". Even so, in summary "this is an exceptionally interesting car which, in its suspension and overdrive, has set a fashion that the world is now following."

Chapter Nine

THE 540K

1936-1939

Some writers have suggested that Mercedes' wealthier customers began to demand even more power and performance almost as soon as the 500K reached the showrooms, but the truth is probably more prosaic. The engineers at Stuttgart had almost certainly begun work on a more powerful version of the supercharged straight-eight engine as soon as the 5.0-litre type had been signed off for production, simply because they could. The mood in Germany was upbeat by the middle of the 1930s; nobody can have doubted that the market for a more powerful 500K would be there when the car was ready.

Both the bore and the stroke of the M24 engine were increased, the former by 2mm and the latter by 3mm, to 88 x 111mm. The new dimensions gave an engine of 5401cc, to which Stuttgart gave the name of M24 II; the 5.0-litre type became an M24 I in retrospect. There was also a change to the air intake for the supercharger; some engines had the same long horizontal air cleaner as the 5.0-litre engines but with the feed pipe to the blower relocated ahead of the front exhaust header, while on others the supercharger had its own small vertical air cleaner in front of the blower casing. By the German tax rating system of the time, the engine was rated at 5363cc, and this figure usually appears on the chassis plate.

Peak power went up by 15% to 115PS at the same 3400rpm without the supercharger engaged; kicking the blower into action deliv-

1937 540K
Special Roadster

ered 180PS at 3400rpm, 20PS or 12% more than the 5.0-litre engine had mustered. Maximum speed with the new engine went from 160km/h (100mph) to 170km/h (105mph) – but these claims from the factory were conservative. Most cars were probably capable of some 5mph more than the advertised figure, just as the 500K models had been.

The new engine was ready by summer 1936, and it was announced at the Paris Motor Show that October. The car it powered was called a 540K, and as production got under way, a few favoured customers had 5.4-litre engines fitted into their existing 500K cars.

There was of course more to the new 540K than an extra 400cc of engine capacity, even though the car was always intended to be based on the 500K and inherited its W29 works designation. Redeveloped under Gustav Rohr, who had been recruited from Adler when Hans Nibel had died and Max Sailer had taken over the top engineering job in the car division, its chassis now had improved swing-axle rear suspension with transverse compensating springs that stiffened the suspension in roll but did not adversely affect the soft ride. The three-speed gearbox with separate overdrive was also replaced, by a lower-geared four-speed type with direct top gear and synchromesh on the top three gears. The axle gearing was taller than on the 500K, and there was now a choice of just two ratios.

The standard wheelbase length of 3290mm

On the 5.4-litre engine, the supercharger was again located alongside the front of the cylinder block, but this time the air filter arrangements were different: there was a vertical filter instead of the horizontal tubular type of the 500K engine.

was unchanged from the earlier car, as was the short wheelbase of 2980mm. However, in practice it looks as if the short-wheelbase cars did not become available until 1939. There were also two variants of the standard chassis. One had the radiator mounted directly above the front axle, and this was normally used for the Cabriolets B and C, Saloons and Tourers. The other was the "sports" chassis, with its radiator set 185mm (7.3in) behind the axle, and the engine bulkhead and bodywork all moved a corresponding amount rearwards. This was used for the two-seater Cabriolet A, but also seems to have been used for some other bodies to special order. Early examples of the 540K had the same track dimensions as the 500K, but later examples had wider tracks.

As had been the case with the 380 and 500K

chassis, the 540K chassis were built up at Untertürkheim and were then delivered to the Sonderwagen department of the Sindelfingen body works to have their bodies constructed. Each body was coachbuilt by hand, and although there certainly were standard designs shown in the catalogues, Sindelfingen was as prepared to make variations to suit the customer's requirements as was any independent coachbuilder of the period.

Some cars were probably returned to Sindelfingen for modifications or even updates to the original specification, and all these factors make it difficult to trace the evolution of the 540K, although it is possible to pinpoint certain changes over the years. Photographs show, for example, that the early 540K cars had three-piece front bumpers, but from 1938 they usually had a one-piece type. The three-piece bumpers were usually faced with a rubber strip, which could be black or white and was matched on the rear bumper. A white strip was often, but not invariably, used when the car had a white steering wheel. However, some of the earliest cars built in 1936 had the twin rubber strips more usually associated with the 500K; the transition from one style to the next seems to have been gradual. From 1937, rear wheel spats became available on some Sindelfingen bodies.

One unexplained change that occurred around this time was highlighted by Jan Melin's researches in the Daimler-Benz archives. In 1937, documents began to record the model type of the 540K as W129 rather than W29. (Note that the number was later re-used, as R129, for the 1989-2001 SL sports car.) Melin says that the new number was definitely not used only for the short-chassis cars, which are always referred to as W29 Kurz (short). One possible explanation is that Daimler-Benz found the old two-figure codes awkward for some reason, and wanted to standardise on three-figure codes, but there is no firm evidence of this. Today, the Mercedes-Benz archive website uses the W129 code only for the experimental 5.8-litre 580K models (see below).

The major changes in the cars' appearance came for 1938. Much of the lightness and grace

This 540K show chassis was carefully prepared with elements of the engine, gearbox, differential and radiator cut away to show the internals. The paired rear coil springs are clearly visible.

of the classic mid-1930s styles disappeared (and this was most noticeable on the Special Roadster) as heavier-looking wings and one-piece front bumpers arrived for the standard Sindelfingen designs. The 1938 cars also had their bonnet side air vents painted in the body colour rather than chromed, although the older style was still available to order and seems to have been retained on cars built for export. Later still, the very last 540Ks had a new radiator grille with a less obvious vee, which tended to make the car look wider.

There were some big changes for the 1939 cars, too. To meet new German regulations, the stop and tail lights and rear reflectors were modified. An improved clutch mechanism was fitted, together with wider front brakes and larger dampers. Most important, perhaps, was the introduction of a five-speed gearbox with overdrive top gear and a new, taller, 2.8:1 final drive. This combination allowed a 90mph cruising speed at 2700rpm without the supercharger engaged.

Production of the 540K had ended in 1939, even though no replacement model was yet ready. After the outbreak of war in September 1939, the market for such cars was in any case going to be severely reduced. Nevertheless, a few examples of the 540K remained unsold by October 1940, and Jan Melin found a document dated 10 October which revealed that the works still had five brand-new cars – three with Cabriolet A bodies, one Combination Coupé and one Saloon. There were also either two or three unbodied chassis at the works as late as 1942, when they were used to meet part of an urgent order from the German government.

The "factory" bodies: standard wheelbase

The catalogued bodies embraced a variety of different types. In the beginning, there were nine different options on the standard chassis: Cabriolets A, B and C; a two-seat Roadster; a 2-3 seat Coupé, a two-door Saloon; a two-door Tourer; the streamlined Autobahnkurier; and the Special Roadster. Not all of them lasted the course. The Roadster, the Coupé and the Cabriolet C were all slow sellers and were withdrawn for 1938, and the Tourer disappeared from the catalogues a year later. In 1937, a new Combination Coupé was introduced, which was in effect a Cabriolet A whose convertible top could be removed and replaced by a hardtop.

Yet few Sindelfingen bodies were exactly alike: wing shapes, colour combinations and body decoration could all be varied; spare wheels normally mounted on the tail could be relocated to the front wings; and if the standard chassis with its forward-set radiator was used in place of the "sports" type, the proportions of bonnet and body could be varied. It was even possible to have the radiator set ahead of the front axle, to achieve yet another variation in appearance.

Autobahnkurier models

The streamlined Autobahnkurier coupé body shown on the 500K chassis at the 1934 Berlin Show remained rare, and although it was offered at the start of 540K production, it was no longer catalogued after 1937. There is some confusion about how many were built on the 540K chassis. The figure of two is generally quoted, but many historians have counted the final 500K Autobahnkurier for the Shah of Iran as a 540K because it was fitted with the new 5.4-litre engine. Daimler-Benz has claimed that a third 540K Autobahnkurier might have been built, but at the time of writing had not clarified this.

The car which seems to have been the very last Autobahnkurier was not delivered until October 1938 (some sources claim 13 September), when it went to the internationally-renowned Spanish opthalmologist, Professor Ignacio Barraquer. It was a gift from an oriental potentate whom he had treated successfully,

This was almost certainly another show chassis. As on the 500K, the twin outside exhaust pipes converged before passing through the chassis side rail and into the main exhaust system.

This Autobahnkurier is clearly in the same vein as the car that was shown as a 500K at the 1934 Berlin Show, but is actually very different. It is configured as a coupé, with no window behind the doors, and the wings follow more orthodox Mercedes lines. There is also an opening fabric roof. The annotation on the negative clearly states that it has a 5.4-litre engine, but whether this is really a 540K or a late 500K with the 5.4-litre engine is just not clear. It is certainly not the Barraquer car.

and featured an extra window behind each door, with the separate pontoon-type wings then typical of other 540K models. Barraquer used it for a number of long journeys, including a famous drive through North Africa from Libya to Cairo and then to Alexandria. The car stayed in the Barraquer family until 2004, when it was sold and restored to concours-winning condition in the USA.

Cabriolet A models

The two-door, two-seat Cabriolet A was built on the "sports" chassis with set-back radiator in order to give it a more dramatic appearance. Although the general lines of the body followed those established for the Cabriolet A on 500K chassis, the 540K did look different thanks to a more modern style of wings with side valances. Doors were always rear-hinged, and the hood

was a rakish affair with the tiny rear window slit so typical of German cabriolets in the 1930s.

The Cabriolet A was available from the start of 540K production in 1936 through to the end of production in 1939. The cars could be fitted with rear-wheel spats, and one notable survivor (on chassis number 154081) was built with them in 1937 for the Maharaja of Indore. From 1938, fatter and heavier-looking wings were fitted, the spare wheels moved from the tail to the wings, and the soft-top came with a built-in radio aerial as standard. Jan Melin's figures show that 83 Cabriolet A bodies were built at Sindelfingen, although this total appears to include the Sport-Cabriolet A bodies built for the short-chassis cars (see below) as well as the Cabriolet A types built on the standard chassis. Three 540K Cabriolet A cars remained unsold at the Daimler-Benz works on 10 October 1940.

The dashboard of the Autobahnkurier had essentially the same layout and design as that on other 540K models. Although this period photograph has undoubtedly been touched up, the inlaid panel has an effect more like mother-of-pearl than figured wood.

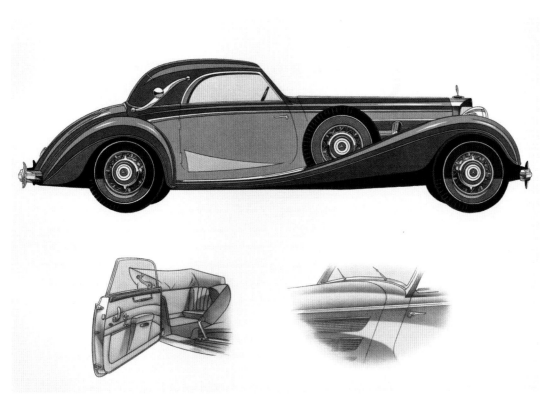

This is the early Cabriolet A body as Mercedes-Benz liked to present it, in a sales catalogue. The two-toning certainly helps the body to look lighter than it really was.

This is how it really was: the red car is an early 540K Cabriolet A from the Mercedes-Benz Museum collection. The depth of those doors makes the car look both solid and heavy. With a two-tone split disguising their size, the car looks very different. The wing-mounted spare nevertheless tends to make the body look shorter and more dumpy than the earlier 500K style with spares on the tail.

Not every Cabriolet A was the same, of course. This 1936 car, pictured in the ownership of collector Peter Heinz Kern, has a set-back radiator and the bonnet with the vertical louvres associated with the 1934-35 500K models.

This interesting Cabriolet A was the work of an unidentified independent coachbuilder and was new in late 1936. The streamlined grille arrangement cannot have pleased Stuttgart very much, although the large three-pointed star emblems on the rear spats helped to identify the chassis maker.

The inside view: this overhead picture of a Cabriolet A makes clear how spacious the passenger cabin really was.

The standard Cabriolet A body had an attractive lightness about it, despite those deep sides and the huge folded hood. The two-tone colour scheme certainly lifts this French-registered 1936 540K model out of the ordinary.

With the hood up, the Cabriolet A was arguably even more attractive. Those yellow headlamps were demanded by French lighting regulations.

Provenance : the car carries both a Sindelfingen coachworks badge and a body number plate.

The car's identification plate shows the actual engine capacity of 5401cc instead of the smaller size used for German tax ratings. Details of the original owner are shown on the factory build record.

The standard mother-of-pearl instrument panel is set in a wooden dashboard, and a cream steering wheel with blue horn ring perfectly sets off the two-tone leather upholstery, clearly designed to match the bodywork.

This is the casing of the supercharger; above it is the trunking leading from the vertical air intake.

Top up or top down, this 1937 540K Cabriolet A presents a tidy appearance, but the flamboyance of the earlier cars has gone, to be replaced by something approaching sobriety.

Spare wheels were no longer mounted on the tail, but were carried more soberly alongside the engine bay. There was nevertheless still room for the two outside exhaust pipes on the right-hand side.

Despite increasing sobriety elsewhere, the exquisite instruments in their mother-of-pearl panel remained in the specification

Nevertheless, seeing that front end approaching in the rear-view mirror would quickly persuade most drivers to move over. The car remained imposing from any angle, exuding both good taste and an aristocratic sense of supremacy.

The identification plate here gives the 5363cc "fiscal" engine capacity.

Would-be buyers of a Cabriolet B might well have been persuaded by this page from a 540K sales catalogue. Although the illustrations are drawings, and suffer from a little bit of idealisation, they do give a good idea of the real thing.

... and this is the real thing. The car has modern amber turn signal lamps front and rear. Unusually, it was supplied with right-hand drive.

Cabriolet B models

The Cabriolet B was by far the most popular body style on the 540K chassis, with 190 examples built at Sindelfingen. It was a rather upright and formal two-door style with front-hinged doors, four seats and an extra pair of side windows for the rear seat passengers – not at all the kind of body associated in the popular mind with the 540K chassis today. It was available right through the production run, from 1936 to 1939. For 1938, the Cabriolet B body was redesigned with a more bulbous rear end reminiscent of the W150 Grosser models; the car also became shorter, with an overall length reduced from 5250mm (206.7mm) to 5032mm (198.1in).

Cabriolet C models

The Cabriolet C was the least popular of the cabriolet bodies on the 540K chassis, and the last example left Sindelfingen in 1937 after only 32 had been built. Cabriolet C bodies had two front-hinged doors and a formal-looking hood to give headroom for rear seat passengers, who nevertheless had to manage without their own side windows. One Cabriolet C was delivered in 1936 to King Farouk of Egypt, and this car still survives.

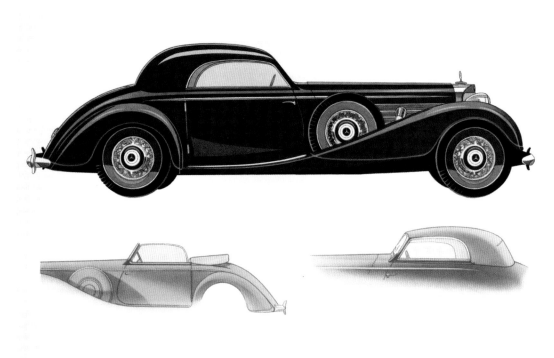

Another page from the 540K sales catalogue shows the so-called Combination Coupé. This had a removable hardtop which could be replaced by a folding canvas hood. The pictures give a good idea of the result, but no doubt the difficulties associated with swapping tops were a key reason why this design was never popular.

These pictures show a later iteration of the coupé design, with the revised wing lines adopted towards the end of the 1930s.

Combination Coupés

The Combination Coupé ("Kombinations Coupé") introduced in 1937 can only barely be described as a production model because so few were built. One body appears to have been fitted to an older 500K chassis (which also received a 5.4-litre engine at the same time), and Jan Melin could find evidence that only two were built altogether. One of those remained unsold as late as October 1940. The body fitted to the 500K seems to have been different from that on the 540K.

The Combination Coupé was an interesting concept, as it was essentially a Cabriolet A that could be fitted with a removable hardtop and so turned into a closed coupé. With the hardtop on, it was as good as indistinguishable from a 540K coupé. A series of pictures taken at Sindelfingen show that the convertible top first had to be removed (it was anchored to the bodywork by a series of long pegs, probably with securing bolts), and that the operation required two men. Although the idea was ingenious, in practice the difficulty of swapping one top for the other probably made it rather impractical and may have been a deterrent to customers. The known 1937 car had rear wing spats.

Did Sindelfingen ever really build a 540K in this colour? The artist's imagination has run riot in this sales catalogue illustration of the 540K coupé, and the effect of that colour would have been far greater in the mid-1930s than it is today.

Coupés

The Coupé was a particularly attractive body built on the sports chassis with the set-back radiator. It was in effect a hardtop version of the Cabriolet A, with the same rear-hinged doors and sloping tail, where the spare wheel was concealed under a removable cover. It came with two seats in the front and the option of a sideways-facing seat in the rear; if the seat was not fitted, the rear of the passenger compartment was configured as a luggage carrier, and was supplied with a set of fitted luggage. Only 7 Coupé bodies were built at Sindelfingen before the model was withdrawn at the end of 1937, although a Special Coupé with four seats, a divided windscreen, rear wheel spats and a low roofline was shown in Paris in 1938.

The bumpers on this 540K Special Coupé built in 1939 are quite different from the standard items, although the wing line is essentially that found on the later cars. The rear wings are nevertheless more enveloping than the standard type, making the car look as if it is squatting on its haunches. The additional window behind the door suggests a two-door saloon more than a coupé, and the trim details at waist level are special.

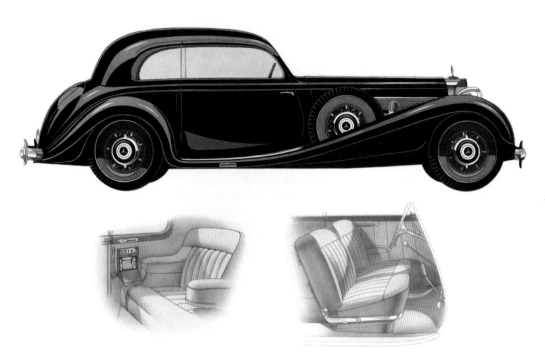

Roadsters

The Roadster, sometimes called the Normal or Standard Roadster to distinguish it from the Special Roadster, had essentially the same body as the 500K Roadster that preceded it. However, the 540K versions had the valanced wings always associated with those cars, which tended to make the Roadster look heavier and less sporting. It was built on the standard chassis, with radiator above the front axle, normally had a single-piece windscreen, and carried its twin spare wheels exposed at the tail. The body was available only in the 1936 and 1937 seasons and was not a popular choice: Jan Melin found that only four Roadster bodies were built at Sindelfingen for 540K chassis.

Saloon models

In the beginning, there were both four-door and two-door saloon bodies for the 540K, but the four-door was not a strong seller and soon disappeared from the catalogues; it was probably available only in 1936, and just five bodies of the type were built. Despite its rather upright lines, the two-door saloon had a quite light and sporting appearance. In 1939, at least one example was built to special order with a lower roofline, spare wheels in the tail instead of

Just visible at the bottom of the scuttle panel above the wing is Sindelfingen's coachwork badge. This is a late two-door saloon, with the restyled wing lines and rear-wheel spats.

Although the popular perception is that all 540Ks were open cars, there were in fact more of these two-door saloons than there were Special Roadsters. The lines are beautifully balanced, and the car was less ostentatious than the roadsters while lacking none of their performance. Quite clear here is the wheel "lean" associated with the swing-axle rear suspension. Note also the opening rear window and the metal strips on the boot lid that allowed an additional trunk to be strapped to the outside without damaging the paintwork.

The front view is no less impressive, although the mirrors mounted on brackets above each spare wheel strike a jarring note.

As always, the details mattered. These are the characteristic Mercedes rear lights, and the easy-grip fuel filler cap.

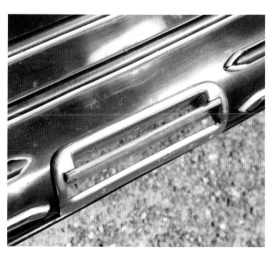

A delightful characteristic of Sindelfingen's own bodies was the boot-scraper on each running-board. Owners did not want mud on their carpets...

The identification plate and body number plate are vital in establishing the car's authenticity.

The big eight-cylinder engine was identical to that in the other 540K models.

A multiple fuse box like this one was not common on lesser cars even 20 years after the 540K saloon was built. Third from the right at the bottom is the fuse for the direction indicators ("Winker").

The upholstery in this car is high-quality cloth rather than the leather seen in the open cars. The general arrangement of the dash is similar but less ornate, and the rear seats with their central and side armrests look like a special place to be.

Daimler-Benz has never been quite as logical about its model designations as it likes to pretend, and when the 540K chassis was used for some special armoured saloons for the Reichs Chancellery in 1942, it changed from a W29 (or, later W129) type to a W24 type. That designation had been used earlier for a long-wheelbase model that might have replaced the 770! The two-door saloon body was neat but unspectacular - probably deliberately, to avoid drawing unnecessary attention. The bonnet panels reverted to vertical slats for ventilation.

The Special Roadster started off looking like the last 500K models in 1936, but gradually evolved. This is one of the early models, still with those delightfully shaped wing valances and an exposed spare wheel in the tail.

alongside the bonnet, and rear-wheel spats. A total of 28 two-door saloon bodies was built for the 540K chassis, and at least one of them (on chassis number 154100) was exported to the USA when new in February 1937. There is sometimes some confusion about names here: some later two-door Saloons seem to have been called Coupés on occasion. One Saloon body remained unsold at the Stuttgart works on 10 October 1940.

Special Roadster models

As it had been for the 500K chassis, the Special Roadster was always the glamorous top of the range model of the 540K. It was also the most expensive of the "standard" types available from Sindelfingen, with a price of 28,000 Reichsmarks, or some 27% more than was asked for most of the other 540K styles. All the Special Roadsters were built on the "sports" chassis with its set-back radiator, and just 25 bodies were built between 1936 and 1939.

The first 540K Special Roadsters were barely distinguishable from the 500K types that preceded them. However, the design did not stand still. The 1937 cars had deeper doors with shorter exterior handles, and they also had a more streamlined tail which allowed a single spare wheel to be concealed under a removable metal cover that sat flush with the bodywork; if the cover was removed, a second spare could be stowed on top of the first, but standing proud of the bodywork. The 1938 models then sadly lost most of the lightness and grace that had distinguished the early Special Roadster bodies, taking on redesigned wings without the quirky inset valance, and a more bulbous-

This catalogue illustration shows the final iteration of the Special Roadster, as introduced in autumn 1938. Comparison with a contemporary photograph shows that the artist did take some licence: the area where exhausts emerge from the bonnet side is not strictly accurately represented, and the step for the dickey seat (behind the door in the photograph) is absent. These later cars had lost the lightness of touch that characterised the earlier Special Roadsters; the flamboyant wing valances and chrome flashes had gone, and the reshaped tail was simply bulky.

looking tail. The standard dickey seat also came with entrance steps that folded down out of the body sides just ahead of the wings. This design was continued for 1939, at the end of which 540K production ceased.

Among the best known 540K Special Roadsters is the one delivered to Hermann Goering in 1937, on chassis number 154081. The car was ordered at the Berlin Show on 20 February, with armour-plated side panels and bullet-proof glass. This meant that the side windows were fixed in position and the divided windscreen had a metal top frame that was absent from the standard type. It was painted in Goering's favourite colour of metallic Air Force Blue, carried his family crest on both doors, and was

With the top up, the Special Roadster looked more like a fighter plane than ever. This one – an early car, as the wing design reveals – is a right-hand-drive example equipped with a long-range fuel tank on the passenger's side running-board. The spare wheels are also specially mounted under metal covers in the wings.

Dating probably from 1937, this car still has the chrome flashes on its wings but with different rear lights and bumpers. The stylish metal cover for the spare wheel is pictured in place, although - as the smaller picture shows - only one spare could be carried in this condition.

nicknamed "Der Blaue Gans" (the Blue Goose). It also had a specially enlarged driver's seat to suit Goering.

The car was found by US Army troops at Berchtesgaden in May 1945, and it was subsequently used as a command vehicle by Major General Maxwell Taylor. It then spent some time as an exhibit on a victory bonds tour in the USA before entering private ownership, and has since been restored to original condition.

New in 1937, this 540K
Special Roadster was
delivered to Sir John
Chubb of the British
lockmaking family, and
originally had right-
hand drive. It was
subsequently owned by
US car designer Brooks
Stevens and was
converted by Mercedes-
Benz to left-hand drive.
In 1995, it joined the
collection of Bernie
Ecclestone.

The high-door, long-tail body style would disappear at the close of the 1937 season, but is generally considered the most desirable of the Special Roadster styles.

The use of chrome accents on the wings was exquisite, and marked these cars out from earlier types with full-length chrome strips.

This car underwent a nut-and-bolt professional restoration in the 1980s, and the attention to detail shows. It is a past class winner at the annual Pebble Beach concours event. Note the machine-turned finish of the engine top cover, not seen on earlier cars.

Once again, the body proudly carries the Sindelfingen coachworks plate. The identification plate shows the German fiscal engine size, even though the car was delivered new in the UK. There seems to have been no consistency about this: the French 540K cabriolet pictured earlier had the correct 5401cc capacity on its identification plate.

The dash top roll differs from that in earlier Special Roadsters, but the mother-of-pearl instrument panel is still present. The white steering wheel and shift grip contrast elegantly with the red leather of the upholstery. The door trims, as always, incorporate map pockets.

The later Special Roadster body was less ornate than earlier iterations, but was still beautifully proportioned. This is a 1938 example on the 540K chassis. The wings are valanced but lack the chrome trims of earlier cars; a step for the dickey-seat is let into each side of the body; and the bumpers have white rubber facings. The spare wheel well is here covered by a hinged cover.

Huge headlamps with a single central driving lamp characterise the front end; the shape of the sidelamps was unchanged from earlier cars.

The horns – chromed, of course – were mounted on the bulkhead on these later cars. Note also the 540K engine's characteristic vertical air intake for its supercharger.

Cause of confusion: although the engine capacity of 5363cc shown is the size for German tax purposes, the 540K engine actually had 5401cc.

IDENTIFICATION NUMBERS, W29 540K MODELS

Generally speaking, chassis and engine numbers for these cars matched. A replacement engine would have its number prefixed by A (for "Austausch", exchange).

These figures were established by Jan Melin and are taken from his book, *Mercedes-Benz, The Supercharged 8-cylinder Cars of the 1930s, Volume 1.*

Number(s)	Total	Remarks
130901-130950	50	
154061-154160	100	
169311-169410	100	
189381-189430	50	
408331-408430	100	18 cars in this sequence were earlier 540Ks renumbered when rebuilt with Aktion P armoured bodies
421985-421989	5	Special short-chassis cars
	405	If the 18 renumbered Aktion P chassis are subtracted, the total is 387

Jan Melin has also identified two sequences of numbers that were allocated to the 540K but were cancelled in 1941. These were 439766-439790 (25 cars) and 449511-449540 (30 cars).

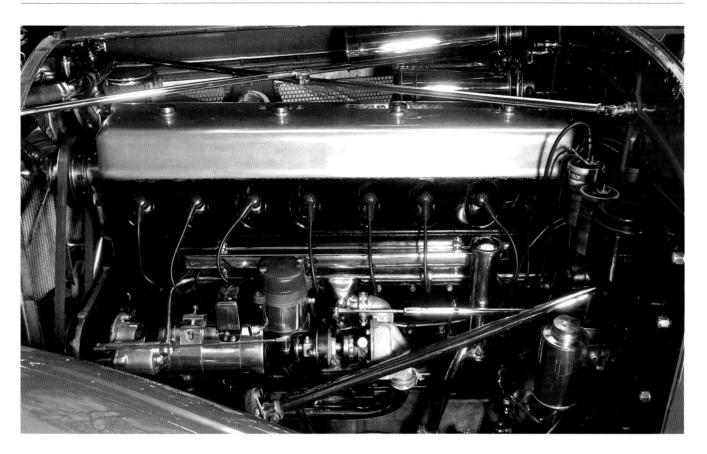

The modern coils strike a rather jarring note; one coil was always carried as a spare.

As always, the spoked wheels had a huge central "spinner", usually painted to match the body, and there were chromed balance-weights around the rims.

Large and plushly upholstered seats contribute to an inviting cockpit. The seat backs hinged forwards to give access to luggage space behind. Just visible at the bottom of the scuttle panel is the Sindelfingen coachwork plate.

It was distinctly snug in the dickey-seat of a Special Roadster, but again thick seats with leather upholstery gave at least an impression of luxury.

The instrument panel was beautifully finished, with an array of matching dials and switches.

The heavy wood-rimmed wheels of the Type S and its descendants were long gone by the time of the 540K; this steering wheel has a slim white rim and a large chromed horn ring.

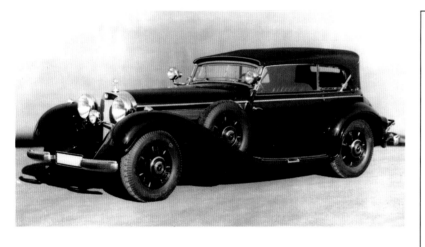

With the top up, the Tourer looked large and imposing, and in the unrelieved black paint of this example, more than a little forbidding. Perhaps that was the idea – other drivers would move over instinctively. This car has a demister panel behind the windscreen and was built in 1937 specially for Dr Robert Ley, the chief organiser of the National Socialist Party.

Tourer models

This was the body style known to Daimler-Benz as the "Offener Tourenwagen" (open touring car), and it had two doors, four seats and removable rear side windows. The convertible top was a very square-rigged design and the exterior support arms for the hood folding mechanism stood in front of those rear side windows when the hood was erected. On the 1936 and 1937 cars, the door windows had a vertical rear edge. The body was redesigned for 1938, with two very marked changes. First, the convertible top now folded down completely into the bodywork behind the seats, where it was concealed under a metal tonneau cover. Second, the door windows now had a curved rear edge and the removable side windows

---

BODY TYPES

Jan Melin's researches uncovered the following data concerning the body types built at Sindelfingen and fitted to the 540K.

Cabriolet A	83
Coupé	7
Cabriolet B	190
Combination Coupé	2
Cabriolet C	32
Autobahnkurier	2
Tourer	12
Saloon (4-door)	5
Roadster (standard)	4
Saloon (2-door)	28
Special Roadster	25
Chassis	29

---

were redesigned to suit. Not many of either body design were built: there were just 12 Tourer bodies in all between 1936 and 1938, and the model was dropped from the 1939 range.

The "factory" bodies: short-chassis cars

As with the 500K, it is not possible at present to be certain how many short-chassis 540K models were built, although Jan Melin's researches have suggested that there were only five of them, all built as a single batch towards the end of production in 1939. Stuttgart advertised the availability of Sport-Roadster and Sport-Cabriolet A bodies, but it is likely that there were very few of either. As on the 500K, the short-chassis cars had the radiator mounted much further forwards in the frame than the standard cars.

The two-seater Cabriolet A design on the short chassis was broadly similar to that on the standard chassis, but the body was necessarily shorter. This was most obvious just behind the doors, where the space between hinge pillar and rear wing was minimal. The short-chassis cars also carried their spare wheels alongside the bonnet in order to leave room for luggage in the tail.

There may have been no more than one Sport-Roadster, a very special car built for Adolf Hühnlein, leader of the National Socialist Motor Corps (NSKK) and in charge of all German motor sport activity. The car was exhibited at the 1939 Berlin Motor Show and had helmet-type wings and vertical bonnet louvres, with a two-tone colour scheme. It has sometimes been described as a 500K that was fitted with a 5.4-litre engine, and sometimes as a 580K (see below). All the records that Jan Melin found in the Daimler-Benz archives confirmed that the car was a short-chassis 540K on chassis number 421985, although Melin concedes that it might have been fitted with a 5.8-litre engine at a later date but that the fact was not noted in factory records.

Although no short-chassis Special Roadster was catalogued, one such car was built at Sindelfingen in 1939 as a special order for the

German industrialist Alfried Felix Alwyn Krupp von Bohlen und Halbach. This car was barely used before being laid up when war broke out in September. It was taken as war booty in May 1945 and went to the Netherlands.

Bodies by independent coachbuilders

Daimler-Benz figures reveal that 29 540K models were supplied as bare chassis to be bodied by outside coachbuilders. Of those, no fewer than 12 were delivered to the Berlin coachbuilder, Erdmann & Rossi. Among these were a Roadster-Cabriolet with fascinating "see-through" rear wheel spats that appeared on the coachbuilder's stand at the Berlin Motor Show in 1938; it later became part of the famous Schlumpf Collection and still survives. One of the remaining 17 chassis was bodied in 1937 as a Sport Cabriolet by Voll & Ruhrbeck, the Berlin

Few 540Ks were built on the short chassis. This 1939 Sport Roadster was a special example for NSKK leader Adolf Hühnlein. Note how the radiator is set much further forward than on the standard-wheelbase cars.

This is a Cabriolet A on the short chassis, again dating from 1939. Just visible here are the headlamp shells, which are painted rather than chromed. Other pictures of this car show that it had the flatter radiator seen only on very late models.

The special 1938 streamlined research car looked so little like a Mercedes that Stuttgart obviously felt obliged to paint a large three-pointed star on its nose. The car was built for high-speed tyre testing, and had a 5.4-litre engine without supercharger.

coachbuilder best known for its avant garde designs. This car now survives with one of the experimental engines intended for the 600V models (see Chapter 11).

When Michael Frostick trawled through the sales records of the British Mercedes Company for his book *The Mighty Mercedes*, he found references to seven cars that had been bodied in England. There may have been others: the records are incomplete. The ones he discovered, with chassis numbers and the dates recorded in the ledger, are as follows.

256883	November 1937
267838	December 1937
269503	February 1938
269504	1939
271790	February 1938
277023	May 1938
277277	June 1939

Particularly interesting is that 269504 was bodied by Freestone & Webb for the German Embassy in London – a gesture possibly intended as a demonstration of friendship at a time when British Prime Minister Chamberlain was attempting to buy time through a policy of appeasement with Hitler. At least one other car was bodied by Freestone & Webb, and one was bodied as a Cabriolet C (two doors, four side windows and four seats) by Offord in London. This latter car still survives.

The 540K "long-wheelbase"

The 540K story is further complicated by Stuttgart's construction in 1936 of a small number of long-wheelbase Tourers that were known as 540K types. These were specifically intended as parade cars for the German government, and despite the 540K name really had little more than the supercharged 5.4-litre engine in common with the W29 540K models. They even had a project special designation of W24 and are discussed in more detail in Chapter 10.

The Jaray streamliner, 1938

In 1938, a special streamlined body was built for high-speed tests conducted by the Dunlop tyre company. This was fitted to a 540 chassis – a 540K without its supercharger. The body was built at Sindelfingen and used principles outlined by Paul Jaray.

The Aktion P cars, 1943-1944

On 27 May 1942, Reinhard Heydrich, the "Reichsprotektor" (Governor) of Bohemia and Moravia, was attacked by a team of Czech and Slovak soldiers trained by the British and sent by the Czech government in exile. He died from his injuries a week later. Almost immediately, the Reichs Chancellery ruled that senior officials in future must only appear in public in armoured vehicles. This ruling was known as "Aktion P"; the P stood for "Panzer" (armoured) and "Aktion" is probably best translated as Project.

Orders were placed with Mercedes for a number of armoured saloons that were to be distributed to the governors of occupied territories and to others thought to be at risk of assassination. The order probably did not specify the type of car in detail, but simply gave the outline requirement; it would have been up to Stuttgart to decide how best to meet the specification. Different sources give different versions of the story: some say that the order was for 40 cars and that Mercedes met it with 20 on 540K chassis and a further 20 on 770 chassis, while others suggest that just 20 cars were ordered and that the order was fulfilled with 17 540K models and just three 770s.

One way or another, Stuttgart had a problem with the 540K cars. The model had gone out of production by 1942, although a few unused chassis were still lying around at the works. Some sources claim that there were two of these; others claim three. One way or another, the deficit was made up by confiscating existing cars from their owners. So either 17 or 18 cars were returned to the works to be rebuilt as armoured saloons to meet the Aktion P requirement. Their original bodies were removed and scrapped; those who claim the total of used chassis was 18 argue that there were six Cabriolet A, six Cabriolet B, and six Saloon types. All were on the standard 3290mm wheelbase.

All the Aktion P cars were redesignated as W24 types, using the works code allocated to the cancelled successor to the original 770 models in 1936 (see Chapter 10). Quite why this was done remains unexplained. The cars were fitted with neat but unspectacular two-door saloon bodies to a design by Hermann Ahrens. Their bodies were armoured with 2.3mm steel panels to resist small-arms fire, with 30mm thick glass in the side windows and 35mm armoured glass in the windscreen. There was also an armoured plate that could be raised inside the car to protect the rear window. Surprisingly, they retained their standard 17-inch wire-spoked wheels and were not fitted with armoured disc wheels such as those used on the 770 parade cars, but the tyres were special bullet-proof types. Overall weight is said to have been 2930kg. There is photographic evidence that one of the Aktion P armoured bodies was fitted to an engineless chassis and was tested under fire from a variety of weapons. This body was presumably additional to the 20 supplied to the German government on complete cars.

The Aktion P 540K armoured saloons were delivered in 1943 and 1944, and their known users included the following:

Heinrich Abetz	Effectively German Ambassador in Paris
Herbert Backe	Minister of Food and, later of Agriculture
Hans Frank	Governor-General of Poland
Karl Frank	SS leader in Czechoslovakia
Joseph Goebbels	Propaganda Minister
Arthur Greiser	Governor of Poland
Heinrich Himmler	Head of the SS
Ernst Kaltenbrunner	SS General
Erich Koch	Gauleiter of East Prussia and Reichskommissar of the Ukraine
Albert Speer	Minister of Armaments and War Production
Alfred Rosenberg	Minister for the Occupied Eastern Territories
Arthur Seyss-Inquart	Reichskommissar in the Netherlands
Josef Terboven	Reichskommissar for Norway.

Another car was given by Hitler to Ante Pavelic, leader of the Independent State of Croatia. After the war this car was captured and used first by Ivan Krajacic (Croatian Minister of the Interior), and then by Marshal Tito, the Yugoslavian Prime Minister.

The cars used by Hans Frank and Karl Frank have both survived with their original bodywork. The Prague Technical Museum has the Karl Frank car on chassis number 408417, and the car that was used in Poland by Hans Frank (408400) has been restored and was last known to be in the hands of a German collector. A third car, on chassis number 408372, was rebodied as a Cabriolet A after the war and survives in that guise. The car used by Seyss-Inquart appears to have been 408387.

Jan Melin discovered documentary evidence that a further 17 armoured saloon bodies were ordered on 5 November 1943 but could find no evidence that they were actually delivered.

BUILD VOLUMES

As is usual with Mercedes-Benz production figures from the 1930s, there are several different opinions about how many 540K models were built. This book argues for an overall total of 387 cars, including just five short-chassis types. These figures do not include the 5.4-litre 500Ks or the 1938 unsupercharged 5.4-litre streamlined research car.

The Daimler-Benz Global Media website gives the total as 319, which is clearly wrong. Jan Melin argues for a total of 419 – but he includes the late 5.4-litre 500K cars in his figure.

Melin's researches show that Stuttgart calculated the figure as 406 in 1940, and broke that figure down into calendar-year totals as below. Werner Oswald repeated these totals in his 1984 book, *Mercedes-Benz Personenwagen, 1886-1984*.

1936	97	**1937**	145
1938	95	**1939**	69

New calculations by Mercedes-Benz in the 1960s and 1970s were based on the original 1940 list, but to that added 38 short-chassis cars, noted as W129 types. Oswald repeats these figures:

1936	4	**1937**	12
1938	14	**1939**	8

Jan Melin argues that the production figure for the short-chassis cars is included within the overall total of 406.

The 580K

Stuttgart was quite clearly looking at a further development of the supercharged eight-cylinder engine by the end of the 1930s. This was a 5.8-litre enlargement of the existing M24 engine, with a bigger bore (95mm) and shorter stroke (100mm) than the 5.4-litre type. It was known as a W129 II type. Cars with the 5.8-litre engine may have been known as W129 types, although Jan Melin's researches suggest that the W129 designation appeared earlier and was a replacement for the original W29 designation of the 540K.

There were supposedly a dozen prototypes, 10 built in 1939 and two more in 1940, before Daimler-Benz suspended work on the new car. Some sources believe that Adolf Hühnlein's 1939 short-chassis 540K was fitted with a 5.8-litre engine, and there has been some suggestion that 5.8-litre engines left over from the development programme were used in some of the Aktion P cars that were built in 1942. All of this remains to be proved.

Figures supplied by Mercedes-Benz show that the 5.8-litre engine was rated at 130PS unsupercharged and at 200PS with the supercharger, in each case at 3400rpm. The maximum torque was 439Nm (324 lb ft) at 2200rpm, which would have given little in the way of improved acceleration as compared to the 5.4-litre engine, but the additional power enabled the 580K to reach a higher top speed of 180km/h (112mph).

Jan Melin mentions three documents said to exist which might shed some more light on the so-called 580K, but that he has never been able to find them in the Mercedes-Benz archives. Werner Oswald states that 17 examples of the 5.8-litre engine are known to have been built.

The front compartment of the 1937 Cabriolet A looks as inviting today as it must have done when it was new.

SPECIFICATIONS, 540K
(W29 AND W129)
1936-39

Engine:
5401cc eight-cylinder with 88mm bore and 111mm stroke
Overhead valves and side camshaft
Nine main bearings
Coil ignition
Compression ratio 5.2:1 (some engines with 6.5:1)
Single Mercedes-Benz twin-choke updraught carburettor
Roots-type supercharger driven by gear from crankshaft
115PS at 3400rpm
180PS at 3400rpm with supercharger engaged
432Nm (318lb ft) at 2200rpm

Gearbox:
Four-speed (1936-1938), with synchromesh on upper three gears. Ratios 3.90:1, 2.28:1, 1.45:1, 1,00:1.
Five-speed (1939). Ratios 3.65:1, 2.25:1, 1.48:1, 1.00:1, 0.80:1.

Axle ratio:
3.08:1 or 3.60:1 (1936-1938)
3.50:1 (1939)

Chassis and suspension:
Box-section steel chassis frame
Independent front suspension with coil springs and wishbones
Double-joint swing-axle with dual concentric coil springs and (1936-38) auxiliary compensating spring

Brakes:
Hydraulic operation on all four wheels, with Bosch-Dewandre vacuum servo

Wheels and tyres:
17-inch wire spoked wheels with 6.50 x 17, 7.00 x 17 or 7.50 x 17 tyres (1936-38);
7.50 x 17 tyres standard (1939)

Weights and measures:
Overall dimensions
(standard wheelbase models):
Roadster 5000-5350 x1880 x 1530mm
Cabriolet B and C
5250 x 1900 x 1630mm
Saloon 5020-5250 x 1880 x 1660mm
Tourer 5100-5360 x 1880 x 1600mm
Overall dimensions
(short wheelbase models):
Roadster 4480 x 1880 x 1530mm
Cabriolet A 4650 x 1900 x 1480mm
Wheelbase 3290mm (standard) or 2980mm (short-chassis)
Track 1535mm (front),
1547mm (rear); some cars with
1515mm (front) and 1502mm (rear)
Weight 1800kg unladen; 2850kg (maximum permissible, standard wheelbase)

Maximum speed 170km/h (105mph)

Fuel consumption 29 litres/100km (8.1mpg)

SPECIFICATIONS, EXPERIMENTAL
580K MODELS
1939-40

Engine:
5800cc eight-cylinder with 95mm bore and 100mm stroke
Overhead valves and side camshaft
Nine main bearings
Coil ignition
Compression ratio 6.5:1
Single Mercedes-Benz twin-choke updraught carburettor
Roots-type supercharger driven by gear from crankshaft
130PS at 3400rpm
200PS at 3400rpm with supercharger engaged
439Nm (324lb ft) at 2200rpm

The 5.8-litre engines appear to have been used in otherwise standard 540K chassis. They drove through five-speed gearboxes to final drives with 3.20:1 gearing, a 3.08:1 gearset being the alternative.

Maximum speed was claimed to be 180km/h (112mph) and fuel consumption was 30 litres per 100km (9.46mpg).

THE W129 DESIGNATION
The 540K was initially known as a W29 type, and there are three different theories about the later W129 designation.
- Jan Melin's researches showed that the designation began to appear in Mercedes-Benz records in 1937, and he speculated that it was introduced because the engineers wanted to standardise on three-figure project codes.
- The W129 designation may have applied only to the experimental 5.8-litre cars, because the 5.8-litre engine was a W129 II type.
- The "official" Mercedes-Benz explanation, as implied on the company's archives web site, is that the W129 code applied only to the short-chassis cars.

Chapter Ten

OFFICIAL TRANSPORT

The 770, 1938-1943

Dating from 1936, this is an early W24 model. Most cars had pressed-steel disc wheels like the ones seen here. On this car, the rear bumper seems to have been on extendable brackets, to allow for the - frankly hideous - demountable luggage boot to be fitted.

By the middle of the 1930s, it was clearly time for the 770 to be updated. Not only were there new competitors on the market, but there was also new technology available, and the buyers of cars at the top end of the market invariably expect their purchases to reflect the latest and best of what is available. The 770 had been adopted as a parade car by senior members of Germany's ruling Nazi party, so there were also good reasons for delivering a modernised design. These were not necessarily political: putting the latest Mercedes-Benz technology into a car that would be seen by thousands of people at public rallies and other events was likely to be as effective at advertising the company's products as racing successes.

By the time work began on the replacement for the W07 770 models, the leadership of the

engineering department had changed. Hans Nibel had died suddenly in November 1934, and from 1 January 1935 the top job in the Design Office and Testing Department passed to Max Sailer, who had made his name racing for Daimler before the 1914-18 war. So the new car was designed on his watch, no doubt with considerable input from his deputy, Fritz Nallinger.

The W24 prototypes

The original plan for a replacement, drawn up presumably during 1935, was rather different from what eventually happened. This original plan called for a new model that would replace both the W08 Nurburg 500 saloon and the W07 770 Grosser Mercedes. It was to be developed under the works code of W24.

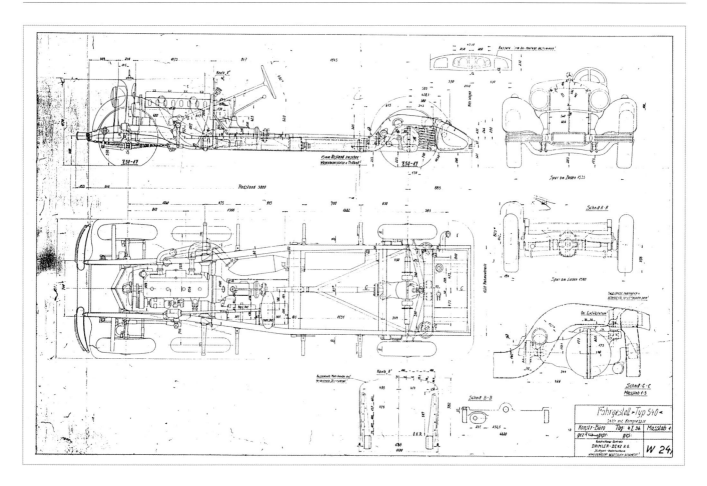

The first two prototypes of the car were built with 5-litre engines, but it is not clear whether these were further-developed 4918cc M 08 engines from the Nurburg saloon or super-charged 5018cc M24 engines from the 500K. The coincidence of M24 and W24 does rather suggest the latter, and it would have been logical to use the newer engine from the 500K in a new prestige model. However, the 5.4-litre version of the M24 engine was also running at the Untertürkheim works by this stage, and it appears that this was fitted to all subsequent prototypes. Some of the engines, and possibly all of them, had what looks in photographs like a finned sump to aid cooling of the oil.

The cars were designed around a longer wheelbase than that of the existing production 770, perhaps mainly to provide more space

This general arrangement drawing of the W24 chassis is dated 4 January 1936. Interesting is that it is described as a Type 540; the K is nowhere to be seen, even though the sub-title refers to the engine as a "5.4 ltr mit Kompressor". The car was usually called a "540K Lang" (long) within Daimler-Benz.

One car was built at the Mannheim plant. This is it; features include the spoked pressed-steel wheels.

IDENTIFICATION NUMBERS, W24 500K AND 540K MODELS

When they were built, chassis and engine numbers for these cars matched. A replacement engine would have its number prefixed by A (for "Austausch", exchange)

These chassis numbers and production figures were established by Jan Melin and are taken from his book, *Mercedes-Benz, The Supercharged 8-cylinder Cars of the 1930s, Volume 1.*

Number(s)	Total	Remarks
86123-86124	2	5.0-litre engines
130141-130150	10	5.4-litre engines; only 6 built
	12	The actual build total was 8 cars. Note that the 20 Aktion P cars built on 540K chassis in 1942-43 were also known as W24 types

Jan Melin has also identified a sequence of numbers (128878-128885, eight in all) that were allocated to W24 engines only. It is not clear whether these were 5.0-litre or 5.4-litre types.

---

within the body. With 3880mm (152.7in) rather than 3750mm (147.6in) between axle centres, the difference was not only worthwhile but also appropriate to a car of this nature. Curiously, however, the new chassis was designed with the box-section side members that were now old technology at Stuttgart: it did not have the immensely strong chassis architecture seen on the latest Mercedes family saloons, with its oval tubes and diagonal cross-bracing. It also had a conventional beam front axle with semi-elliptic leaf springs, but the rear end boasted a sophisticated De Dion-type independent set-up with coil springs. This was mainly the work of Hans Gustav Röhr, recently recruited from the Adler company to the position of Technical Director. The brakes had a Bosch-Dewandre vacuum servo, and there was a centralised chassis lubrication system. The wheels were pressed steel discs with 17-inch rims (although at least one car had perforated disc wheels and the last one had wires), the original tyres were 7.5 x 17, and both front and rear ends had anti-roll bars.

Three of these cars, all bodied as Tourers, appeared on the Mercedes stand at the Berlin Motor Show in March 1936. At least one of them, an eight-seater, seems to have been presented to the German government immediately afterwards for use as a parade vehicle. An internal memorandum seen by Jan Melin and dated April 1936 reveals that all was still well by that date, and that the engineers had confidence in the qualities of the new W24. However, over the next couple of months, things began to go wrong. In July 1936 the project was abandoned, and the decision was taken to build an all-new Grosser 770 Mercedes instead, which would

replace only the existing 770 and not the Nurburg saloon as well. Of the planned batch of ten 5.4-litre W24 prototypes, probably only six were completed.

What had gone wrong? In the absence of documentary evidence, we can only guess, but it is clear that there were alternative plans within Daimler-Benz even as early as autumn 1935, when an internal memo proposed the W148 model (see Chapter 10) as a replacement for the Nürburg saloons, and possibly also for the W07 as well. One possibility is that the W24 and W148 projects were run side by side to see which showed more promise. Another is that there were some internal conflicts associated with the appointment of Hans Gustav Röhr as the new Technical Director of the Passenger Car Division.

It may also be that the W24 car did not fully meet the needs of the German government – who were, after all, likely to be a major customer. Perhaps the possibility of an armoured version had been investigated, and either the chassis or the engine proved not up to the task. Perhaps there was some other dissatisfaction with the car presented to the German government. One way or another, the car was not under development for long enough to be given a proper model designation for public use. Documents show that it was often referred to at Daimler-Benz as a "540K (long wheelbase)" – which, of course, it was not. The only other information of any consequence so far uncovered is that all the cars were recalled during 1937 to be fitted with wider 8.25 x 17 tyres.

All the known W24 cars were Tourers, and at least one seems to have had its body built at the Mannheim plant rather than at Sindelfingen. All of these cars eventually found their way into Government use, and three in particular turn up regularly in photographs taken at Party events in 1936-38. These had registration numbers IA-103708, IIA-48234 and IIA-56388. The last W24 to be completed (in 1936) was delivered in January 1937 to Dr Robert Ley, a Nazi Party official who was head of the German Labour Front. Just one car is known to have survived.

BUILD VOLUMES

Jan Melin's researches in the Daimler-Benz archives show that there were probably no more than 8 examples of the W24 model out of 12 chassis numbers allocated. Daimler-Benz themselves are wont to quote the figure of 78 for the model, a figure which seems to have come from nowhere at some time in the 1960s or 1970s. As Melin says, this seems a highly unlikely figure for a model which was built only in prototype form, and was abandoned after six months.

Adding to the confusion is that the W24 designation was also used for the armoured Aktion P saloons on 540K chassis built for the German government in 1942-43. However, even adding their total (20) to the maximum of 12 suggested by the Daimler-Benz chassis numbers gives just 32, which is nowhere near the figure of 78.

HANS GUSTAV RÖHR

Hans Gustav Röhr seems to have had a rather unhappy time during his period as Technical Director of the Cars Division at Daimler-Benz between 1935 and 1937. His previous job had been as technical chief of Adler, where he had made his name with advanced suspension concepts and front-wheel drive layouts.

Röhr left Adler in 1935, and Emil von Strauss, Chairman of the Daimler-Benz Supervisory Board, moved rapidly to secure the services of this gifted engineer for the job of Technical Director, vacant since the sudden death of Hans Nibel in November 1934. However, he moved so rapidly that he failed to discuss the matter first with Wilhelm Kissel, Chairman of the Management Board. This ensured that Röhr would have difficulty from the moment he joined the company in September 1935; Kissel refused to allow him the place on the Management Board normally accorded to the Technical Director of the Passenger Car Division.

Röhr brought with him to Daimler-Benz not only some exciting new ideas but also a number of former Adler colleagues, including his long-time collaborator Joseph Dauben. However, he very quickly encountered considerable resentment from the old guard at Daimler-Benz, partly perhaps because he had been recruited from outside rather than from inside the company, and also because his radical new ideas looked as if they would set the Car Division on a radically new course. There were political influences at work, too. His wife was French, and she was quite openly opposed to the Nazi regime. As a result, Röhr was viewed as a security risk; special arrangements were made within Daimler-Benz to ensure that neither he nor any member of his team had any involvement with military projects.

In this intolerable climate, Röhr pressed on with designing a series of front-wheel drive cars with "boxer" engines of modular design. There were to be four-cylinder (W144 130VB), six-cylinder (W145 190VB) and eight-cylinder (W146 260VB) types, and at the top of the range was to be a W147 400V with a separate design of V8 engine. However, on 10 August 1937 Röhr died from pneumonia contracted during a trip to the Nürburgring in an open cabriolet. He was just 42 years old. Work ceased almost immediately on his front-wheel-drive cars, and the prototypes are said to have been destroyed as the old guard once again took over at Daimler-Benz. Today, Röhr's name is rarely even mentioned in official histories of the Daimler-Benz company.

The W150 models

So from mid-1936, the plan to replace the Grosser W07 model focused on an all-new car with the works code of W150. It is not at all clear who oversaw the development programme, but there is a distinct possibility that Technical Director Hans Gustav Röhr was kept at arm's length. As the panel above makes clear, Röhr was kept away from anything to do with military projects, and the new Grosser Mercedes was destined from the start to be used by the German government and therefore also the German military.

As a result, although the new suspension designs incorporated into the car were undoubtedly inspired by Röhr, the names generally associated with the W150 are those of Fritz Nallinger and Max Sailer. Nallinger had been Hans Nibel's deputy, but he was considered too young and inexperienced to take over as Technical Director when Nibel died in 1934 (Nallinger would have been in his mid-thirties) and retained the deputy's position under Röhr. Sailer had been a racing driver at Daimler before the 1914-18 war, but had always remained employed as an engineer as well. He had become head of the Design Office and the Testing Department on 1 January 1935.

The W150 project must have started over the summer of 1936, and there would have been certain assumptions from the start. Among these would have been that the car would have a new chassis frame based on oval tubes rather than on the box sections that had featured on both the Grosser W07 and on the abandoned W24 replacement. These had entered the picture at Daimler-Benz a couple of years earlier, and were first seen on the new 170V model that was announced at the start of 1936. With diagonal cross-bracing instead of conventional ladder-type cross-members, this new design of chassis promised to be both immensely rigid and considerably lighter than earlier types.

Although the diagonal cross-bracing was not adopted for the W150, the chassis was redesigned with oval-section tubular side-members and six cylindrical cross-members. As far as dimensions were concerned, it looks as if the car was intended from the start to have the same 3880mm wheelbase as the abandoned

W24 models. Whatever the reasons for their demise, it was clear that this new size – up from the 3750mm of the W 07 – was well suited to the requirements of the parade cars favoured by the German government. And, as it would turn out, almost every example of the W150 would be built for the German government, either for its own use or as a gift to foreign rulers and governments supportive of Germany.

To this new chassis was added a completely new suspension system, with independent springing for all four wheels. Röhr had been a leader in independent suspension design at Daimler-Benz, and his deputy, Fritz Nallinger, was an enthusiastic devotee of the same principles. So at the front, the new W150 chassis had coil springs and wishbones, and at the rear there was a De Dion-type arrangement, again with

Everything about the car spoke of its massive construction, although the details were skilfully handled. The twin flag posts on this car mark it out as one destined for the German government.

Both of these chassis seem to have been prepared for show purposes. Wire wheels were not common on the W150 770K, as most bodies were too heavy. The massive construction of the frame is obvious; the black-painted chassis lacks several items, such as brake pipes and, apparently, the inner spring of the concentric pair on the rear axle.

These two pictures may well show the same car, but the colour one is much more recent and depicts one of the Mercedes-Benz Museum's exhibits.

coil springs. The differential was bolted to the penultimate cross-member at three rubber-bushed points, and there was a V-shaped anti-roll link which was connected to the middle cross-tube by a rubber doughnut. Track and camber remained constant under all conditions, and within Daimler-Benz this suspension arrangement was usually known as the "parallel wheel axle".

At least one show chassis seems to have been prepared with wire wheels, but in practice the production models all seem to have had steel disc wheels. The weight of a completed W150 was probably one reason for this, although disc wheels were in any case becoming more popular by the end of the 1930s, and would have been seen as the latest thing in design. In due course, there would also be some special reinforced disc wheels for the armoured models. As on the earlier 770, all wheels were centre-lock types.

There was more new technology in the braking system. Rod-operated brakes were

simply old technology by the mid-1930s, and so the W150 went over to an all-hydraulic system. The wheel brakes were manufactured in Germany by ATE-Lockheed, and as on the W 07 models (and on cars such as the 500K and 540K), the system incorporated a vacuum servo.

As for the engine, it is all too easy to assume that it was a mildly re-worked version of the 7.7-litre supercharged eight-cylinder from the earlier Grosser Mercedes. It did indeed retain the same bore and stroke dimensions and the same overall architecture, with a single side camshaft driving overhead valves, but it thoroughly deserved its new designation of M150. The cylinder block was now made completely of alloy, and there were no fewer than three geared oil pumps to optimise the lubrication system. The exhaust valves were now sodium-cooled, an automatic ignition control system replaced the old type adjustable from the steering wheel, and the water pump was now driven directly by the oil pump shaft.

With a 6.1:1 compression ratio, there was a minor increase in unblown power to 155PS, but the maximum power available with the super-charger engaged jumped by 30PS (about 15%) to 230PS. The whole thing was beautifully finished in the best Mercedes tradition: the block and accessories were in black enamel, with machine-turned aluminium panels to give a striking contrast, and chrome plating for the fan and the brass tubing as well. All examples were supercharged, and there seem not to have been any plans to offer an unsupercharged version. For a start, there had been little interest in unsu-percharged versions of the earlier 770, and then

there was the small matter of additional weight on the new car. The typical production example was some 900kg heavier than its predecessor – and there were armoured versions to consider as well.

Also new was the gearbox. Out went the three-speed with overdrive type of the old Grosser model, and in came an all-synchromesh four-speed gearbox. Power was transmitted through a single plate disc clutch. For good measure, the original W150 design also had what was in effect a two-speed axle, with selectable gearing that gave an overdrive ratio. Very little information is available about this, but it seems to have proved unsatisfactory, and from 1939 the cars were fitted instead with a single-speed axle and a five-speed overdrive gearbox. Maximum speed with the five-speed gearbox was 145km/h (90mph) unblown and 170km/h (105mph) with the supercharger engaged.

The new W150 was first displayed at the Berlin Motor Show that opened on 18 February 1938. Once again there was a range of body styles from the Sindelfingen works, although it was slightly more restricted than before. The basic Pullman limousine with division and the seven-seat open Tourer were still there, and in addition there were four-door Cabriolet D and six-seat Cabriolet F models. The cars were certainly intended initially for customers other than the German government, just as their predecessors had been; chassis 429317, for example, was ordered as a Cabriolet F in June 1939 by a pen manufacturer called Soennecken AG in Bonn. However, the outbreak of war prevented it from being delivered. Retained by Daimler-

Benz, the car was given a new body in 1941 when the German government ordered a Grosser Mercedes Tourer and was presented to Field Marshall Mannerheim in Finland.

There were some quite strong visual similarities between these new 770s – for the cars retained the name of the one model they replaced – and the later versions of the old Grosser Mercedes. However, all the bodies had been redesigned, and the enclosed limousine in particular had a passenger cabin that strongly suggested the influence of the General Motors "turret-top" design introduced in 1935. Overall height was reduced, by about 30mm on the enclosed limousine. Helmet-shaped front wings were a distinguishing feature, and the big radiator grille was now very slightly raked backwards.

The cars shown at Berlin in 1938 had ornate two-bar front and rear bumpers, but all the later ones seem to have had single-bar bumpers; both types had rubber facings, and the single-bar types had over-riders as well. Some, and perhaps all, of the Berlin show cars were returned to Sindelfingen to be re-worked. The one eventually registered as IIA-148/68, for example, returned to the factory after the show, came out again to be shown to Hitler in Berlin on his birthday on 20 April 1938, went back to Stuttgart for more work and was then finally delivered to the Reichs Chancellery in Berlin.

The bodies

All the bodies on the W150 chassis were built in the Daimler-Benz works at Sindelfingen, and no bare chassis seem to have been supplied to

Only five examples of the Cabriolet D body were built on the 770 chassis.

Soviet Union. In 1989, it was bought by an American and completely restored, appearing at the 2008 Pebble Beach concours in an attractive maroon rather than white, as originally built.

Cabriolet D
Just five examples of the Cabriolet D body were built between 1938 and 1940. This was a four-five seater car, with three windows on each side. Some of these bodies were armoured.

Cabriolet F
There were only seven examples of the Cabriolet F body, all built between 1938 and 1940. The Cabriolet F had two windows on each side of the body, and a standard cabriolet-type roof with external chromed hood irons. When folded, this roof made a huge and ungainly package at the back of the car. There was fixed seating for five, and two additional jump-seats could be folded out when needed. Some of these cars may have been armoured.

One 770 Cabriolet F, on chassis number 429314, was left in Czechoslovakia at the end of the 1939-1945 war. It was seized by the Czechoslovak state, and in 1952 was rebodied as an open parade car by the coachbuilder Sodomka at Karosa for Minister General Cepicka.

independent coachbuilders; nevertheless, Jan Melin found that one chassis was not bodied at Sindelfingen. Cars used by Government officials in Germany had a red spotlight mounted on the driver's side window pillar, and there are many pictures of these vehicles in Blaine Taylor's book, *Hitler's Chariots, Volume Two, Mercedes 770K Grosser Parade Car.*

The details of the Sindelfingen bodies are as follows.

Cabriolet B
The only Cabriolet B model built was a special order, commissioned by the German government as a gift for the Crown Prince of Persia. Built on chassis number 429319 in 1940, this was an elegant looking car with spats over the rear wheels. However, the war prevented it from being delivered, and it remained in Germany. The car was seized in 1945 as war reparations by a Russian General and was taken back to the

The Tourer was ideal as a parade car. This one was used in that capacity by Adolf Hitler, seen here at the Olympic Stadium in Berlin on 18 May 1939. Note the additional bright trim around the spare wheel housing, and the flag carried on a standard on the far side of the bonnet. The cushion of the front passenger-side seat was arranged to tip up to provide standing room for parade use.

BODY TYPES, W150 MODELS

Melin's researches uncovered the following data concerning the body types fitted to the W150 770:

Cabriolet B	1
Cabriolet D	5
Cabriolet F	7
Tourer	46
Saloon	10
Pullman Limousine	18
Chassis only	1

Pullman Limousine

The Pullman Limousine was designed to carry seven passengers in the same seating configuration as the Cabriolet F. The car had three windows on each side, and some examples were built with spats over the rear wheels. There were 18 Pullman Limousines in all, of which nine were armoured. One of the unarmoured cars (150006/0030, the last W150 to be built) was presented to the Turkish President Ismet Inönü at the Chankaya Palace in Ankara by German Ambassador Franz von Papen, the former German Vice Chancellor. The car was sold to a US buyer in 1967, and has subsequently returned to Germany.

Saloon

The W150 Saloon was never a "catalogued" model. Ten examples were constructed in 1943 in response to a demand from the German govern-ment for armoured vehicles. These cars, like the 540K models ordered at the same time (see Chapter 9), were for Aktion P and all were armoured. The body was a neat four-door design with two windows on each side and, unlike all the other W150 designs, it did not have the spare wheels mounted alongside the bonnet. The final examples were not bodied and delivered until March 1944.

Tourer

The Tourer was the favourite parade car of German officialdom between 1938 and 1945. It was also the most numerous of the W150 types; no fewer than 46 examples were built. The Tourer had a similar seating configuration to the Cabriolet F, but the cushion of the front passenger seat could be folded up on most examples so that a state official could stand up in the car. The fabric top was also very different, lacking external folding arms and being more square-rigged at the rear. There were three windows on each side of the body, but only the two in the doors could be wound down; the rearmost window was held in place by brackets and could be lifted out.

Many of the Tourer bodies were armoured. In addition to the steel plate and armoured glass, they had a metal shield behind the rear seat that could be wound up to protect the occupants from shots fired behind the car. The car most frequently used by Hitler after July 1940 had a more sweeping wing line than was standard – something of a throwback to the designs used on the 770s of the mid-1930s.

Grand and typically heavy-looking, this is the Cabriolet F body on a W150 770 chassis. Just seven examples were built.

Several 770s have been claimed as used by Hitler, and the authenticity of some of those claims has been thrown into doubt. This car was certainly used by a senior member of the German government: it is shown here in preservation with armoured screens erected behind the rear seats.

Armoured W150s

All the bodies on the W150 could be ordered with custom touches to suit the buyer, and all could be ordered with armour protection. As things were to turn out, the majority of these second-generation 770s were armoured. The armoured models had their own designation of W150 II. They were almost incredibly heavy, with an overall laden weight which has been quoted as 5420kg – something in excess of five tons – although it is not clear whether that was for an open tourer or a Pullman limousine. The outer body panels were made of aluminium, but this was lined with 18mm armoured steel, and all the glass was a 40mm thick armoured type. It consisted of five layers of glass; a central layer of 13mm glass was sandwiched between two layers of 9mm glass, and these in turn were sandwiched between two layers of 4.5mm glass. The covers for the side-mounted spare wheels were also armoured, presumably to give additional protection to the engine bay, and it appears that a characteristic of the armoured versions was special bonnet sides with a series of hinged ventilation doors instead of the long air inlet on the standard cars. To compensate a little for the extra weight of the armour, the wings were made of aluminium. There was an electro-magnetic door locking system to prevent the doors being opened from the outside – a sort of early version of today's central locking.

These armoured 770s also had specially strengthened versions of the standard 8.25 x 17 tyres, or a bullet-proof tyre which contained 20 individual cells so that deflation of one cell would not reduce mobility by causing full deflation of the tyre. The wheel-and-tyre combination was said to be so heavy that changing a wheel required two strong men. The drivers of cars equipped with these tyres were advised to limit their speed to 80km/h (49.7mph) because the tyres would not cope with higher speeds.

The bullet-proof tyres also gave an uneven ride because no way of balancing them had yet been developed, and Hitler himself famously preferred not to ride in a car with such tyres because the jarring ride upset his weak stomach. The special tyres were wider than standard, so they increased the 770's tracks and also gave it a larger turning circle. Without the encumbrance of these special tyres, the armoured 770s were otherwise said to be capable of 140km/h (87mph), which was a very high speed for such a heavy car; stopping from that speed on the standard drum brakes would probably have convinced the driver not to test the car to the limit again.

Even these armoured behemoths may not have been the ultimate versions of the W150. Among the legendary documents in the Mercedes-Benz archives is one that supposedly records the construction of five very special versions with experimental engines that would have given a top speed of between 180 and 200km/h (112-124mph). These had twin dual-choke updraught carburettors, a higher compression ratio of 7.2:1, and twin superchargers. Although the power output of 160PS at 3600rpm unblown was nothing special, the peak power of 400PS at the same engine speed with both superchargers working hard must have been sensational. Exactly why these cars were developed is not clear; perhaps the Mercedes engineers were looking for a way of delivering better performance for the heavy armoured versions of the W150. It is regrettable that no further reliable details of their specification have so far come to light.

Numbers

Just 88 examples of the W150 were built between 1938 and 1943, and the peak year for

---

IDENTIFICATION NUMBERS, W150 MODELS

Generally speaking, chassis and engine numbers for these cars matched. A replacement engine would have its number prefixed by A (for "Austausch", exchange).

These chassis numbers and production figures were established by Jan Melin and are taken from his book, *Mercedes-Benz, The Supercharged 8-cylinder Cars of the 1930s, Volume 1.*

Number(s)	Total	Remarks
189737-189744	8	Pilot-production run
189774-189798	25	
429311-429335	25	
150006/0001-150006/0030	30	See note below
	88	

The chassis numbers of the final batch of 30 cars are interesting because they have a different pattern from all the others. Instead of a six-digit number, they have a prefix code (150006) that seems to incorporate the type-code number (W150), and this is then followed by a serial number. Why "006"? The reason is simply not known. Also interesting is that the engine numbers of this final batch did not all match the chassis numbers: chassis number 150006/001, found in Iran in 2003, had engine number 150006/13, and the two numbers were carried on separate plates alongside the main identification plate on the bulkhead.

PRICES

The price of an individually-finished car like the 770 was inevitably affected by the amount of custom-finishing required. Nevertheless, catalogue prices were quoted for the W150 models, as below. No prices were quoted for armoured variants; they were "Auf Anfrage" (On Request).

Chassis	30,000 RM
Pullman Limousine	44,000 RM

Also available as complete cars from the factory were an Open Tourer with seven seats, a four-door Cabriolet D and a six-seat Cabriolet F.

---

production was 1939, when 44 cars were built. However, it looks as if several more than that had been planned. Jan Melin identified four "Offener Tourenwagen" (Open Tourer) models ordered but not built; they were recorded with Commission Numbers 397364-397367 but no chassis numbers were allocated. In addition, he notes that a further batch of 25 chassis numbers (439408-439432) were allocated to W150 cars but were not used. Finally, he discovered that the German government ordered ten armoured W150 bodies on 17 September 1943. These may have been intended as replacements for unarmoured bodies on W150 chassis already in service, and were to be a mixture of Saloons and Tourers. However, Melin found no evidence that they were ever delivered. As the Daimler-Benz factories were instructed to stop production of passenger cars in 1943, this is not surprising.

Around 25-30 W150 cars are thought to have survived. Many were abandoned in the occupied territories at the end of the 1939-45 war and remained there until their new "owners" could be

The special Cabriolet B for the Crown Prince of Persia was built in 1940 but was never delivered to its intended owner.

BUILD VOLUMES

Mercedes-Benz state that 88 W150 models were built between February 1938 and mid-1943. Only the pilot-build cars for the Berlin Show seem to have been built at the start of 1938, and volume production (if it can really be called that) began in September that year. The final chassis seem to have been constructed in November 1943, but the last cars were probably not bodied and delivered until March 1944.

Of these cars, just five supposedly had the twin-supercharged engine.

Werner Oswald gives the following breakdown of build volumes, year by year:

1938	13
1939	44
1940	1
1941	1
1942	10
1943	19

persuaded to part with them. A number have subsequently ended up with collectors in Germany, the USA and Russia. Those supposedly used by Hitler have acquired a special value, and it is not always easy to authenticate their use: one Cabriolet F (429317), given by Hitler to Marshal Mannerheim of Finland, was erroneously believed to have been Hitler's own parade car for many years. Some suffered an ignominious fate: one of the cars used in Norway, for example, was said to have received no offers when put up for sale and was eventually scrapped. Others are or have been in museums in Canada, France, Germany and the USA.

More than 65 years after the end of the Second World War, Germany has still not forgotten the horrors of the Nazi regime and those who own or handle cars used by senior figures in that regime often prefer to remain anonymous. When cars change hands, they frequently do so out of the public view. None of that prevents cars with Nazi connections commanding especially high prices, and in 1973 a car wrongly identified as Hitler's favourite (it was actually the Mannerheim Cabriolet F) set a new price record at auction. In 2009, no fewer than six former Nazi parade 770s were sold as a group, including the armoured cabriolet

---

SPECIFICATIONS, 770 (W150)
1938-43

Engine (1):
7655cc 8-cylinder with 95mm bore and
135mm stroke
Overhead valves and side camshaft
Nine main bearings
Twin-plug cylinder head with dual ignition
by coil and magneto
Compression ratio 6.1:1
Single Mercedes-Benz twin-choke
carburettor
Roots-type supercharger driven by gear
from crankshaft
155PS at 3000rpm
230PS at 3200rpm with supercharger
engaged
Torque figure not available

Five cars supposedly built with
special engine:
Compression ratio 7.2:1
Two twin-choke updraught carburettors
Two Roots-type superchargers
160PS at 3600rpm
400PS at 3600rpm with both superchargers
engaged
Torque figure not available

Gearbox:
Four-speed with overdrive (1938-39). Ratios
not known.
Five-speed (1939-43). Ratios 3.76:1, 2.26:1,
1.435:1, 1.00:1, 0.713:1; reverse 3.3:1

Axle ratio:
4.11:1

Chassis and suspension:
Oval-section steel chassis frame
Independent front suspension with coil
springs and wishbones
De Dion rear suspension with coil springs
(1938-39) or dual concentric coil springs
(1939-43)

Brakes:
Hydraulic operation on all four wheels, with
Bosch-Dewandre vacuum servo

Weights and measures:
Overall dimensions 6000 x 2070 x 1800mm
(6000 x 2100 x 1900mm for armoured
versions)
Wheelbase 3880mm
Track 1600mm (front), 1650mm (rear);
on armoured models the tracks were 30mm
wider
Weight 4200kg for standard cars;
5420kg for armoured models
(maximum permissible)
Maximum speed 145km/h (90mph)
unsupercharged and 170 km/h (105mph)
supercharged for standard models;
180-200km/h (112-124mph) for twin-super-
charger models; armoured models were
limited to 80km/h (50mph) by their tyres

Fuel consumption 30 litres/100km (9.5mpg);
armoured models 40 litres/100km (7mpg)

---

delivered to Hitler in 1935. Their buyer was rumoured to be a wealthy Russian.

Driving the W150
In *Car* magazine for March 1980, Gordon Wilkins remembered his 1939 drive of a W150 limousine which had been brought over to the UK. "It was a superb car," he remembered, "finished in typical Mercedes-Benz style, with ebony interior woodwork inlaid with pewter stringing. The frantic scream of the blower was utterly inappropriate amid such luxury. During

my time with this car, I came up behind a woman in a Hillman Minx, and the sudden blast of sound as I powered past startled her so much that she put both her semaphore indicators out simultaneously and nearly turned her car over.

"I wanted to try for maximum speed at Brooklands, but the company representative who brought the car from Germany had strict instructions not to allow the blower to be engaged for a full lap. I had to be content with a short sprint down the Railway Straight, which produced a timed speed of 108mph."

Chapter Eleven

ABORTED PLANS

Though quite convincing, this is not a real car but an April 1940 scale model of a Limousine-bodied W148 600V. The car would have had a 6-litre V12 engine; some sources say it would have been supercharged, others disagree.

D aimler-Benz's plans for successors to the great supercharged eight-cylinder models of the 1930s simply faded out during the 1939-45 war. By the time the company emerged at the other end of that period, its factories were in ruins, and the market for hugely expensive and glamorous saloons and grand tourers had ceased to exist. Not until the early 1950s did the company begin to think about entering that market again, and by then both the eight-cylinder engine and the supercharger were in the past. The cars of the 1950s would not go beyond six cylinders, and instead of supercharging they would use the new technology of fuel injection.

Nevertheless, there is no doubt that plans were in place during the late 1930s. As early as autumn 1935, an internal memorandum proposed building a new car called the W148 as a replacement for the unsupercharged eight-

cylinder Nürburg saloons, and possibly also for the W07 Grosser Mercedes as well. As noted in Chapter 10, there was a contemporary plan to do exactly the same thing with the W24 model; some W24 prototypes were built in 1936 and abandoned the same year, but the W148 project stayed the course – up to a point.

The 600V (W148) models

The plan was for the W148 to be built on a 3620mm wheelbase, which was 50mm shorter than that of the Nürburg and 130mm shorter than that of the Grosser W07. The engine was to be a new design called the M148, which was drawn up as a 6-litre V12 with 80 degrees between cylinder banks, and this was to be available both with and without a supercharger. Figures discovered by Werner Oswald show that in unsupercharged form it delivered (or was expected to deliver) 170PS at 3600rpm and around 285lb ft of torque at 2000rpm. There can be no doubt that a V12 configuration had been chosen because there were V12s already available in Germany from Mercedes' rivals in the top luxury class, Horch and Maybach.

Then in October 1937 came a decision not to supercharge the M148 engine. The W148 car

This general arrangement drawing of the M148 V12 engine appears to show an unsupercharged version. Note the location of the twin carburettors in the vee; their traditional position on the in-line engines had been alongside the block.

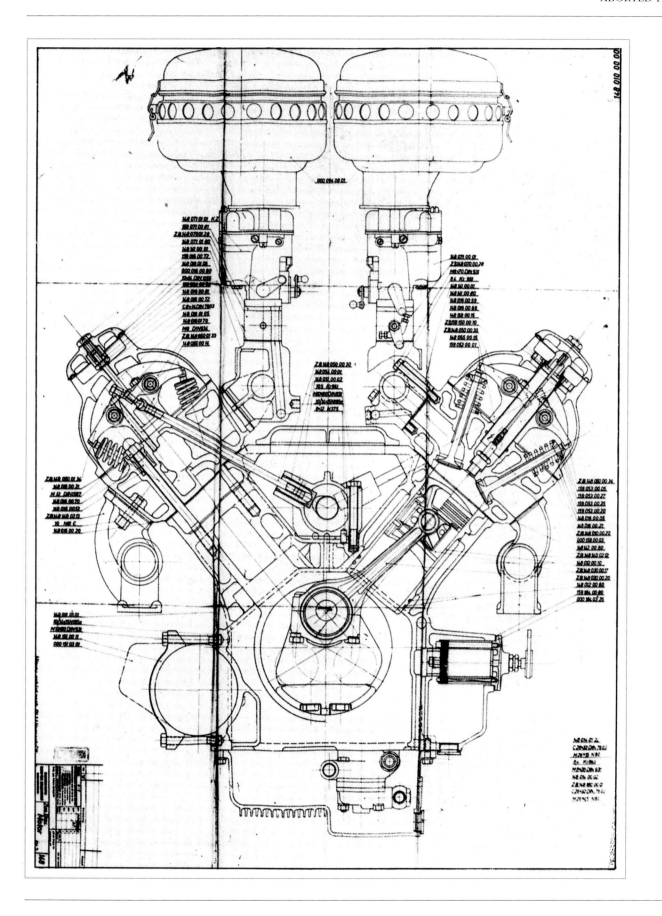

Two prototype W148 cars were built, one with a Cabriolet F body and the other as a Saloon.

would go ahead with the 170PS version of the V12, and the engine would be adapted to suit a new project, W157, which was intended to deliver a replacement for the then-current 540K. It seems likely that development problems had arisen with the V12 engine – certainly they did later on – and this may have influenced the course of events. In practice, it appears that no full prototype of the W148 was built until 1941, when somewhere between four and eight vehicles (see panels) were built. Photographs of two cars – a saloon and a Cabriolet F – have survived as proof of their existence. The Cabriolet was completed on 12 May 1941, and the Saloon followed on 9 July.

It appears that the plan then was to call the car a 600V. The V may have been a redundant reflection of the V used for the contemporary 170V models; it had initially been introduced to indicate that they had front engines (the V stood for "Vorn", front) and to distinguish them from

IDENTIFICATION NUMBERS, W148 600V MODELS

Generally speaking, chassis and engine numbers for these cars matched. A replacement engine would have its number prefixed by A (for "Austausch", exchange)

These chassis numbers and production figures were established by Jan Melin and are taken from his book, *Mercedes-Benz, The Supercharged 8-cylinder Cars of the 1930s, Volume 1.*

Number(s)	Total	Remarks
439811-439813	3	
448176-448182	7	
	10	The actual build total was 8 chassis, but some more engines were built for military use and delivered to the German Army.

BODY TYPES, W148 MODELS

Jan Melin's researches revealed that at least four bodies were ordered for prototype W148 chassis. These were as follows.

Cabriolet D	2
Cabriolet F	1
Pullman Limousine	1

SPECIFICATIONS, 600V (W148) PROTOTYPES ONLY, 1941-42

Engine:
6020cc 80-degree V12-cylinder with 82mm bore and 95mm stroke, type M148
Overhead valves and single central camshaft
Four main bearings
Single-plug cylinder head with dual ignition by coil and magneto
Compression ratio 6.3:1
Single Solex 32 IFF downdraught carburettor
170PS at 3600rpm
386Nm (284.7lb ft) at 2000rpm
(No figures available for supercharged version)

Gearbox:
Five-speed. Ratios 3.76:1, 2.26:1, 1.435:1, 1.00:1, 0.713:1; reverse 4.0:1

Axle ratio:
3.60:1

Chassis and suspension:
Oval-section steel chassis frame
Independent front suspension with coil springs and wishbones
Double-joint swing-axle with dual concentric coil springs

Brakes:
Hydraulic operation on all four wheels, with Bosch-Dewandre vacuum servo

Wheels and tyres:
17-inch steel disc wheels with 8.25 x 17 tyres

Weights and measures:
Overall dimensions
5870-6000 x 2070 x 1800mm
Wheelbase 3780 or 3880mm
Track 1600mm (front), 1650mm (rear)
Weight 3200-3400kg
Maximum speed 160km/h (99.4mph)
Fuel consumption 32 litres/100km (8.8mpg)

the 170H cars with rear engines of the same capacity (H stood for "Heck", rear).

There were plans to build several different bodies on the 600V chassis. In April 1940, a series of 1/5th scale models were built as a first stage, and photographs of these have survived. Among them were Saloon and Pullman Limousine types, both with a six-light configuration but the latter with a larger and more bulbous boot. The models were built with rear-wheel spats on one side, and on the other without spats but with a new design of large hubcap.

Werner Oswald has published some specification details of the W148 cars, although the tables in his *Mercedes-Benz Personenwagen, 1886-1984* show that he believed a supercharged W148 was among the 1941-42 prototypes. One way or another, the W148 had an oval-tube chassis frame with an independent front suspension similar to that on the W150 Grosser models and a new swing-axle rear suspension. The wheelbase was either 3780mm or 3880mm, which made these cars much larger than originally planned, and their overall size was much the same as that of the Grosser W150.

Nevertheless, figures suggest that they were very much lighter. Their gearboxes had five speeds with an overdrive fifth and the same ratios as used in the W150. Jan Melin notes that Hitler's chauffeur, Erich Kempka, test-drove a W148 and found it sluggish. Oswald cites a discussion between Hitler and Reichsminister Albert Speer on 22 March 1942, when Hitler said that he had no interest in the Daimler-Benz 12-cylinder car – although that comment may well have referred specifically to the 600 GFA project that is discussed at the end of this chapter.

BUILD QUANTITIES, W148
As noted in other tables, it looks as if there were 8 W148 chassis, of which perhaps only four were bodied. Nevertheless, figures published by Werner Oswald (and probably taken from documents drawn up by Daimler-Benz in the 1960s or 1970s) suggest there were 12 cars. Of these, 8 were built in 1941 and the remaining 4 in 1942.

This is again a scale model, apparently made at Sindelfingen in August 1940 and showing a six-light W157 600K saloon in one-fifth scale.

The 600K (W157) models

As already explained, the earliest trace of the W157 project so far discovered was in October 1937, when it was described as a replacement for the 540K, using a derivative of the 6-litre V12 engine that was then under development. This new derivative would be called the M157 engine, and it would be supercharged. Meanwhile, the W157 chassis was planned with a wheelbase of 3400mm, which was 110mm longer than the 540K's.

By this stage, it must have been clear that development of the V12 engine was not proceeding smoothly. Jan Melin uncovered evidence that Daimler-Benz expected the development of the engine to take longer that that of the chassis, and so approval was given to testing the new W157 chassis with a 5.4-litre super-

charged engine. An internal memorandum from September 1938 shows that the Development Department intended to build a W129 (a designation associated with the 540K, see Chapter 9) to a new design and with 5.4-litre engine. The car was intended as a forerunner of the W157 and appears to have been drawn up as what we would now call a "mule" prototype – a hybrid constructed from a mixture of existing W129 and prototype W157 parts. It was to have a 3390mm wheelbase, 10mm shorter than the original planned dimension.

Again we are indebted to Jan Melin for the information that the Daimler-Benz Board expressed its disappointment during 1939 that nothing definite had yet come from the V12 engine project. The development programme had been running for three years and (as far as we can now tell) there were still no prototype cars with V12 engines, even if there were engines running on Unterturkheim's test-beds.

IDENTIFICATION NUMBERS, W157 600K MODELS

Generally speaking, chassis and engine numbers for these cars matched. A replacement engine would have its number prefixed by A (for "Austausch", exchange).

These chassis numbers and production figures were established by Jan Melin and are taken from his book, *Mercedes-Benz, The Supercharged 8-cylinder Cars of the 1930s, Volume 1.*

Number(s)	Total	Remarks
439821-439822	2	(439822 not built)
448171-448175	5	
	7	The actual build total was 6 chassis.

BUILD QUANTITIES, W157

As noted in other tables, it looks as if six W157 chassis were built, but only five were bodied. Nevertheless, Werner Oswald confidently published figures (probably taken from documents drawn up by Daimler-Benz in the 1960s or 1970s) that suggested there were 12 cars. Of these, 4 were built in 1941 and the remaining 8 in 1942.

The proposed W157 Cabriolet C design was also tried out as a 1/5 scale model.

There was to be a two-door coupé body on the W157 600K, as well.

BODY TYPES, W157 MODELS
Jan Melin's researches revealed that five bodies were ordered for prototype W157 chassis. These were as follows.

Cabriolet A	1
Cabriolet B	2
Roadster	1
Saloon	1

Melin suspects that this expression of disappointment lay behind the creation of one or more prototypes that were given further-developed, 5.8-litre, versions of the M24 six-cylinder engine (see Chapter 9). The Development Department may well have felt that it would be wise to have a fallback plan in place for a 540K replacement in case the Board began to take a closer interest in their work.

Meanwhile, work continued on the W157. Melin discovered documents indicating that an M157 engine was to be fitted to a W150 for testing, but it is not clear if this ever happened. In August 1940, a series of four one-fifth scale models of planned W157 derivatives emerged from the Sindelfingen body works, perhaps as a way of indicating to Daimler-Benz top management that something was still happening on the project. They consisted of a Roadster, a Coupé, a Cabriolet C and a six-light Saloon. The overall design picked up on cues introduced with the W150 770 models and was

generally unsurprising. Most were made with rear wheel spats on one side and an exposed wheel on the other, to show alternative appearances. The Roadster, however, did not translate well onto this new chassis, and the design

The Roadster design looked heavy and not very sporting in 1/5 scale.

The Cabriolet B design for the W157 600K was built up as a running prototype.

looked heavy. It would not have been a worthy successor to the Special Roadsters on 540K chassis. Then in 1941 some prototypes appeared at last – probably six in all, of which maybe only five were bodied. The bodies built

for them were a Roadster, a Saloon, a Cabriolet A and two examples of the German public's favourite Cabriolet B.

Werner Oswald revealed that these cars had oval-tube chassis, again with the independent front and rear suspension systems used on the W150 and W148 cars. However, they had much narrower tracks than the W148s and shorter wheelbases of 3280mm or 3415mm. They had the same five-speed overdrive gearbox as the W148s, but their M157 engines delivered a lot more torque than the M148 types, with 415lb ft of torque at 2200rpm. (Small wonder, then, that Hitler's chauffeur Erich Kempka remembered this car as much better than the W148 when he test-drove it.) Peak power was down, at 155PS, but with the supercharger engaged this rose to a very healthy 240PS that gave the car a maximum speed of 190km/h (nearly 119mph). Some sources claim that there were some final experiments with a fuel injection system, technology which, like the supercharger itself, had been pioneered on the company's aero engines.

The 600 GFA and the W173 650

The W148 and W157 appear not to have been the only Daimler-Benz projects to have used the V12 engine, although they were the only ones to use it in supercharged form. In his *Catalogue Raisonné, 1886-1986*, Jürgen Lewandowski produced evidence that the 6020cc unsupercharged version was planned for a vehicle known as the 600 GFA that had project code W148 II G. This was to be a cross-country

SPECIFICATIONS, 600K (W157) PROTOTYPES ONLY, 1941-42

Engine:
6020cc 80-degree V12-cylinder with 82mm
bore and 95mm stroke, type M157
Overhead valves and single central camshaft
Four main bearings
Single-plug cylinder head with dual ignition
by coil and magneto
Compression ratio 6.3:1
Single Solex 32 IFF downdraught carburettor
Roots-type supercharger driven by gear
from crankshaft
155PS at 3600rpm
240PS at 3600rpm with supercharger
engaged
563Nm (415lb ft) at 2000rpm

Gearbox:
Five-speed. Ratios 3.76:1, 2.26:1, 1.435:1,
1.00:1, 0.713:1; reverse 3.0:1

Axle ratio:
4.11:1

Chassis and suspension:
Oval-section steel chassis frame
Independent front suspension with coil
springs and wishbones
Double-joint swing-axle with dual concen-
tric coil springs

Brakes:
Hydraulic operation on all four wheels, with
Bosch-Dewandre vacuum servo

Wheels and tyres:
17-inch steel disc or wire spoked wheels
with 7.50 x 17 tyres

Weights and measures:
Overall dimensions 5000 x 1900 x 1700mm
Wheelbase 3280 or 3415mm
Track 1475mm (front), 1500mm (rear)
Weight 2000kg
Maximum speed 190km/h (119mph)
Fuel consumption 35 litres/100km (8.1mpg)

vehicle intended as a replacement for the six-wheel Mercedes-Benz G4 (W31) cars that Adolf Hitler and other senior Nazi Party officials used when travelling away from main roads. Lewandowski claims that the project dated from 1942, but it seems clear that no prototype was ever built. This may well have been the vehicle to which Hitler was referring in his 1942 conversation with Albert Speer mentioned earlier.

Lewandowski also claimed that there were three or four prototype cars built with a different V12 engine, this time with a 6.5-litre swept volume and a 60-degree angle between the cylinder banks rather than the 80-degree angle of the 6-litre engine. There were some carry-overs: the 95mm stroke of the new engine was the same as that of the old, but a larger bore of 85mm was responsible for the bigger displacement.

This new model was built during 1942, was again unsupercharged, and delivered 130PS. It was known as the W173 or 650, and had a huge 3880mm (152.7-inch) wheelbase. Lewandowski did not say whether a supercharged derivative was also considered.

End of the road
By 1942, Daimler-Benz had more pressing demands on its engineers than the creation of new low-volume cars for officialdom and the ultra-rich. In 1943, the company was instructed to stop building cars altogether (and, somewhat humiliatingly, ended up with a contract to build thousands of Opel Blitz lorries for the German Army). Nothing more was heard of the W157, or of the W148, and the prototypes seem to have simply disappeared.

Yet not quite everything was lost. One prototype M157 V12 engine survived the war, at some time having been built into a 540K that carried a Cabriolet C body by Voll & Ruhrbeck. The car appears to have been updated at Stuttgart with late 540K features such as a five-speed gearbox and an improved braking system. It has since been partially restored, in its original colour of metallic blue, and has been seen at classic car shows.